FIVE MINUTES
TO MIDNIGHT

FIVE MINUTES TO MIDNIGHT

HOW BRITAIN SURVIVED
THE 2008 BANKING CRASH

MICHAEL HARRISON

In memory of Geoff and Anne Harrison   ·

Hartington Press

Copyright © Michael Harrison, 2020

The right of Michael Harrison to be identified as the
Author of this work has been asserted in accordance
with the Copyrights, Designs and Patents Act, 1988.

ISBN 9798555787781 (paperback)
Available as an ebook.

The book is typeset in Caslon, a font first designed
in 1722 by William Caslon and renowned for its
work-like qualities and pleasant open appearance.

CONTENTS

The Gathering Storm		1
Day 1	The Clock Starts Ticking	28
Day 2	Man the Lifeboat	47
Day 3	Bradford & Bingley Breakup	52
Day 4	Meetings with the Bank Manager	56
Day 5	The Irish Bombshell	63
Day 6	Breakfast at Number Ten	71
Day 7	Whose Plan is it Anyway?	77
Day 8	The Risky Reshuffle	81
Day 9	HBOS on the Brink	87
Day 10	The Osborne Ambush	93
Day 11	Stock Market Meltdown	100
Day 12	The Balti Bailout	112
Day 13	Prepare to Pack your Bags	134
Day 14	Thunderbirds Are Go	150
Day 15	Waiting on the World	160
Day 16	Nice Day for a Drive-By Shooting	171
Day 17	Who Blinks First	182
Day 18	Where the Hell is Victor?	190
After the Storm		195
Where Are They Now?		203
Bibliography		207
Acknowledgements		208
Index		209

The Gathering Storm

Until a certain pandemic re-wrote history, Alistair Darling could pinpoint beyond peradventure the exact moment he realised the British banking system – and, by extension, the entire UK economy – was facing its gravest existential crisis in a century. It was at 10.30am on Tuesday, 7 October 2008 and the then Chancellor of the Exchequer had just come off a telephone call with Sir Tom McKillop, the chairman of Royal Bank of Scotland.

What McKillop had to say made Darling's blood run cold. Unless RBS received an emergency injection of cash from the Bank of England in the next two hours it would be bust by the end of the day. This was not just any financial institution. This was not another Northern Rock by a different name. This was not one more regional bank or former building society brought low by the hubris of its management and the terrible mismatch between their overblown ambitions and actual business acumen. This was not even the UK's own version of Lehman Brothers. This was RBS. This was Britain's biggest bank. This was the world's biggest bank.

If RBS went under there was a serious danger it would take the rest of the British banking industry with it. First HBOS and then Lloyds, followed by Barclays and then perhaps, God forbid, the mighty HSBC. The contagion would be rapid in its spread and devastating in its consequences.

The Chancellor and his Prime Minister, Gordon Brown, knew they were staring down the barrel of a full-blown economic disaster. And that disaster promised to escalate very quickly into a political crisis. And from that crisis beckoned consequences for British society that no politician could contemplate with any equanimity.

In the same way that the world is struggling today to contain a pandemic and cope with its economic fallout, they had to discover a vaccine and they needed to find it fast. What could they do to inoculate the economy against the deadly disease that had been incubating inside the banking system? Where was the antidote and, even supposing one could be found, would it work?

Then, as now, the world's financial system was suffering toxic shock and risked going into complete cardiac arrest. Then, as now, fear and uncertainty had replaced optimism and self-belief. Consumer confidence had evaporated and the economy was on the brink of a crisis brought about by a collapse in demand – as opposed to the collapse in supply we are witnessing today. Then, as now, the country was being led by a largely untried and untested Prime Minister and Chancellor. And then, as now, their parliamentary opponents were torn between supporting the Government in the national interest and making political capital out of the crisis.

Brown and Darling had only been in their respective posts for a little over a year and now they were facing the biggest challenge of their political careers. Brown himself had spent a record ten years as Chancellor auditioning for the role of Prime Minister and had only found the time to get married when he was one year short of 50. If the country's financial titans were looking for someone to save them, then Brown, the son of a Church of Scotland minister and scourge of the capitalist classes, was hardly the most obvious candidate. After all, had he not nailed his colours to the mast on his first day as Labour Chancellor by imposing a windfall tax on the fat cats running Britain's privatised utilities in order to redistribute wealth to the young and unemployed? And had he not kept the UK out of the single currency, much to the frustration and sometimes anger of large swathes of the business community?

What he also possessed, however, was a wealth of political experience and a deep understanding of the mechanisms by which the world's financial systems functioned. And in Darling, he had a seasoned ally with bags of ministerial experience well used to dealing with crises. To the outside world, the Chancellor probably came across as another saturnine Scot who enjoyed nothing more than listening to the music of Leonard Cohen. But as Transport Secretary in July 2005 he was the man in the hot seat when London's tube and bus networks came under attack from suicide bombers.

So, Brown and Darling made for an impressive duo whose respective skills complemented one another's. But were they up to the task of preventing the world's biggest bank from collapsing and taking the UK economy with it?

With its cash machines empty, RBS's three million customers would be unable to withdraw money and without liquidity of its own, no other bank would be prepared to let RBS piggyback on their ATM networks. With the doors closed to RBS's 8,000 branches, thousands of companies up and down the country would be unable to transact their day-to-day business. They would not be able to lodge their takings or borrow money. They would not be able to pay their suppliers. Most seriously, they would not be able to pay their employees. And without money, how would those families pay for food, transport and medicines for their children?

As Brown would later recount, how would the Government cope with and contain the civil unrest that could follow, in the unlikely event that he was still in Downing Street and in power? Troops on the streets? Civil liberty in limbo? A nation in lock down? It seemed as impossible to imagine then as it does today.

Had RBS succumbed that afternoon then, in truth, it would have been the story of a death foretold. Like a tsunami gathering strength far out to sea, the UK banking crisis had been a long time a coming. Like vessels being swept away as the tidal wave races towards land, several smaller banks had already capsized and gone under. And like that eerie moment of quietude when the waters suddenly ebb and the sea appears to retreat back upon itself just before the tsunami crashes, there was a stunned silence among those in the room with Darling as they listened solemnly on the speaker phone to the chairman of RBS spelling out the mortal threat faced by his bank.

That threat had its origins 3,000 miles away on the other side of the Atlantic in what was to become known as the US sub-prime mortgage scandal. Sub-prime mortgages were a polite term for lending to poor people. They were low interest rate loans advanced to home buyers with little or no credit history, very often for 100 per cent of the purchase price and sometimes more than 100 per cent. They came into vogue in the early 1990s and grew in popularity over the following decade. In 1995 the US sub-prime market was estimated at $65 billion. By 2007 it had mushroomed to $1.3 trillion and accounted for one in every ten American mortgages.

When interest rates rose and the American economy turned down, as it inevitably would, many of these sub-prime homeowners found themselves stranded, without a job or the means to make their repayments. As a result, millions of householders defaulted on their loans. The financial impact was catastrophic, but it was not limited to the American economy. So colossal had the sub-prime market become that financing on a truly global scale was required to feed the beast. Sub-prime loans were parcelled up by fee-hungry investment bankers and sold onto other banks and external investors in other countries where they were divided up again and repackaged for further onward sale in the form of what became known as Collateralised Debt Obligations or CDOs. These were financial instruments, portfolios of bonds and credit default swaps that produced fabulous returns, but which also carried with them a vertigo-inducing degree of risk. To compound the complexity, the inventors of the CDO then created something called a CDO-squared – a new financial instrument which invested in tranches of the original CDO.

These esoteric and arcane financial instruments had been created inside the walls of perhaps no more than 40 global financial institutions. Their creators did not truly understand them and their bosses, the men and women who ran the great bulge bracket firms on Wall Street, comprehended even less. But having created them, they also enthusiastically traded in them.

The net position in this giant global casino was always zero because for every winner there was also a loser. Although the sub-prime market represented only a small sliver of the overall global financial trading market, the bets these traders placed on it were enormous. In New York's Washington Square, elderly gentlemen can be seen playing chess and inviting all-comers to take them on for $10 a game. As the former Governor of the Bank of England Mervyn King observed, it was as if the traders of these financial instruments had descended on Washington Square and decided to wager hundreds of billions of dollars on the outcome of a $10 game of chess. Colossal bets on a game offering the tiniest of returns. To make the gamble worthwhile, the wall of cash had to be enormous.

Whilst all bets were won or lost within the group of banks, from the outside it was impossible to know who was long and who was short, which bank was losing money and which bank making money. And so the capital markets and the fund managers decided not to lend to any of them or anyone else. Thus was born the credit crunch which was to stop the financial markets in their tracks in September 2007.

Along with their counterparts in Europe, Asia and elsewhere, British financial institutions enthusiastically stuffed their portfolios with CDOs. But some went further and decided to give themselves direct exposure to the US sub-prime market. HSBC paid a cool $15 billion in 2003 for one of America's biggest sub-prime lenders, Household International – a decision which rebounded hideously on the bank in 2008 when it was forced to take a $3.2 billion charge against loan defaults in its US business.

RBS had entered the game even earlier, planting its flag in US sub-prime territory in 1988 with the purchase of Citizens Bank, a New England-based lender. Citizens was the bridgehead that allowed RBS to expand further into the US with the acquisition of the Pennsylvania-based Mellon Bank's retail operations in 2001 and then in 2004 Charter One, which operated in Illinois, Ohio, Indiana and Michigan. By this time RBS, through Citizens, had become America's twelfth largest bank with $131 billion in assets and 1,500 branches.

Back home, RBS had not rested on its laurels either. In 2000 it bought NatWest for £21 billion after emerging victorious from a takeover tussle with the rival suitor Bank of Scotland, its Edinburgh neighbour. Although the deal was led by RBS's chief executive Sir George Mathewson, it was his deputy, an accountant by the name of Fred Goodwin, who impressed the City with his determination and drive to win the bid battle. Goodwin was made CEO a year later and followed up the NatWest purchase with an even more audacious deal in 2007 – the €71 billion ($96 billion) takeover of the Dutch bank ABN Amro by a consortium of RBS, Fortis of Belgium and the Spanish bank Santander. Although RBS's share of the purchase price was a more modest €14 billion, it inherited two-thirds of ABN's balance sheet comprising the riskiest assets – commercial loans, CDOs and property investments – that were tied up in the Dutch bank's US subsidiary, LaSalle, and its worldwide investment banking activities.

Sir Philip Hampton, who was subsequently hired as RBS chairman to help clear up the mess left behind by Goodwin, described ABN Amro as 'the wrong deal, at the wrong price at the wrong time'. The due diligence undertaken by Goodwin amounted to two lever arch files and a CD, according to the FSA.

That did not seem to matter to Goodwin at the time. In buying ABN Amro, he had again seen off a rival bid for the bank – this time from Barclays – which was satisfaction in itself. But in the testosterone-fuelled world of international finance, it had also enabled him to achieve one of his other prime objectives – to leapfrog J P Morgan and transform RBS into the world's biggest bank with a balance sheet worth a staggering £1.9 trillion. That was £400 billion more than the output of the entire UK economy.

Goodwin came to be admired and feared in equal measure by his counterparts in the banking world. He acquired the nickname 'Fred the Shred' because of his supposedly ferocious approach to cost-cutting (in fact it was a misnomer, the number of jobs shed at RBS on his watch was modest). But he had also described the act of scooping up smaller and weaker competitors as 'mercy killings' and, in that respect, he was guilty as charged. Under his watch, RBS completed 25 'mercy killings' in five years.

Goodwin had wasted no time shaking up RBS. Shortly after taking over he decided that a bank with a mission to become one of the biggest and most powerful financial institutions in the world needed a headquarters that matched its ambitions. So he forsook its original head office – a Palladian mansion on St Andrew's Square in the centre of Edinburgh – and built a brand new one at a cost of £350 million on the site of a former mental asylum in Gogarburn on the outskirts of the city close to the airport. Reputedly, Goodwin personally supervised the location of the kitchen supplying the director's dining room so that his culinary favourite, scallops, were served at precisely the right moment and perfectly cooked. Complete with its own mock high street sporting a coffee shop, chemist's and hair stylist, Gogarburn was reminiscent of another monument to corporate hubris – Waterside, the ersatz headquarters that British Airways had built for itself close to Heathrow and which became known to local taxi drivers as Ayling Island after its then CEO Bob Ayling.

As he built the business, Goodwin had accumulated the other corporate baubles that went with running the world's biggest bank – a private suite at the Ritz costing £700,000 a year, a fleet of 12 chauffeur driven Mercedes limousines and a corporate jet which allowed him to follow the Formula One circuit wherever it was in the world. He had also hired a trio of 'global ambassadors' in the shape of Sir Jackie Stewart, Andy Murray and Jack Nicklaus. The three sporting heroes were paid £1 million a year to burnish the RBS brand and promote its name. But that was a rounding error compared with the doubling in debts and inter-bank borrowings to £500 billion that Goodwin presided over between mid-2007 and October 2008.

Emboldened by Goodwin's extraordinary success at RBS, a host of wannabe UK banks sought to emulate his strategy, built on high-risk lending and growth at a breakneck speed buoyed by acquisitions wherever possible. Halifax, the former building society-turned bank, bought the insurer Clerical Medical and a 60 per cent stake in the wealth manager St James Place Capital and then, in turn, merged itself with Bank of Scotland in 2001 to create HBOS. Despite warnings from its own compliance officers, HBOS went on to sanction some of the most reckless lending ever witnessed in British banking in the form of self-certified mortgages, commercial real estate loans and borrowing backed by sub-prime mortgages. Much of the business was done under the supervision of Peter Cummings, the head of HBOS's corporate division. Some of it was tinged by fraud and corruption. By the time the bank hit the buffers in 2008 some £63 billion of its assets equivalent to 10 per cent of the balance sheet were classified as high risk.

Smaller UK banks raced to keep up with their bigger and better-funded counterparts. Northern Rock, another former building society which decided that its fortunes lay in being quoted on the stock market rather than mutually owned by its members, was at the front of the pack. The Rock, or rather the Crock as would become known, expanded at a dizzying pace offering homeowners mortgages worth 125 per cent of the value of their property. But there was one small technical challenge: where to get hold of the funds in the first place in order to advance these extraordinarily generous loans.

Historically, 90 per cent of the mortgages offered by Northern Rock had been funded by deposits from retail savers. By January 2007, this ratio had fallen to 33 per cent and on the day that it finally collapsed nine months later on 14 September, it had shrunk further to just 20 per cent. Northern Rock had been reliant on the international financial markets for the remaining 80 per cent of its funding. But the credit crunch brought about by the US sub-prime crisis had effectively cut off this financial supply line. And so Northern Rock became the bank that quite literally ran out of money. A similar fate may well have befallen Alliance & Leicester, another plucky little demutualised building society, had it not been swallowed up in July the following year by Santander.

Ironically, the immediate cause of Northern Rock's demise had been a report the previous evening on the BBC Ten O'clock News by its Business Editor Robert Peston revealing that the Bank of England was poised to step in to provide the company with emergency funds. His report also sought to reassure the bank's customers that, although serious, this was a crisis of liquidity, not solvency. The bank was in trouble, but it was not going bust. In the end the distinction was academic, as was demonstrated by the television pictures the following day of savers queuing around the block outside Northern Rock branches to withdraw their money. If a bank cannot get access to liquidity it is generally because the market fears it is under-capitalised and a bank that lacks capital is an insolvent bank. Solvency was the fundamental problem. Lack of liquidity was merely a symptom.

Following the collapse of Northern Rock, Brown became increasingly fixated by the need for banks to be able to lend, not only to one another, but more importantly to the real economy. And a kernel of truth began to lodge itself in his thinking which only grew more self-evident as the months passed by. It was less about liquidity and more about capital. If banks had too many under-performing toxic assets on their balance sheets, then by definition they were under-capitalised and that would cast a question mark over their solvency and impair their ability to raise money to lend to their customers.

Over the Christmas of 2007 Brown tested out his thesis on a small number of advisers and confidantes, including Shriti Vadera, his newly-appointed minister for international development. Vadera was in many ways an outsider. In 1972 and aged just ten, she was forced to join the exodus of Ugandan Asians fleeing their country and the wrath of Idi Amin. Her family, which had owned a small tea plantation, initially sought refuge in India and then came to the UK, where the young Shriti was educated at Northwood College and then Somerville College, Oxford before deciding to make her career in the City. There, she made her name as a hard-driving investment banker with SG Warburg who did not take prisoners.

Now she was in government and she was the eyes and ears of the Prime Minister across Whitehall. She had been monitoring events and her diagnosis too was that the global banking system was beginning to freeze up because of the sheer extent to which balance sheets were riddled with toxic asserts. Vadera would become a central and controversial figure when the dramatic operation to rescue Britain's banks was launched months later

Having conducted a trial run of his theory, Brown then wrote an article in the *Financial Times* in February 2008 fleshing out his ideas, saying banks had to declare their losses and clean up their balance sheets. He understood they were carrying assets in their books at the wrong price and did not trust each other. But it was not a problem that afflicted only Northern Rock. By then the lack of resilience of the whole banking system had become truly jaw-dropping. Historically, around a third of any bank's balance sheet had consisted of liquid assets such as short-term government securities – assets which could be turned instantly into cash which they could use to fund their lending operations. By September 2007 that figure had fallen to 1 per cent. Northern Rock's debts were 80 times its equity. The normal ratio for most companies is between one and three.

So, the banking sector was headed straight into the perfect storm. On the asset side of the ledger, they had very few liquid assets and on the liabilities side it was mostly borrowed money. At the same time, the banks were lending huge sums of money short-term. Ordinarily, they would be able to roll those loans over but in the autumn of 2007 that stopped happening because no-one wanted to loan to a bank that might be on the verge of insolvency. The only place to turn was the Bank of England and its fellow central banks.

It was not as if policymakers and regulators weren't alive to what might happen in the event of a major UK banking failure. Between 2006 and early 2007 the Economic Secretary to the Treasury Ed Balls had, at the request of Brown, led a series of exercises involving the Treasury, Bank of England and Financial Services Authority – the so-called Tripartite – to simulate just such an event. The exercises were held at the Bank of England's conference centre inside its imposing Threadneedle Street headquarters in the heart of the City of London.

The purpose of this war gaming was to assess whether such a failure would spread contagion to other banks and thus pose a 'systemic' threat to the entire banking sector. Brown subsequently approached the US Treasury Secretary Hank Paulson and got his agreement to participate in a transatlantic version of the exercise. Paulson obliged and enlisted the help of Ben Bernanke, the chairman of the Federal Reserve, along with the New York Federal Reserve and the Securities and Exchange Commission, the FSA's American equivalent.

There was one major flaw in the exercises: they were missing a key participant – the banks themselves. The politicians had decided it was better not to involve the bankers in case news of the simulations leaked and spooked the markets into believing a major financial institution really was on the brink of collapse. Brown later acknowledged that this had been a serious omission because it left unanswered one crucial question: in an actual crisis how would the bank or banks involved respond? Nor did the simulations cover scenarios involving multiple, simultaneous bank failures or stress test the way in which individual banks were interlinked and reliant upon one another for short-term credit and overnight lending.

As Brown also came to realise, the danger of one bank collapse producing a domino effect across the financial sector was compounded by the existence of a vast shadow banking system made up of entities that were neither regulated nor bound by conventional banking rules, trading in esoteric and often dubious financial instruments. During 2008 a total of $50 trillion in credit cover was available from the global financial industry – more than the combined income of every man, woman and child on the planet. Of course, had that credit been called on the industry would not have been able to deliver.

The war-gaming inside the Bank of England had also overlooked another important consideration. At the end of the exercise, there was a 'lessons learnt' session. The Governor of the Bank, Mervyn King, was sat in the audience. He stood up and asked Balls whether a mechanism existed for dealing with a bank that did fall over in a timely and speedy manner. There was no such mechanism. The Government did not have powers as such to take control of failing banks and there were no adequate protections in place to protect the interests of depositors.

Despite all the war gaming and simulations, a certain complacency continued to prevail, at least in the UK. The Bank itself was not immune. It had a large team dedicated to maintaining the financial stability of the economy staffed by clever people. Their job was to scan the horizon for potential threats to the smooth operation of the banking system. Accordingly, the team would produce lengthy lists of new risks it had identified, often running into double figures. However, what was really required, but not being provided, was a cool assessment of the one or two very big threats the financial system faced and the resilience and robustness that needed to be built into the plumbing of the system to negate those risks.

Sub-prime was a case in point. The Treasury's view as late as August 2007 – just a month before Northern Rock became Northern Crock – was that the sub-prime crisis was essentially a US problem which would not contaminate the UK banking system. In addition, the Treasury's approach to regulation – as evidenced and exercised by the FSA – was to focus on the health of single banks and whether they had adequate capital ratios. In other words, that they possessed a big enough financial buffer to withstand a run on the institution if things got sticky.

In any event the received wisdom – accepted by politicians and regulators alike – was that globalisation and the ability of large multi-national banks to obtain liquidity and capital from many different sources in many different parts of the world spread the risk. In fact, the opposite was the case. The way that banks and financial institutions borrowed from one another and bought each other's debt instruments concentrated and intensified the risk, rather than dissipating and reducing it. Although its ultimate demise was not a 'systemic' threat to the UK's banking system, Northern Rock in its own small way proved the point.

It also put Brown's government on notice that what had happened to a medium-sized retail bank in the north-east of England could happen on a much larger scale to a much bigger bank. Such thoughts were no doubt on Alistair Darling's mind when he received a house call from an unexpected visitor in the week before Christmas 2007. Darling had been Chancellor for just six months. He opened the door of his beautifully proportioned Georgian villa in the Morningside district of Edinburgh and standing there in the driveway was Fred Goodwin.

Goodwin was a near neighbour and lived less than a mile away but the two men did not know one another despite having spent much of their lives in Edinburgh – one as a budding banker of growing repute, the other as a constituency MP. Darling and his wife Maggie, a former prominent Scottish journalist, preferred the company of their other illustrious near neighbours – the writers J K Rowling and Ian Rankin, author of the Rebus detective series.

Because of the impromptu nature of Goodwin's visit to the Darling residence that day, the two men were able to talk alone. There were no private secretaries or bag carriers present to minute their conversation and report back to Cabinet or boardroom. Darling asked Goodwin what was on his mind, and he replied that the Bank of England urgently needed to inject more liquidity into the banking system. At that point, it had provided around £10 billion of financial support.

Darling then asked why the markets seemed to be singling out RBS for especially close scrutiny and harsh treatment if this was a system-wide problem. Goodwin replied that the pension fund managers and banking analysts who tracked RBS did not believe it had sufficient capital, but they were wrong in thinking that. The conversation ended with the two men exchanging polite festive greetings. After he closed the door, Darling wandered back into the kitchen where Maggie was preparing some of her hearty but delicious homemade soup. 'How did that go?', she asked her husband. Darling replied that he had the distinct impression RBS was in more difficulty than Goodwin cared to admit.

Goodwin's house call in Edinburgh coincided with a hardening in resolve at the Bank of England. It was also around Christmas, 2007 that the Governor became clear in his own mind that something had to be done about the lack of capital held by the UK's banks. He had flagged his concerns the previous June when he delivered his annual address to the Lord Mayor's Banquet for Bankers and Merchants of the City at the Mansion House, the Square Mile's spiritual home just a hundred yards from the Bank's own headquarters. He had warned his audience of bankers and financiers about his serious concerns over the quality of the assets they were holding – CDOs and CDOs-squared. He told them bluntly that in his view they were under-capitalised and questioned whether they were 'really so much cleverer than the financiers of the past'. Extraordinarily, he was booed by some of those in the hall for his troubles. Nothing quite like that had ever happened before to a Governor of the Bank of England. They were accustomed to communicating instructions to investment banks with a raise of one eyebrow, not being drowned out by the catcalls of nouveau rich derivatives traders.

The UK's approach to tackling the mounting problems in the banking sector were not helped by the problematic relationship between the FSA, whose job it was to regulate individual banks and financial institutions, and the Bank of England, whose remit was to guard the broader financial and monetary stability of the country. Nowhere was this friction greater than at the top of the two organisations. Sir Callum McCarthy, the chairman of the FSA, and King were alike in many ways – spikey, iconoclastic, intellectual. Neither suffered fools gladly but nor did they see eye to eye. King liked McCarthy and yet their personal relationship had become increasingly strained following the collapse of Northern Rock which was seen partly as a failure of regulatory oversight by the FSA.

The atmosphere within the Tripartite was by now quite toxic. It was not helped by the Government's inability to find a buyer for Northern Rock and the subsequent need for the taxpayer to take over the bank. Because there was no mechanism, as King had earlier pointed out, for dealing with a failed bank – or putting it into resolution as it is technically known – the Government had no choice but to introduce a new law enabling it to nationalise not just Northern Rock but any bank. It was as if Tony Blair's New Labour had never abolished Clause IV of the party's constitution committing it to public ownership of the means of production, distribution and exchange and had instead reverted back to its socialist roots. Trust between the three component parts of the Tripartite eroded. They briefed brazenly against one another.

They were also at odds over the best remedy for the malaise: whether to inject money into the system as a whole (the Bank's preferred solution and the approach adopted by the European Central Bank and US Federal Reserve) or support each failing bank as the need arose (the FSA's and Treasury's modus operandi). King mistrusted the latter approach, arguing that if a bank came to believe it had a free pass and would always be bailed out by the taxpayer, then it would be encouraged to take excessive risks in the pursuit of short-term shareholder gain. A concept known as 'moral hazard'.

As 2008 dawned, the storm clouds were gathering in greater force and the harbingers of a sharp economic downturn were there to be seen. The strains on European and US banks were also becoming more pronounced. In late January, the Federal Reserve was forced to cut US interest rates twice in one week in an attempt to inject more life in the American economy. That same week, Brown brought the French President Nicholas Sarkozy, the German Chancellor Angela Merkel, the Italian Prime Minister Romano Prodi and the President of the European Commission, José Manuel Barroso, together in London to discuss a concerted plan to force Europe's banks to disclose their losses more promptly and clean up their balance sheets more effectively.

Then, six weeks later, came the first in a series of 'thunderclaps' which were to reverberate around the international banking community. On 14 March Bear Sterns, the seventh largest investment bank in America, collapsed under the weight of its exposure to CDOs and other toxic assets held by its in-house hedge funds. Despite the offer of a $25 billion loan from the Federal Reserve Bank of New York, Bear Sterns could not be kept alive. Shorn of its toxic assets, the little that was left of the bank was bought by JP Morgan Chase for $240 million – a far cry from its stock market valuation of $18 billion only a year earlier.

The failure of Bear Sterns set alarm bells ringing amongst regulators on both sides of the Atlantic, demonstrating as it did what could potentially happen to a seemingly healthy bank in the space of 12 months. By then the Tripartite had developed a sliding scale of options for how it might deal with a failing UK bank depending on how critical its condition and how systemic it was to the proper functioning of the banking system. It contained seven separate levers. At the bottom end of the scale, regulators would consider relaxing capital and liquidity requirements or seeking a buyer for the troubled institution. If neither of these were appropriate or feasible, then the next two options were the secret provision of emergency liquidity support and loan guarantees. If this was not sufficient, then straight loans not requiring any collateral in return could be made available. If none of the above worked, then the penultimate lever was the injection of capital from the taxpayer. Lever number seven was full public ownership. When the UK banking system went critical six months later, the authorities had to pull six of the seven levers.

As the sub-prime crisis spread beyond Bear Sterns and into the rest of the finance sector, previously healthy banks watched as their balance sheets were hollowed out like some financial equivalent of the flesh-eating disease necrotising fasciitis. At the same time the real economy was also slowing rapidly. The US and UK economies in particular had become heavily reliant upon the housing, consumer and financial services sectors with the latter alone contributing a quarter of the UK Exchequer's corporate tax take. Mounting losses by the banks meant declining tax revenues while the downturn in housing sales and consumer spending resulted in lower stamp duty and VAT receipts. In order to stimulate the economy, the UK needed to maintain public spending which in turn meant a rise in government borrowing to £100 billion a year and more.

By April 2008, the sub-prime crisis contagion had spread to other bank lending and assets including commercial property. Company debt was adding $1 trillion globally to the banking industry's exposure. At the meeting in Washington that month of the Group of Seven industrialised nations, the G7, the US Treasury Secretary Hank Paulson arranged for the world leaders to be joined at dinner by the heads of a number of European and US banks. All of them warned of looming difficulties.

The same month RBS announced that it intended to raise £12 billion by offering new shares to existing investors at a deeply discounted price. HBOS unveiled plans to raise £4 billion through the same mechanism. RBS also put its two insurance businesses, Direct Line and Churchill, on the block. The money was needed to fill a £6 billion hole in its balance sheet left by the credit crunch and the excessive amount of CDOs and other toxic assets that the bank had taken on. Contrary to what Goodwin had told Darling only four months earlier, the bank was indeed short of capital.

Brown could see that the banks were under stress and having difficulty persuading the markets to support them. So he convened a meeting of UK bank chiefs in Downing Street that same month to canvass the idea of a Special Liquidity Scheme under which the Bank of England would make available up to £186 billion for them to draw upon. To access the scheme, they would have to lodge securitisable assets with the Bank at least equal in value to the cash they received. The idea was that the banks would use this additional funding to increase lending to businesses and, in turn, stimulate economic activity. The Governor grudgingly agreed. For once, Brown and the bankers were on the same side – they both felt the Bank should have launched the scheme at least three months earlier.

RBS managed to get its £12 billion share issue away successfully when the offer closed in June. But HBOS's £4 billion capital raising was a flop with its own shareholders who subscribed for less than 10 per cent of the shares being sold, obliging the underwriters, Morgan Stanley and Dresdner Bank, to take up rest. Barclays meanwhile announced its own plan to raise £4.5 billion. But it too was given the cold shoulder by its own shareholders, who bought only 19 per cent of the shares allocated to them, forcing the bank to turn to the Gulf state of Qatar and a handful of Chinese, Japanese and Singaporean investors to take up the slack.

So, all the financial underpinning had failed to do its job, either for the banks or the broader economy. The net effect was akin to pushing water uphill. The credit crunch continued to intensify, confidence in the UK housing market slumped to a 30-year low, oil prices continued perversely to soar to a high of $148 a barrel resulting in a dose of stagflation where prices continue to rise even as the economy goes into reverse. And the financial health of a clutch of UK banks continued to deteriorate. By late summer RBS, HBOS, Bradford & Bingley and Alliance & Leicester were being monitored on a daily basis by the FSA and the Bank of England.

Alliance & Leicester was the first to accept that it could not survive on its own. It was saved from the same fate as Northern Rock after Spain's Santander agreed to buy the former building society turned bank in July.

But the failure of the HBOS share sale was a bigger and more worrying litmus test as far as the FSA was concerned. If the bank's own shareholders were not prepared to stand by it, then perhaps it no longer deserved to have an independent future. Over the summer months, therefore, the FSA's McCarthy instructed his officials to conduct a discrete search for a buyer for HBOS. His officials began by scouring the international financial markets for a buyer, contacting a score of potential overseas purchasers. No-one was interested. Despite the obvious anti-trust hurdles that a sale to a domestic buyer would face, the FSA was forced to begin looking for a rescuer within the UK.

Luckily, there was one interested party and it had already begun to test the political waters. In July the chairman of Lloyds, Sir Victor Blank, had privately approached Gordon Brown to sound him out about a much bigger and bolder merger deal than Santander-Alliance & Leicester: how would the Government respond if his bank were to buy HBOS? By then, the two banks had been in secret merger discussions for several weeks. Lloyds had already been blocked from buying Abbey National and warned off bidding for Northern Rock on anti-trust grounds. Blank wanted to know whether a tilt at HBOS would receive the same response from the competition authorities.

Blank was a larger than life character, both literally and metaphorically. Six feet four inches tall and broad in the beam too, he was one of the City's best-known characters. Stockport born and bred and brought up by his father after his mother died from ovarian cancer when he was only 12, Blank went on to study modern history at Oxford. He began his professional career as a lawyer becoming, aged 26, the youngest partner in the history of the law firm Clifford-Turner (now Clifford Chance). He left the law after 15 years to join Charterhouse Bank where he rose to become chairman after which he also chaired Mirror Group Newspapers and Great Universal Stores, the owner of Argos and Homebase, before finally becoming chairman of Lloyds in May, 2006. He even had his own coat of arms.

Brown warmed to Blank. He also concluded that if HBOS was struggling so hard to raise capital on its own that its management was prepared to throw in the towel, then other banks would also be in need of more capital – or a friendly white knight to rescue them. But where would that capital be found? Whilst he was on holiday in Suffolk that summer, Brown spent more and more time puzzling over the conundrum of capital and where it might come from. He also picked up Ben Bernanke's essays on the Great Depression and saw more than a passing resemblance between conditions then and now. Vadera, who by now had become a junior minister in the Department for Business, Innovation and

Skills, had written a paper on the subject of under-capitalised banks which she sent him. This in turn prompted a lengthy email exchange between the two of them. The subject matter in the header field was framed as a question: 'Is it capital?'

Finally, Brown invited Vadera up to Suffolk for a brainstorming session with his Permanent Secretary Jeremy Heywood where they talked amongst other things about Bernanke's ideas for quantitative easing – it was that kind of holiday. Their conclusion was that any financial rescue which took diseased assets off the banks's hands and put them into public ownership would not succeed if it stopped there. The problem was much more fundamental than that. When she left, Brown told her that the Treasury was by necessity focused overwhelmingly on dealing with banks as they failed one by one. Number Ten was best placed to stand back, see the big picture and decide what the solution was for the entire financial sector. He also asked her to make a discrete tour of oil-rich sovereign wealth funds in the Gulf to see whether they might be the source of the new capital which Britain's banks needed so badly.

She consulted Michael Klein, a hotshot investment banker and rainmaker who had worked for the US bank Citigroup for three decades and was well-connected in the Middle East. He helped her navigate the region, advising on which funds would be more receptive than others and which to steer clear of because they had already got their fingers burnt by participating in earlier capital raisings. She accepted the mission from Brown even though she was sure it was already too late in the day to be asking them. But Brown wanted to be sure that there was no other source of money.

Whilst Vadera was touring the Gulf states, Brown returned to London where he sought the advice of the economist Gavyn Davies on his diagnosis of what was wrong with the global banking system and how best to re-boot the world's economies. Although he had been a senior partner in that symbol of rapacious capitalism Goldman Sachs, rising to become the firm's international managing director, Davies was a lifelong Labour supporter who had also contributed some of his not inconsiderable wealth to the party's coffers.

By mid-summer, the Fed had cut US interest rates from 5 per cent to 1.25 per cent. But to Brown's chagrin the Bank of England (which had been given its independence by him when he became Chancellor in the first Labour government) persisted in keeping UK rates high. Even though the UK economy was technically in recession, they were still at 4.5 per cent.

Growing tensions were not only apparent between the Bank of England and Number Ten. Relations were also becoming increasingly strained with Brown's neighbour in 11 Downing Street. When he appointed Darling as Chancellor in June 2007, Brown had candidly told his fellow Scot that he might need to replace him at some point. Twelve months later, Darling had cause to wonder whether the Prime Minister was about to do precisely that. That July, Darling had given an interview to *The Times* in which he warned that the downturn would last longer and prove deeper than expected, that growth would be lower and slower than forecast and lastly that the problems in the UK banking sector were more deep-rooted than most people imagined. The headline over the piece was 'Prophet of Gloom'. Darling had said much the same in an interview with the New Statesman a month earlier. Both pieces appeared without too much fallout.

But it was a third interview, given in August to *The Guardian's* star feature writer Decca Aitkenhead that was to prove a political and financial depth charge. Darling had agreed to the interview at the urging of one of his special advisers, Catherine MacLeod, herself a former political editor on *The Glasgow Herald*. The idea was to help set the narrative for his Chancellorship but also lift the skirt a little to reveal the personality beneath. It took place on a gloriously sunny afternoon while the Darlings were holidaying in a croft house on the island of Lewis. The interview had been intended as a colour piece for *The Guardian's* Saturday magazine and had been due to run on the eve of Labour's annual conference in Manchester the following month. But the paper decided to publish it two weeks early because of what Darling had told Aitkenhead when they met that afternoon: that the UK was facing its worst downturn in sixty years. And the story was not tucked away in a weekend supplement. It was the paper's front-page splash and it ran under the provocative headline: 'Economy at 60-year low'.

The explosion could be heard almost immediately from the Prime Minister's office where Brown's attack dog, his high-profile special adviser Damian McBride, went on the offensive, declaring the interview to have been a disaster. Brown, unbeknown to his next-door neighbour, had tasked his small inner circle to work up a strategy built around a quite different narrative – that the UK economy was poised to recover and bounce back over the next six months. That was the story they had seeded with the media during the Press hurdle at the back of the plane bringing Brown home from the closing ceremony of the Beijing Olympics four days earlier. In fairness, the Bank of England, International Monetary Fund and respected independent economic forecasters such as the National Institute for Economic Research, had been saying much the same.

But Darling's comments blew the gaffe and left the Treasury and Number Ten in an even more heightened state of mutual suspicion. Relations were not helped by the other piece of scuttle bug doing the rounds in Westminster – rumours that Brown was facing a potential leadership challenge. The repercussions would be felt a few short weeks later when the Chancellor and Prime Minister sat down to plan the rescue of the British banking system and convince other world leaders to adopt their blueprint.

At the Bank of England, King was also painfully aware of just how strained relations had become between Numbers Ten and Eleven. His only point of contact in Downing Street was with Darling and he worried that his message and his views might not be getting through to the Prime Minister. King had gotten to know Brown well during his long years as Chancellor. But he realised that he had not exchanged a single solitary word with Brown since he had become Prime Minister a year earlier. And so on his own initiative, King sent a private note to Brown asking to come and see him to explain his acute concern at the state of the country's banks. The result was to be a series of regular working breakfasts over the summer with the Prime Minister in Downing Street at which King set out his analysis and his solution. He called it his BRP standing for Bank Recapitalisation Programme and began sending papers to Brown expanding on his prognosis.

Brown was slightly puzzled by the Governor's new-found enthusiasm for intervening in the banking sector. Earlier that year King had given a speech in which he warned against governments bailing out banks because of the 'moral hazard' it risked inviting. Now here he was suggesting that the state spend tens of billions of pounds taking controlling shareholdings in many of the country's banks .As much as he admired the Governor, he decided that he preferred the counsel of his close friend and ally Vadera.

By September 2008, the UK's Special Liquidity Scheme was in full swing. By the time it had run its course in another 18 months UK banks would have taken £185 billion from the scheme in the shape of Treasury bills capable of being traded immediately for cash. In the US, Treasury Secretary Paulson was working meanwhile on his $700 billion Troubled Assets Relief Programme or TARP as it was known – a scheme whereby the US government would purchase the bad assets of its banks and sell them on at knock down prices, enabling those same banks to begin borrowing and lending again.

Paulson had to break off briefly from TARP to rescue the country's two biggest mortgage providers, Fanny Mae and Freddie Mac with a $200 billion bail-out. And then came the big one: the collapse of Lehman Brothers. On Monday, 15 September the US bank filed for Chapter 11 bankruptcy protection, burdened down by $60 billion of toxic assets. The collapse of Lehman's was significant for the global financial industry because it massively increased the reluctance of banks to lend to one another. A side product of Lehman's demise was that the great Goldman Sachs and Morgan Stanley had to go out and raise capital from Warren Buffett and Mitsubishi respectively.

More parochially, it was also important for the UK. About half the bank's business went through London where Lehman's employed 5,000 people. Many of them could be seen the following morning carting their belongings away from the bank's Canary Wharf offices in black plastic bin liners.

Nationalising Lehman's was not an option for Paulson because he had used up too much of his political capital trying to push TARP through Congress. Bank of America had its arm twisted to rescue the bank but resisted the pressure. Paulson and the chairman of the New York Federal Reserve, Tim Geithner, turned instead to the UK where Barclays had lodged an interest in buying Lehman's. Barclays would have needed the approval of its shareholders to undertake such an enormous and high-risk transaction. Paulson suggested that the UK government temporarily suspend such shareholder rights to allow the emergency rescue of Lehman's to proceed. Moreover, the US Treasury Secretary expected the Bank of England and not its own Federal Reserve to provide dollar liquidity to Lehman's US operations. Unsurprisingly, the Americans received short shrift. Darling, supported by McCarthy at the FSA, refused to allow Barclays to proceed on the not unreasonable grounds that if no other US financial institution would touch Lehman's with a barge pole why should a UK bank buy it, potentially exposing the UK taxpayer to huge and unquantified liabilities? Paulson recalls that when Darling told him of the UK's decision he justified it by saying 'We don't want to import your cancer into Britain'. After coming off a remarkably similar and equally fruitless call with McCarthy, Geithner put it more succinctly: 'We're fucked,' he told his aides. In the end, Barclays did buy some of Lehman's healthy assets, but for a song and without any of its liabilities.

But where there is despair there is also, sometimes, hope. On the same evening that Lehman's collapsed on one side the Atlantic, a conversation took place on the other side which would save the UK's fourth biggest bank from a similar fate. Citigroup, the giant US investment bank, was holding a full board meeting the following morning in London and had decided to host the great and the good of British politics and finance to drinks and dinner the night before in the grand surroundings of Spencer House, the ancestral home of Lady Diana Spencer. Gordon Brown turned up for the drinks reception and immediately made a beeline for the Lloyds chairman Sir Victor Blank. The Prime Minister had an answer to the question Blank had posed two months earlier. Not only would the Government not block a Lloyds/HBOS merger, it would positively support and welcome such a move. Brown was desperate to avoid HBOS becoming another failed bank. Even though he had introduced legislation in the wake of the Northern Rock collapse giving ministers the power to nationalise ailing banks, it was the last thing Brown wanted to do. Far better that HBOS was taken under Lloyds's wing, even if it would drive a coach and horses through competition policy by gifting Lloyds well over a quarter of the UK mortgage and retail banking market.

But Blank had better move fast. The Treasury was on the point of informing HBOS that it would have to close to new business if it could not find a buyer. It had been due to issue the notice the following day, 16 September. Had it done so, it would have been the death knell for HBOS, provoking a run on the bank that would have made Northern Rock's experience a year earlier look like a minor glitch with a handful of its ATMs.

With that Brown left the reception, having talked to few other guests – much to the chagrin of Digby Jones, the former director-general of the CBI turned government junior business minister. He had been brought into government as part of Brown's mission to create an administration of 'all the talents' but also to act as a bridgehead between Labour and a business community traditionally wary of socialist-leaning politicians. To Jones, the reception had been a golden opportunity for Brown to reach out to this suspicious constituency. In the event, it was an opportunity wasted.

At the time, it was widely reported that Brown had used the encounter with Blank to strong-arm Lloyds into saving HBOS. In fact, nothing could have been further from the truth. Three days later on 18 September the merger of the two banks was duly unveiled with Lloyds agreeing to pay 232p a share for HBOS, valuing the bank at £12.2 billion. The Government also imposed a ban on the 'short-selling' of bank stocks – a practice used by dealers to make quick profits by artificially lowering the value of their shares.

Importantly, Lloyds was paying for the deal, not with cash but with its own shares. HBOS shareholders would receive 0.83 of a Lloyds share for every share they held in HBOS. There was none of the razzmatazz usually associated with mega-mergers. Everyone knew this was a rescue in all but name. Blank therefore eschewed his chauffeur driven Audi A8 and instead arrived at the press conference squeezed into his G-Wiz electric vehicle alongside his driver Bill. The sight of Blank exhaling deeply as he extracted his long frame from the tiny car made most of the front pages the next day.

The markets also breathed a huge sigh of relief. Perhaps there was life after Lehman's after all. The next day Paulson formally unveiled his TARP programme, bank shares soared and London and Wall Street saw record stock market gains with the FTSE100 index of leading shares ending the day 8.8 per cent higher.

Armageddon averted. Crisis over. Or so they hoped. Like that brief lacuna before the tsunami makes landfall, when all is momentarily calm, it was to prove a cruel and false dawn.

It took just 48 hours for the mild euphoria which had greeted the announcement of the Lloyds/HBOS deal to evaporate. It was replaced by a mood of renewed anxiety amongst banking regulators, politicians and policymakers. On Saturday, 20 September, Adair Turner took over as chairman of the FSA, a job he likened to being made captain of the Titanic after it had hit the iceberg but before it sank.

Although he styled himself as a 'technocrat', Turner was a formidable operator. A former President of the Cambridge Union, he cut his teeth at BP and Chase Manhattan before joining the rarefied ranks of the management consultancy McKinsey and then going on to become the voice of British business as Director-General of the CBI where he championed UK membership of the euro.

Turner had not been due to assume the position at the FSA until the Monday but his predecessor McCarthy had phoned him the previous week and asked whether he could start a couple of days earlier. So febrile and uncertain were the times that the FSA could not risk the post of chairman going unmanned even for a weekend.

It matched the fevered atmosphere in Westminster, where the financial crisis was ratcheting up the pressure on Brown to warp factor ten. Addressing Labour's annual conference in Manchester the following week Brown told delegates that while he was all in favour of apprenticeship programmes, now was not the time for a 'novice'. Brown had intended it as a reference to the Opposition leader David Cameron, but the media took it as a veiled warning to his Cabinet colleague David Miliband to get his tanks off the Prime Minister's lawn.

It was just as well that Turner had begun work at the FSA early because that Sunday morning the phone rang at his Kensington mews house. His wife Orna answered it and told him it was Hector Sants, chief executive of the FSA, on the line. Although he had spent his career in the City as an investment banker, Sants had only been in the top job at the FSA for a year himself so the two most senior officials at Britain's principal financial regulator were relatively untested.

Sants apologised for ringing so early but said Turner had better get to the office because there were major problems brewing with two Icelandic banks that had major UK operations and hundreds of thousands of British savers. Orna, whom Turner had met and married in 1985 when they both worked at McKinsey, was used to weekends being interrupted by corporate crises as she served on a number of company boards herself. She waved him off as he headed for the FSA's Canary Wharf headquarters. She did not see him until the following morning.

It was a baptism of fire for Turner but not an unexpected one. He knew that the organisation he had inherited was, rightly or wrongly, proud of itself and the work it had done to ensure the banks under its charge had adequate amounts of capital on their balance sheets. But he also knew that it lacked strength in depth. With the benefit of hindsight, it also became painfully apparent that those capital ratios as they were known were hopelessly inadequate. Moreover, the FSA was entirely focused on regulating the industry institution by institution with the result that nobody was looking properly at the bigger picture and the levels of leverage in the banking system as a whole. As Turner saw it, the main threat lay in systemic risk, not the actions or inactions of individual banks, but there was a dearth of the proper intellectual analysis and policy response that necessitated.

Turner knew in his bones that the challenge he had just taken on would prove the most demanding but also the most exhilarating of his professional career – much more satisfying than riding industry's hobby horse at the CBI. Much of the global economy, including that of Britain, was on the brink of plunging into a depression on a par with that of the 1930s and a small handful of players were about to be tasked with stopping that from happening.

They had a little over two weeks to save the financial world from disaster. This is how they did it.

Day 1 – Friday 26 September

The Clock Starts Ticking

If there is a financial equivalent of the Doomsday Clock, then it began to tick down towards midnight for Britain's banks on the evening of Friday 26 September 2008. Two highly significant events occurred that night. First, the two most powerful City regulators in the country pulled the plug on Bradford & Bingley, a struggling building society turned bank. Second, and with the express authority of the Prime Minister Gordon Brown, the Chancellor Alistair Darling ordered a team of senior officials from the Treasury, Bank of England and Financial Services Authority – the Tripartite – to begin work in earnest on a plan to rescue the rest of the UK banking industry from oblivion. They were told they had a little over a fortnight to execute the plan and that failure was not an option.

After many months of prevarication, sticking plaster solutions and misplaced Panglossian optimism there was agreement at last that drastic action of a sort never witnessed before in the UK's financial services sector was necessary if the banks, and by extension the British economy, were to be saved.

The heads of the Tripartite – Darling, the Bank Governor Mervyn King and the FSA's chairman Adair Turner – had already met on two successive evenings earlier that week. On the Wednesday they had gathered in Number 11 Downing Street so that the newly-appointed Turner could be formally introduced to the other two men. Afterwards he accompanied King back to the Bank of England's Threadneedle Street headquarters to share a bottle of red wine over dinner in one of the three private dining rooms next to the Governor's office on the first floor. It was an opportunity for the two men to speak openly without anyone else in the room intermediating or limiting their conversation. King had liked Turner's predecessor, Callum McCarthy, but the two men had a fractious relationship and the Bank Governor was not sure McCarthy had appreciated the sheer scale of the difficulties facing the banking sector. It was also therefore a chance to reset the relationship between the Bank and FSA.

The dinner had been arranged a couple of months earlier following the announcement of Turner's appointment. It was the first time that King had had the opportunity to work with Turner, but he knew from reputation that the new FSA chairman had the ability and intellectual capacity to understand the bigger picture and the wider problems the banking sector was facing. The two men also shared a similarly dim view of investment banking, regarding much of it as socially useless 'casino banking'.

But King thought Turner was likely to be constrained in his new role by the nature of the organisation he had inherited and its set, institutionalised view of the world. Nor did he know the strengths of the team below him. The FSA was fixated on requiring banks to operate with a certain capital ratio or buffer that ensured that their balance sheets were fireproofed against the lending risks they took on. The problem with this was that the simplest way to hit the FSA's ratios was to shrink the balance sheet rather than raise new capital. The smaller a bank was, the less capacity it would have to lend and that meant it would take longer for the banks to act as engines of the economy to get the country out of the recession it was facing. Neither Brown nor King wanted that.

As he entered the Bank past the pink-jacketed and bowler-hatted butler on the front door and walked across the Roman mosaic in the front hall to the stairs that would take him up to the Governor's rooms, or Parlours as they are known, on the first floor, Turner wondered what exactly King wanted to speak to him about so badly.

He did not have to wait long to find out. King had become increasingly alarmed, almost to the point of obsession, that the UK's banks did not possess enough capital to support the multi-billion pound risks they were carrying on their balance sheets. Over their dinner that evening of sea bass and ravioli, King expanded on his theory, telling Turner that the problem did not lie with just one or two badly-run institutions. It was quite unlike the plight of the blue-blooded investment bank Barings, which the Bank of England had decided it could afford to let fail 14 years earlier after it was brought to its knees by the activities of a lone rogue trader, Nick Leeson. This time, the entire banking system was screwing up on a scale the country had not witnessed since 1914.

He had warned Darling of this not long after he had moved into Number 11 in one of the monthly chats that the two men held to discuss the state of the economy. He told Turner how he had repeated his concerns in a series of papers prepared by Bank officials and sent over to Brown and Darling in subsequent months. He advocated a compulsory, industry-wide scheme whereby every bank in the country, including those which were healthy and solvent, would be required to take capital from the Government, leaving them majority or part-owned by the taxpayer. King's argument was that this would avoid individual banks from being stigmatized and prevent the financial markets picking off the banks one by one, starting with the weakest. It would also send a very clear signal to the markets that the Government would do 'whatever it takes'.

Alistair, the Governor explained, was very easy to deal with but he was concerned that Brown had lost confidence in him. The Chancellor was calm and he had a good sense of humour. But his approach to dealing with a crisis was to get everyone together in one room, establish what was the lowest common denominator, the thing that everyone could agree on, and then get consensus on how to deal with it. That was never going to work in the banking crisis because the only solution was to recapitalise the banking system, with or without the consent of the banks, in a way that avoided stigmatising any one institution. Compunction would be necessary.

Warming to his theme, King told Turner about something that had happened a couple of years earlier which had convinced him stigma was the issue which concerned individual bank CEOs almost more than anything else because of its effect on confidence and ultimately the solvency of the institutions that they were in charge of. The example he gave was a new system for lending money that the Bank had introduced in 2006 which reduced volatility in overnight interest rates. What was special was that it allowed the banks themselves to decide how big on average the reserves needed to be that the Bank held on their behalf on a monthly basis. King had thought when the crisis began, the banks would ask it to hold much bigger amounts of cash. To his surprise, in September 2007, they did not ask for more cash at all because they were worried that when this became apparent to the outside world and their competitors they would be stigmatised as being vulnerable institutions.

They also felt that if one bank alone issued more equity it would also be stigmatised. The only way this was going to work, therefore, was through a collective compulsory scheme, involving the country's top six to eight banks. If it remained voluntary then some banks would clearly need more than others but banks such as HSBC would opt out entirely on the grounds that they had plenty of support from their Asian customers and did not need any new equity. What would then happen was that the next most secure bank would also opt out so in turn each bank would decide not to take part. A voluntary scheme, therefore, risked not working at all or going off half-cocked.

King knew that what he was advocating was contrary to Darling's philosophy about how to manage the crisis. It was much more consistent with Brown's view but Gordon was always hesitant to force the issue. He would agree in the abstract but was unwilling to say to the banks 'you are all in this'.

The Bank Governor also knew that the logical conclusion of his solution might be the complete nationalisation of one of more of the UK's banks. That did not unduly concern him. They could be restructured free of interference from private sector management, the casino banking activities that King mistrusted so much could be sold off and they could be returned to the private sector in timely fashion. Sweden had done much the same with its banks in the 1990s and indeed King had arranged for the architect of that scheme, the Swedish central bank governor Stefan Ingves, to visit Brown in 2006 when he was still Chancellor, to explain in private audience how it had been done.

Turner left the dinner persuaded that the Governor was correct about the need to recapitalise the banks. But he was yet to be persuaded that compulsion was the route they should go down. At the time the Tripartite was also still examining the possibility of launching a UK-style version of the TARP scheme that Bush and Paulson were promoting as the answer to the ills of America's banks. Under this, the Treasury would have purchased 'non-performing assets' from UK banks at a discount to their face value, giving them increased capacity to borrow funds to then lend out to their customers.

The following afternoon, King, Turner and Darling met again in the Chancellor's second floor office in the Treasury, this time accompanied by Sir John Gieve, one of the Bank's two deputy governors, and Hector Sants, the FSA's chief executive. A number of other Treasury, Bank and FSA officials were also present.

The Chancellor's office was easily big enough to host quite large meetings. When Brown held the post, he had preferred to operate from a much smaller and rather unattractive room which lacked a decent view. It was not much more than a cupboard and the furniture dated from Anthony Eden's days. But it appealed to Brown's nature and probably reflected his conservative with a small c Methodist upbringing. When Darling arrived at the Treasury from his previous Cabinet posting in Trade and Industry he discovered that there was a much nicer and larger office called the Piano Room that George Brown had occupied when he was Labour Chancellor in the 1960s. It was later used to host gatherings of the National Economic Development Council or Neddy as it became known. Darling liked the feel of the room so he moved in. There was enough space to accommodate the Chancellor's desk, a couple of armchairs and coffee table for informal chats and a large oblong table for formal meetings. Darling could also hang his favourite paintings which the custodian of the government art collection had readily agreed he could bring with him for fear of being restructured out of her job.

The purpose of meeting that day was primarily to discuss the plight of Bradford & Bingley and what should be done with the ailing bank. The bank's shares had fallen by 90 per cent in the past year and it was clearly in serious trouble. But inside the Treasury at least the calculation was that the bank did not face an imminent threat.

After the formal meeting, Darling, King and Turner met in private session to talk about the wider problems the banking sector was facing. The Bank Governor took the opportunity to press his case more urgently that unless the whole UK banking system was recapitalised, then there would be more Bradford & Bingleys. The Government, he said, should be focussing on capital, not alleviating the liquidity shortage. In his ever pragmatic way, Darling replied: 'You may be right Mervyn, but dealing with the liquidity issue will at least buy us some time to work out what the hell we are going to do with the bigger problem.'

By now, a broad consensus had begun to develop that the challenge the banks faced was indeed much bigger than a shortage of liquidity. It was a lack of capital, confidence and ultimately solvency. At a conceptual level, King had put his finger on problem. But Treasury and FSA officials and their advisers were much less convinced that compulsion was the best way to proceed. Politically and practically, it was a non-starter. A compulsory recapitalisation programme would be complicated to execute, time-consuming and fraught with legal difficulties. Nor would it avoid the arbitrary stigmatising of some banks as 'unhealthy' because any smart banking analyst would be able to run the numbers in five minutes and work out which were in the most acute distress. And healthy banks such as HSBC were certain to challenge any scheme which trampled on shareholder and ownership rights by allowing the Government to buy stakes in the banks at a discount to their market value. The Treasury and FSA were also concerned that making the scheme compulsory would spook the market so badly that it would have the opposite of its intended effect and oblige the Government to nationalise the entire banking sector. As one adviser unkindly remarked to Darling: 'Like a lot of Mervyn's ideas, it will not survive contact with reality.'

Brown and Vadera sat somewhere in the middle of this stand-off between the Bank and the Treasury. They thought the distinction between voluntary and compulsory was largely academic. If the banks were told they would not get access to life-saving liquidity support from the Bank unless they volunteered to accept capital from the taxpayer, then the scheme became compulsory in all but name. They felt that the much bigger issue was whether to opt for one big bold plan that resolved the banking crisis at a stroke or stick with the Treasury's cautious 'salami-slicing' strategy of dealing separately with each failing bank as it hit the wall. The danger of that approach was that the banking market would stay frozen until the very last bank had been sorted out. Meanwhile, the contagion that had begun in the financial sector would leach deeper and deeper into the real economy.

Number 10 regarded Darling as a great manager of the system who took a civil service brief incredibly well. But because he was not an expert in banking or finance he was always slightly behind the curve and unable to grasp the bigger picture. Brown, by contrast, was that rare thing: an intellectual giant with a brain the size of the planet. He might not be the most practical of prime ministers, but he understood the politics, the economics, the financial imperatives and the international aspects of this existential crisis that confronted western capitalism.

In Vadera, Brown had a banker who understood the technical issues and also saw the big picture. And, unlike her counterparts in the Treasury, she was not dealing with the daily grind of policy execution or else fire-fighting the next mini-crisis. If this meant that Number 10 ended up driving the agenda and treading on toes as it went along, then so be it.

As for the Governor, King simply wanted every bank to take every last penny of their capital from the taxpayer, irrespective of whether they really needed it. HSBC, for example, did not need money but if it did it would have been incredibly expensive as far as the government purse was concerned. The Treasury would have had a fit.

At the same time as King was setting out his stark prognosis of what was needed to stabilise the British banking system, Brown was in New York making the case for something very similar but on a global scale to world leaders attending the autumn meeting of the UN General Assembly. Brown had flown out to New York on the Wednesday, 24 September, accompanied by Vadera and Tom Fletcher, his private secretary for foreign and security affairs. By now, Vadera had been promoted to a new role as junior minister in the Department for Business, Innovation and Skills, where she had special responsibility for economic competitiveness, small businesses and energy. Because she was not yet a Cabinet Office minister, a pretext had to be invented to justify her presence on the trip. Friend of Sarah Brown, the Prime Minister's wife, would not quite cut it but her brief to keep the UK economy competitive provided just enough cover.

Before he presented his plan to his fellow world leaders, Brown wanted to road test it with some of the best brains on Wall Street and in American academia. He was acutely concerned that for the recapitalisation of the UK banking system to succeed, the same medicine had to be applied to banks worldwide. He needed to understand, therefore, where current US thinking stood, not only on the travails of the banking sector but the wider challenges facing the world economy. So that Wednesday evening, he arranged to have drinks with a group of eminent US economists – Paul Krugman, Joseph Stiglitz, Adam Posen – to discuss ways of stimulating activity through increased government spending and tax incentives.

The following day Vadera and John Cunliffe, a senior official in the Treasury's international division who acted as the UK sherpa at G7 meetings, spent the morning doing the rounds of Wall Street. They spoke to Lloyd Blankfein at Goldman Sachs, they spoke to the heads of other investment banks, they spoke to equity analysts who followed the banking sector. They could not tell the US bankers what was in Brown's mind because to have done so would have caused a firestorm on the other side of the Atlantic.

But they did want to know what Wall Street thought of US Treasury Secretary Hank Paulson's TARP plan for relieving America's banks of their toxic assets. Listening to them, Brown's emissaries became convinced that Wall Street did not believe that TARP would be sufficient to resolve the malaise either. The root of the problem was that America's banks were over-leveraged. They were running capitalism without capital.

At 2.30 on the Thursday afternoon, Vadera and Cunliffe regrouped in an apartment in Manhattan's Upper West Side occupied by the UK's then envoy to the UN, Sir John Sawer, to report back to Brown on the results of their soundings on Wall Street. The message was clear: TARP was good as far as it went but it was not sufficient. The intelligence was helpful to Brown because an hour later Tim Geithner, the chairman of the New York Federal Reserve, walked into Sawer's apartment to discuss that very subject.

Brown got down to business immediately. TARP aside, was there any way that the Bush administration could inject capital into its banks too, he wanted to know? Geithner replied that the idea of the US government buying stakes in its banks would be political anathema to many Republicans on the Hill. It was possible, but the task of selling it to the President would be made easier if Britain led the way. He then gave Brown one other piece of information that was to prove crucial to his strategy. Geithner said it was not widely known or appreciated, but there was a clause in the TARP legislation that did indeed enable the US government to buy capital in the country's banks. It was not the intention of the Act, but it was there in black and white. Brown seized on this little nugget of information. Here was a toehold to exploit. If he could get his foot into it, he could force the White House door open a little wider.

With that, he asked Fletcher to cancel their flight home the following day and see if it was possible to squeeze in a meeting with Bush. Brown and his entourage were flying to Washington instead.

Brown then headed for the UN meeting. He could not miss the opportunity presented by so many of his counterparts gathered together under one roof to press home the case for a genuinely global response to the financial crisis. Brazil's President Lula had agreed to hand over the chairmanship of the G20 to the UK early so that was a good start. Brown wanted to use that body as the fulcrum for a global summit.

President Bush had left New York early to return to Washington. But there were still plenty of other world leaders in town. Fletcher spoke to as many of his counterparts in the remaining country delegations as he could and succeeded in organising an impromptu meeting with his boss that evening. And so, in a discreet room off a quiet corridor in the UN the leaders of Brazil, Spain, Portugal, The Netherlands, Denmark, Norway, Australia, Tanzania and Ethiopia met to listen to Brown's blueprint for how the G20 could work together to tackle the global financial crisis. They agreed to support such an initiative provided Brown could sell it to Bush.

When Brown and Darling woke up on Friday morning the news was not particularly heartening in either London or New York. The entire front page of the *Financial Times* was devoted, as it had been for many days, to the global banking crisis. 'Dissenters holding up US bail-out' was the paper's splash story. The headline on the sidebar read 'Pressure grows on Bank to act', referring to the growing strains on the UK banking system.

Nevertheless, the news that TARP was in trouble was actually helpful to Brown and Vadera. The Bush administration's decision to go down the route of buying up the toxic assets of its banks threatened to put a large spanner in their plans. True, the Americans had also recognised it was a balance sheet issue, but they were attacking it by buying up assets rather than injecting equity. Paulson could do that because for all the might of Wall Street the financial sector did not dominate the American economy in the way it did the UK's. Bank assets were equal to only 80 per cent of US national output. In the UK they were the equivalent of 450 per cent. If Brown attempted to do the same as Paulson it would put unbearable strain on the nation's finances and turn London into Reykjavik-on-Thames. And it was not guaranteed to sort out the problem anyway. This was not a dilemma any government could buy its way out of. The banks would remain under-capitalised and starved of liquidity and therefore unable to lend. And that, ultimately, was all Brown was concerned about. He was not worried about preserving the banks per se, only their ability to act as engines of economic growth and recovery.

Brown also thought it was an illogical way to solve the crisis: assets make up some 90 per cent of a bank's balance sheet and capital 10 per cent. So the UK and the US would get much more bang for their bucks by injecting equity into the balance sheets of its banks than by removing toxic assets.

The bigger worry for Brown was that if he were to be seen doing something quite different to Bush then it would make it look as if there was a UK-specific problem. That, in turn, could lead to an attack on the pound and government gilts provoking a balance of payments crisis and sterling devaluation reminiscent of Harold Wilson's in the 1970s when he had to reassure the nation that the 'pound in the pocket remained the same today as yesterday'.

On the Friday morning, Brown carried out his scheduled commitments in New York, addressing the UN General Assembly and a 2,000-strong gathering of the Clinton Global Initiative. Then he made his way to JFK airport. Vadera, for one, was growing in confidence that progress was being made.

Their flight landed in Washington at 3.30pm and by 4.30pm Brown's party was entering the Oval Office. Vadera had broken a finger and so her right hand was in a plaster cast. As Bush reached out to shake hands, he hesitated before taking Vadera's injured limb. 'You should have seen the other guy', she quipped. The folksy exchange appealed to Bush and helped break the ice. The meeting lasted one hour. Bush sat in splendid isolation on a three-seater sofa while Brown and his entourage squeezed themselves onto the three-seater opposite. Despite the nature of the meeting, there was none of the Mr President and Mr Prime Minister business. They addressed each other by their first names. Gordon was anxious and he was also in a hurry because he had a flight home to catch in a couple of hours. And so he launched straight in, giving George a textbook lesson in global financial economics as he sought to explain why TARP was not the answer because the US needed to recapitalise its banks rather than buy up their bad assets. As he talked, Bush's eyes visibly glazed over. 'He might as well have been talking to him about Mars,' said one of those present. But the President did get the broad drift of Brown's thesis – ditch TARP, don't buy bank assets, buy bank shares instead. At the end of his peroration, Bush looked at Brown incredulously and said: 'So, what you're saying is that we'll end up owning the banks? That's all very interesting but Hank looks after that sort of thing. I'll have to speak to him about this.'

However, Bush cautioned Brown that Paulson had been working six straight weekends attempting to get TARP through Congress. He was dog-tired and short on sleep and could not guarantee how receptive his Treasury Secretary would be to the idea.

Bush was nothing if not a wily old politician and he was being asked to go before an already hostile Congress and propose something that was even less appealing than what was already on the table. Brown wondered if he was going around in circles: Geithner had already told him that the politics were too difficult and if he was to make headway he would need to convince Bush. Now Bush was pushing it back to Paulson. Brown had, however, achieved at least one thing: recapitalisation of US banks was firmly on the President's radar.

The discussion then moved onto more comfortable and familiar ground for Bush – domestic US politics. He wanted Brown to know that Obama could be beaten in the forthcoming presidential election. Finally, the two leaders had a brief discussion about the subject Brown had been primed to raise – his proposal for a gathering of the world's twenty biggest economies to agree a coordinated global approach to the financial crisis. Sarkozy and Merkel had promised Brown that if he broached the idea with Bush first, then they would follow up with the President to press home the case. Bush initially said he would prefer to restrict any gathering to the G7, plus perhaps Russia and one or two others. But Brown argued that it needed to be a much bigger affair involving China and India too. Reluctantly Bush finally declared he would support the idea – but only if the meeting was held in Washington because he was not prepared to travel outside the US in an election year. Brown would also have to develop the content for the summit and guarantee that it would produce a 'result' of some kind. Bush would chair the G20 but everything else was being contracted out to Brown. At least he had secured Bush's support in principle.

As Brown was walking out of the Oval Office, he was ushered into an ante-room and handed a pair of faxes that had just arrived from Number Ten. One contained rough Treasury and FSA estimates of how much capital the UK banking system might need. The other one contained the Bank Governor's rather higher estimates. And there was a message from Darling. He needed to speak to Brown urgently because the Government was going to have to nationalise Bradford & Bingley that weekend. Darling was in Dorneywood, the Chancellor's grace and favour residence in Buckinghamshire, having gone there with the intention of spending the weekend in the countryside. He had just come off a conference call with King and Turner – the third meeting of the Tripartite in three days – and the grim conclusion was that the bank could not survive on its own for another day.

To Brown's mind the Bradford & Bingley crisis only served to underscore his argument that the Treasury had its hands full dealing with the day-to-day casualties of the crisis which was why the overall solution to the problem was best left to Number Ten.

Brown placed the faxes in his bag and then climbed into the back of the car taking him to the airport for his British Airways flight home. As they headed away from the White House, Brown turned to his colleagues and said with a smile 'You wanted me to abandon that conversation because he was not really getting it, didn't you'. Three heads nodded in agreement.

Once his aircraft had reached cruising altitude Brown took the faxed documents out of his briefcase and began to write on the back of them. Vadera was perched on the footstool at the end of his bucket seat in first class, ready to take notes. Picking up the thick black felt tip pen that he habitually used since being blinded in one eye in a childhood sporting accident Brown wrote in underlined capital letters RECAPITALISE NOW. With a further flourish, he then added: NO LIQUIDITY WITHOUT RECAPITALISATION. He clearly had in mind the battle cry of the men and women who led America into the War of Independence. It did not have quite the resonance or historic import of 'No taxation without Representation'. But its message was clear: if the banks wanted access to funds to continue their day-to-day activities, then they had to submit to becoming part owned by the taxpayer.

He looked over to Vadera and asked her what she thought. Vadera replied that 'everything was too unpredictable and fragile to call' but it looked like a better option than the TARP scheme on which the Bush administration was pinning its hopes. Brown then asked her to turn his jottings into a coherent plan built around liquidity, capital and loan guarantees. They did not have time to wait and hope that the US would change its mind and fall into line so the UK would have to take the risk and proceed on its own.

At the back of the plane, meanwhile, the Press pack that had been accompanying Brown on his US trip were busy conferring in an attempt to agree what story to file from his White House encounter with Bush. In the main they were political correspondents from newspapers not best disposed towards a Labour government. His director of communications Michael Ellam joked that the meeting had probably been short enough to justify a headline along the lines of 'Bush snubs Brown'.

Back in the UK, Darling was not laughing as he listened to the advice being given him down the line by King and Turner. Having already pumped £3 billion into the failing institution, King told the Chancellor that the Bank was not prepared to provide any more liquidity because in its view Bradford & Bingley was insolvent. Turner said in that case the FSA would have no option but to withdraw the bank's licence to take deposits which in turn meant that the bank would be put into 'resolution' – in other words, taken over by the Government to protect the interests of its depositors. Darling was furious, according to one of his officials. Although there had been a massive amount of contingency planning, the Chancellor had been assured that Bradford & Bingley had enough liquidity to survive until at least the following weekend. That would have given the Treasury sufficient time to organise a more orderly winding up of the bank and perhaps even find a buyer while drawing up a plan for communicating with staff and customers.

In the event, there would only be 48 hours to sort out the mess as Darling would have to make a statement to the markets on Monday morning about Bradford & Bingley. He also realised that time was running out to prevent other, much bigger banks suffering the same fate. And so, before he left Dorneywood that night to drive back to London, he gave instructions for a small Tripartite team to begin work on the great British bank rescue.

Darling realised he would be chained to his desk in the Treasury for the foreseeable future which meant his home life in

Edinburgh would have to be put on hold. Luckily for him, his two children were not a problem: his son Callum had just started university and his daughter Anna was away on a gap year. That allowed his wife Maggie to join her husband in London where she would act as his sounding board and sanity check during the long days and nights that lay ahead.

Nor would there be any rest for the team mandated to carry out the bank rescue. Twenty-hour days beckoned for all of them. The man in overall charge of the team was the Treasury's Permanent Secretary Nicholas Macpherson, a softly spoken and somewhat inscrutable career civil servant. Brought up in East Sussex and educated at Eton and Balliol College, Oxford, Macpherson had briefly flirted with the private sector, experimenting as an economist first at the CBI and then the accountancy firm Peat Marwick, before deciding aged 26 that the Treasury was the place he wanted to work. Macpherson had already been blooded by the Northern Rock crisis in September 2007 and had spent the next 12 months overseeing the two main strands of Treasury activity: preparing for the next collapse of an individual bank and analysing the broader structural problems facing the sector.

No financial crisis is complete, of course, without a set of codenames and the 2008 vintage did not disappoint. The Bank of England called those on its watchlist by the names of birds or animals, depending on whether they were banks or former building societies: so, RBS was Phoenix and Lloyds was Lark whilst Alliance & Leicester was Tiger, HBOS was Fox and Bradford & Bingley was Badger. The Treasury had its own codenames for the banks and their chief executives. The rescue of Bradford & Bingley was given the codename Project Giraffe after a bright green tie sporting a motif of the said animal that Macpherson was wearing the night the bank collapsed.

Occasionally, the use of codenames was the cause of unintended hilarity. Turner was in one meeting with Darling when the two men were discussing Jaguar, the codename that had been given to the Swiss bank UBS. Darling looked up and asked why on earth the Treasury was being asked to bail out a luxury carmaker as well as the country's banking industry, surely it wasn't also in the business of taking deposits and lending money?

If Macpherson was senior commanding officer, then his platoon sergeant in charge of day-to-day operations was Tom Scholar, a rising star in the department who had cut his teeth in Downing Street and the diplomatic service and would himself go on to become the Treasury's Permanent Secretary. The eldest of three boys, the tall and rangy Scholar had an impeccable pedigree – Dulwich College and Trinity Hall, Cambridge – and a head for figures, as befitted the son of a former chairman of the Government's Statistics Board. Scholar was also a civil service lifer, having begun his Whitehall career when he was 24.

At the time he was the Treasury's Director General for Financial Services. Prior to joining the Treasury, he had served as Gordon Brown's Chief of Staff and Principal Private Secretary. Before that he had been the UK's representative on the IMF and World Bank whilst attached to the British Embassy in Washington as Minister for Economic Affairs. Scholar possessed a ferocious work ethic and a formidable brain but, as one admirer Sir Ivan Rodgers, put it, 'Tom wears his intellect lightly, he doesn't lecture people and isn't pompous or po-faced.' With his ability to engage people and 'build atmosphere', he was the perfect man to act as interlocutor between power-obsessed politicians and testosterone-fuelled bankers.

Nor did Scholar have domestic commitments to distract him from the task in hand. He had seen precious little of his Venezuelan wife Fabiola in the eight months they had been married because of the gathering financial crisis and the time he was being required to spend at work. When it became obvious that he would be seeing precious little of her for the duration, she decided to return to Washington where the couple had met, leaving Scholar to lead an unencumbered bachelor life at his apartment in Russell Square, a 25-minute walk from the Treasury building in Whitehall.

The team Scholar assembled beneath him was drawn from some of Whitehall's brightest and best. The three key individuals were Kirstin Baker, Nikhil Rathi and Lowri Khan. Baker, a Cambridge graduate and alumni of the École Nationale d'Administration in Paris, one of France's grand écoles, had joined the Treasury with an initial brief to help co-ordinate public spending. But she soon found herself in charge of the shareholder team overseeing Northern Rock after it was nationalised in March 2008. Sensing in advance that things could begin to move quickly, Scholar had called Baker the previous weekend while she was at her brother's wedding in Bristol. 'Can you be in bright and early Monday morning because it looks like things are going to kick off next week,' he told her.

Rathi was brought up by his Indian parents in Barrow-on-Furness, where his early claim to fame was to be crowned Cumbria Under-12 tennis champion, before going up to Oxford where he took Politics, Philosophy and Economics. Before joining the Treasury to run its financial stability division, he had been a private secretary in 10 Downing Street and head of the Cabinet Office anti-terrorism unit. Khan was the Treasury official responsible for managing its relationship with the Bank of England and was instrumental in the launch of the Special Liquidity Scheme the previous April under which the Bank had begun channelling funds into the banking system.

All three of them were destined for greater things: Baker would go on to become the Treasury's Finance and Commercial Director before leaving the department to chair Competition and Market Authority enquiries and serve as a director on UK Financial Investments, the body which looks after the taxpayer's shareholdings in private sector banks . Rathi was poached from the Treasury to become chief executive of the London Stock Exchange and then chief executive of the Financial Conduct Authority. Khan rose to become the Treasury's Director of Financial Stability.

Baker, Rathi and Khan each recruited a further half dozen officials to help with the heavy lifting. By the time the rescue was in full swing, the Tripartite team would number more than 60, not including the army of lawyers and investment bankers drafted in by the Treasury as the workload piled up.

Over in Threadneedle Street, the key players were Sir John Gieve, deputy governor for financial stability, and the Bank's two executive directors for banking and markets, Andrew Bailey and Paul Tucker respectively. They were supported by the Governor's economic assistant Iain de Weymarn, the head of systemic risk assessment Andy Haldane and Colin Miles, a specialist in financial stability. The FSA team was led by its chief executive Hector Sants.

What Darling had not fully appreciated, was that the Tripartite would be in competition with a rival team drawing up a rescue plan of its own. The captain of this team occupied the address next door and its players comprised an assortment of Number Ten officials, trusted friends of the Prime Minister and investment bankers brought together by his close political ally Vadera. Its star players were Peter Sands, the chief executive of Standard Chartered Bank, and a pair of senior bankers from Vadera's old firm UBS, Robin Budenberg and David Soanes. They were supported by a small retinue of Number Ten staff led by Fletcher, Brown's deputy chief of staff Gavin Kelly and James Bowler, who would go on to become the Prime Minister's Principal Private Secretary before moving into the Treasury when Brown lost office in 2010.

Whilst Darling's team took over office space on the third floor of the Treasury building, one floor above the Chancellor's office, Brown's shadow team were busily ensconcing themselves in 12 Downing Street – ordinarily the residence of the chief whip – where a 'war room' was set up with a horseshoe desk in the middle. It was here that the Prime Minister himself would spend much of his time over the next two weeks.

Although Brown's team was small in comparison to its counterpart in the Tripartite – reflecting the fact that the Number Ten machine is really quite tiny compared to a great department of state such as the Treasury – it was to cause friction in inverse proportion to its size as the clock ticked down.

There was one player, however, who managed to straddle both factions – Tom Scholar. Scholar knew Vadera well, both from his time in Number Ten and the eight years Vadera had spent as a member of the Treasury's Council of Economic Advisers after she left investment banking. Scholar would act as go-between, interlocutor and peace envoy between the two sides.

As Brown's plane flew home through the night sky, Vadera worked to turn his jottings into something more substantive and by the time they landed at Heathrow she had the outline of a plan but it would have to be finessed and then test driven.

Darling, meanwhile, also handed his team the task of sketching out a broad plan of action and timeline for rescuing the banks. He wanted some proposals on his desk by Monday morning. But first there was Bradford & Bingley to sort out. So that evening, Scholar was given one other job: could he invite the chief executives of every major bank in the country to the Treasury the following morning. The Chancellor had an idea he would like to run past them.

Day 2 – Saturday 27 September

Man the Lifeboat

Dawn broke warm and gloriously sunny on Saturday 27 September. The financial world might be going to hell in a handcart but at least the Indian summer had arrived. The last thing anyone wanted to do – politicians, bankers and civil servants alike – was spend the day closeted in stuffy, badly-ventilated rooms in Whitehall deciding the fate of a failed bank.

Gordon Brown had touched down at Heathrow on the red eye from Washington early in the morning. He returned to Downing Street and freshened up in the four-bedroomed flat in Number 11 that the Brown family were occupying. In keeping with the tradition established by Tony Blair when he was in office, the Prime Minister and Chancellor had swapped living accommodation. The flat on the third floor of Number 10 was much smaller but it was still comfortably big enough for Darling and his wife Maggie.

Brown then came down to meet Darling in the White room, one of Number Ten's three state drawing rooms and the place where Edward Heath had kept his grand piano. Many a world leader has sat in the White room, beneath the Turner masterpiece which adorns one its cream walls, discussing great matters of state. But rarely can a more important compact have been agreed than the one that was discussed that morning as

Prime Minister and Chancellor affirmed their resolve to recapitalise the British banking system.

It is remarkable, in hindsight, how tight the decision-making circle was within government. Brown and Darling did not need approval from Parliament for what they were planning to do (unlike Bush and Paulson who had to get TARP through Congress first). Nor did they need the agreement of the rest of Cabinet even though they were preparing to spend hundreds of billions of pounds of taxpayers' money. Apart from the Prime Minister and Chancellor, the only other ministers who were privy to the plan were Paul Myners, who was appointed City Minister mid-way through the rescue, and Yvette Cooper, who was then Economic Secretary to the Treasury and responsible for public spending. 'This is best handled by a small team because no-one else is going to bring anything more to the party,' Darling told Brown. 'No-one will complain.'

Brown and Darling then went on to discuss Bradford & Bingley. The investment bank Morgan Stanley was advising the Treasury on what to do with the bank, a mandate for which it was paid £1.5 million. It thought there was still an outside chance of launching a 'lifeboat' for Bradford & Bingley whereby a group of its high street counterparts would come together and collectively rescue the bank. As it happened, Morgan Stanley was also separately advising HBOS on its takeover by Lloyds although this workstream was being handled by a different team within the bank. Nevertheless, it did highlight how easily conflicts of interest could compromise the process as the bailout of the banking system gathered pace. All too often, ministers would find themselves receiving advice from one bank about what to do with another bank with which it was in direct competition.

Shortly after 11am the heads of RBS, Barclays, Lloyds, HBOS, HSBC and the Nationwide Building Society gathered at the Treasury in response to the invitation they had received the night before. Baker, Rathi and Khan were already at the Treasury preparing the ground for the discussions that Darling would shortly be holding with the assorted banking chiefs. Darling remembers most of them arriving in their country casuals.

John Varley, the chief executive of Barclays, lived at the time in Brook Green, west London but that morning he had been down at the family's weekend home in the Hampshire countryside midway between Andover and Newbury. The son of a solicitor, Varley had initially chosen to follow in the family tradition by joining a law firm after graduating from Oriel College Oxford with an MA in history. But in 1981 when he was still only 25, Varley's life changed: he married into the Pease family, one of the founding Quaker dynasties from which Barclays was formed, in the process becoming brother-in-law to the hedge fund billionaire Crispin Odey. Twelve months later Varley joined the bank and 22 years after that he became its CEO.

That Saturday morning, sat in the Treasury with his counterparts from the other big high street lenders, he was the nearest thing there was to banking royalty. He would also become one the few bankers whose judgment, perspective and calming influence Darling would come to value in the days ahead. Darling had in fact called Varley privately earlier that week to tell him that the Government was looking to rustle up a buyer for Bradford & Bingley and might Barclays be interested. The answer was 'No', Bradford & Bingley did not form any part of Barclays's strategic ambitions which were firmly focused on building up its international investment banking activities. Nevertheless, Varley climbed reluctantly into his car that Saturday to drive to central London.

Eric Daniels, Lloyds's American chief executive, arrived on foot at the Treasury after walking there from his flat in Belgravia. Daniels would need to be handled carefully. The Government was relying upon Lloyds to solve the problem that HBOS had become. Moreover, it was known that Daniels was adamant that Lloyds itself was not going to be pigeon-holed as a troubled bank in need of a state-sponsored rescue.

Born in Dillon, Montana to a German university professor and a Chinese mother but brought up in New Jersey, Daniels was an interesting mixture of cultures. After an education at Cornell University and the Massachusetts Institute of Technology, Daniels joined Citibank in 1975 and worked all over the world before arriving in the UK in 2001 as head of retail banking at Lloyds. He became CEO two years later in 2003. Somewhere along the way, he developed a penchant for wearing two-tone shirts with different coloured cuffs and collars which were to become his sartorial signature, much as a pair of red braces were Varley's. Daniels was quietly spoken and thoughtful but he also possessed a ruthless streak, as he had demonstrated shortly after taking over at Lloyds by clearing out a swathe of the bank's top management.

Goodwin was there too despite the fact that he had told Macpherson only the previous week that he didn't think his board would allow him to buy Bradford & Bingley even though he personally was attracted to the idea. The others in attendance were Graham Beale, the CEO of the Nationwide, and Dyfrig John, the chief executive of HSBC's UK operations. António Horta-Osório, the chief executive of Santander UK, was not there but his chairman Sir Terry Burns was present in another part of the building. Andy Hornby, chief executive of HBOS, had slipped quietly into the building too.

By this time, there was a permanent Press watch outside both the front entrance to the Treasury on Whitehall and the back entrance which could be accessed from St James's Park. Bankers arriving by car therefore entered the building from King Charles Street which runs between the Treasury and the Foreign Office and is closed to the public. From there they could be discretely dropped off in the circular courtyard or drum that separated the two halves of the Baroque-style building.

The lifeboat never got onto the slipway, let alone into the sea. One or two of the bankers were furious that they had been hauled in on a Saturday to the Treasury to be brow beaten in the first place, regarding it as another ham-fisted example of the Tripartite's dysfunctional approach to the banking crisis.

The bankers met in session and then went in to see Darling one by one. Dan Rosenfield, the Chancellor's Principal Private Secretary, was sat next to him. Rosenfield, a Manchester Grammar School boy, raconteur and active member of Britain's Jewish community, ran Darling's private office. In that capacity, he acted as gatekeeper, adviser, bag carrier, intermediary, summariser and conduit to Number Ten and other government departments. He was Darling's eyes and ears in Whitehall and he would have a ringside seat as the drama played out over the following fortnight. He was using a red pen to write down what each of the CEOs thought Bradford & Bingley might be worth and comparing it to the valuations that Morgan Stanley had placed on the bank.

The Chancellor quickly realised from the body language of the CEOs and the length of the conversations that the lifeboat was a non-starter. Even Beale of Nationwide, who had rescued a number of other failed building societies, did not have the appetite, and certainly not if he had just 48 hours to carry out due diligence on Bradford & Bingley. Darling then asked his Treasury officials to leave the room while he conferred with Morgan Stanley.

Darling emerged twenty minutes later and invited the Treasury team and the bank CEOs to re-assemble in the meeting room next to his office. Varley led off, acting as spokesman for the banks. 'It's not viable or feasible,' he said bluntly. With that, most of the bankers left the building. Varley noticed that Daniels was on foot so gave him a lift back to his flat in Belgravia as he left town on his way back home to Hampshire.

The lifeboat had failed but there was still another option. If the Government could split the bank in two and take responsibility for Bradford & Bingley's toxic assets, then it might find a buyer for the remaining healthy part of the business. As it turned out there were two potential buyers. While the abortive lifeboat plan was being explored on one floor of the Treasury, Macpherson was in conversation on another floor with the Santander chairman Burns. The Spanish-owned bank was keen to build its presence in the UK market and he told Macpherson that if the Government took on the bad assets then his bank would be prepared to buy Bradford & Bingley's branch network and deposit book.

The other interested party was HBOS. The bank was desperate for liquidity and therefore keen to get its hands on Bradford & Bingley's deposits. Moreover, there was no absolute guarantee that its merger with Lloyds would be successfully completed. Curiously, the Lloyds CEO Daniels, who had agreed only a week earlier to buy HBOS, was entirely unaware that the bank he was rescuing was negotiating to rescue another bank.

Day 3 – Sunday 28 September

Bradford & Bingley Breakup

On Sunday what had now become a two-way auction of the good bits of Bradford & Bingley moved from the Treasury in Whitehall to the offices of Slaughter & May, the Treasury's external legal advisers, in Bunhill Row on the edge of the City. It would run for the entirety of the day with the two bidders, Santander and HBOS, camped on separate floors of the building. Rathi remained at the Treasury, where Scholar was co-ordinating the overall sale process. Rathi's immediate boss, Clive Maxwell, was despatched to Bunhill Row with a friendly warning to look out for the water feature in the entrance lobby which had been known to catch out more than one unsuspecting visitor. It was his job to keep an eye on the auction and report back on progress. King had sent his Executive Director for Banking, Andrew Bailey, over to Bunhill Row to monitor the progress of the auction for the Bank.

Slaughter & May, a member of the 'Magic Circle' of London law firms, had begun acting for the Treasury when Northern Rock collapsed a year earlier, helping it first with the failed attempt to find a buyer for the bank and then advising the Government on the legislation it subsequently passed giving ministers the power to nationalise not just Northern Rock but any failing financial institution. By the time Bradford & Bingley came around, Slaughter & May's senior partner Charles Randell was working full-time for Darling, seven days a week, 16 hours a day. Discrete, deeply private and measured in virtually every utterance, Randell's style complemented that of the Chancellor perfectly.

The flow of work was non-stop, monitoring how various banks were performing and advising on takeover deals and share offers in the sector. Above all, it was vital to ensure that the detailed commercial law documentation that underpinned what were highly-complex transactions gelled with the public law statutory instruments being used by the Government.

Working alongside Randell were five other partners who made up the core of the Slaughter & May team. They were George Seligman and Sarah Paterson, both insolvency and restructuring specialists, and three corporate finance partners Nigel Boardman, Nilufer von Bismarck and Matthew Tobin. Boardman was a veteran of many City skirmishes and one of the most highly-rated lawyers in the City despite an odd penchant for composing emails in green italics. Below the five partners was a team of 30 more junior lawyers. Not a huge surprise then that Slaughter & May's bill came to £32.9 million when it eventually invoiced the Government.

Because there would be many different moving parts to the rescue, Randell quickly realised there would need to be clear lines of responsibility and division of labour so he stationed himself inside the Treasury where he acted as Darling's principal adviser and strategic thinker, trying to anticipate where the crisis would erupt next and make preparations for it. Seligman and Paterson meanwhile worked on the actual recapitalisation of the individual banks. Tobin was liaison officer with the Treasury and Boardman attended some of the ad hoc meetings convened by Shriti Vadera.

In order to be ready for the auction of Bradford & Bingley that would begin early that Sunday morning, Randell had spent the night on a sofa in a document storage room next to his office on the fifth floor of Bunhill Row. These came to be his sleeping quarters for a great many nights over that period. He was relieved not to be working from the Treasury's offices that weekend. The Treasury's legal department was in the basement beyond the reach of Wi-Fi and mobile signal, the building lacked proper meeting rooms and anyway the catering and accommodation facilities were far superior at Bunhill Row. And not only could they keep the two bidders apart from each other, they could keep them away from the prying eyes of the media.

Slaughter & May had put together a Memorandum of Sale for prospective buyers of Bradford & Bingley but Randell had already warned Darling it would be hard to find a purchaser for the whole business as a going concern. Valuing the liabilities – the bank's deposit book – was a relatively simple exercise. But identifying and valuing a pot of saleable assets would be a fiendishly difficult task.

By now the media has come to a similar conclusion. *The Sunday Times* splashed its front page that morning with a story headlined 'Treasury to nationalise B&B bank', written by its well-informed City Editor John Waples and Economics Editor, David Smith. The headline was only half right. The bad bit of the bank in the shape of its toxic assets was indeed being taken over by the taxpayer. But the good bit – the deposits and branch network – would be sold later that day to Santander. For a bank to be solvent, the assets it owns – its reserves and loans – have to be worth more than its liabilities, which mainly take the form of the cash deposited with it. The difference between these assets and liabilities is what is known as a bank's capital or net worth. Bradford & Bingley had negative net worth and was therefore, quite literally, bankrupt.

Darling decided, quite rightly, that it would be a risk too far to sell the business to HBOS. If the Lloyds/HBOS merger went ahead, then it would leave the combined group with an even bigger share of the UK's retail banking market. If the merger did not go ahead, then Bradford & Bingley would have to be rescued all over again when HBOS fell over.

The bids were in by 11am and it was obvious that Santander was the superior bidder. But, according to one observer, 'there were all sorts of shenanigans going on'. The problem centred around the role of the investment bank Morgan Stanley which was both acting as adviser to HBOS on its merger with Lloyds whilst at the same time advising the Government on the auction of Bradford & Bingley. To complicate matters further, the Prime Minister's Permanent Secretary, Jeremy Heywood, had worked for Morgan Stanley for several years before entering government.

Sensing a possible political controversy – and also being conscious that at some point the National Audit Office would wish to investigate the transaction – the Treasury called a temporary halt to the auction and the bidding was re-opened. The end result was the same but it meant that the identity of the winning bidder did not become clear until early that evening.

When agreement was finally reached with Santander to acquire the business, Maxwell conveyed the news to Scholar who in turn passed it on to Darling, who was now back at Number 11. Armed with the news, Darling went for a walk in the Rose Garden behind Downing Street to think through how he would announce it in the morning. He wanted to escape the claustrophobia of being shut away in the Treasury's offices for most of the weekend. Every inch of the half-acre of gardens behind Downing Street is covered by security cameras and Darling knew he was being watched every step of the way – making him feel a bit like the prisoner of Spandau. But short of walking around St James's park with a police escort, it was the only way he could get fresh air and anyway he felt at home in a garden.

Bailey too was supposed to call King at home to inform him of the winner before any public announcement was made. It was leaked before Bailey had a chance to make the call.

Not for the first time, the Governor ended up hearing the news first from the BBC's Robert Peston. King concluded that the decision could only have been leaked by Number Ten or Number 11. One more example of the disintegration in trust within the Tripartite.

After his garden walk, Darling went back inside Number 11 and called Rosenfield to check what was in the diary for the following day. The two of them mused over what an anti-climax Bradford & Bingley had been. A year earlier, Northern Rock had been a huge story and an enormous wake-up call for the financial markets and Government alike. Now, another medium sized bank had also become insolvent, but it had been sliced up and sold off in the space of 48 hours. In the scheme of things, it wasn't such a big deal – certainly not by international standards. That weekend, Fortis of Belgium was on the verge of collapse and in the US Paulson had unveiled his $700 billion TARP scheme. Rosenfield told Darling that by comparison sorting out Bradford & Bingley had seemed almost routine.

What came next would be anything but.

Day 4 – Monday 29 September

Meetings with the Bank Manager

If the Government was going to persuade the banks against their will that what they needed was a massive injection of taxpayers' money, then it would be important to get a feel for what the banks' opening negotiating position would be. What did they think was their biggest problem and what was their bottom line?

The man that Darling tasked with finding out the answers was Macpherson. He had already been up to Edinburgh the previous week for an audience with Goodwin at RBS's imposing glass, steel and sandstone headquarters out at Gogarburn, which Her Majesty the Queen no less had opened only three years earlier. Everyone knew that RBS was having difficulty raising long-term funding. Many banking counterparts were only prepared to lend to it overnight and, as Macpherson noted on his flight back down to London, a bank that no-one wants to lend to equals a bank that is in trouble.

Of all the visits he made to see bank CEOs, the most resistance he met was at Gogarburn. He came away with the impression that the only person who had a handle on what was going on within the bank was Goodwin himself. And all Goodwin was interested in talking about was the need for more liquidity. Macpherson was told that if the bank was forced to take government capital, it would amount to 'expropriation of shareholder interests on a scale not witnessed since the 1970s or even the 1940s'.

That Monday back in London, Macpherson began a discreet whistle-stop tour of the other major banks, accompanied by Tom Scholar, to see whether he might get a better reception than the one that had greeted him in Edinburgh. In the space of a day he and Scholar visited Lloyds, HSBC and Barclays. They travelled more in hope than expectation.

Whilst Macpherson and Scholar were visiting the boardrooms of Britain's banks, Vadera was conducting some research of her own. Armed with the outline of the plan put together on the flight back from Washington, she began to sound out a small circle of trusted confidantes in the City about Brown's idea of 'No Liquidity without Recapitalisation'. She spoke only to a handful of people in London, including Richard Gnodde, the co-chief executive of Goldman Sachs International, whom Blankfein in New York had recommended she go and see when they had met in New York the previous week. Because of the acute market sensitivity of what was being proposed, Vadera was very circumspect in her conversations. She was predominantly in listening mode. The only man she spoke to in any depth was Budenberg of UBS, whom she had known for many years and trusted implicitly. She swore Budenberg to secrecy, telling him he could not even speak about it to his close colleague Soanes.

Macpherson and Scholar's first port of call was the Gresham Street headquarters of Lloyds where they were met by chief executive Eric Daniels and chairman Sir Victor Blank. After being ushered up to the C-suite on the 8th floor, the four men quickly got down to business.

The bank's main focus, Blank told Macpherson, was shepherding the takeover of HBOS safely through the challenges it would face over the next few weeks. Lloyds was in a strong financial position but was concerned about how it was going to grow its UK market share. Although the Government had waived the usual takeover rules which would have meant an automatic investigation of the HBOS deal by the Competition Commission lasting at least six months and possibly a year, Lloyds still had to undertake due diligence on the business it was acquiring and obtain the approval of both sets of shareholders. Who knew what horrors due diligence might throw up? And then there was the other big concern: how to maintain market confidence in the deal. Even though Lloyds had partly insured itself by paying for HBOS with newly minted shares and not hard cash, the economics of the deal would quickly begin to unravel if the share prices of the two banks started to diverge in any significant way.

Daniels for his part conceded that to the extent they were able to open the bonnet and take a long hard look at HBOS, it clearly owned a high-risk portfolio of assets, especially on the property front. But the chance to buy the bank was a once-in-a-generation opportunity that would not come along again.

What mainly irked Blank and Daniels, however, was the mere fact of Macpherson's visit. To their mind, Lloyds was in fine financial fettle and did not deserve to be bracketed with the likes of RBS. It had some of the lowest costs of funding in the market and a very conservative funding model which did not rely on short-term lending from the commercial markets to fund long-term liabilities (the funding structure that led to the demise of Northern Rock). Nor had Lloyds engaged in the practice of 'warehousing' – creating special purpose vehicles and filling them with high-risk, long-term obligations in the shape of CDOs and the like which had to be funded in the short-term market.

The leadership of Lloyds had little time for the Tripartite, which they viewed as utterly dysfunctional. Mervyn King was overly pre-occupied with moral hazard whilst his American and European counterparts took a much more pragmatic and realistic approach to keeping the markets open and functioning. The draconian restrictions on liquidity and the terms on which it was available were unlike any imposed by other regulators whilst the Treasury seemed to have very little ability to manage the central bank, unlike finance ministries in other countries. As for the FSA, it was completely asleep at the wheel and had very little understanding of investment bank risk which meant its ability to set capital ratios for any given bank was deeply suspect. In other words, it was largely shooting in the dark and using a blunderbuss to boot.

After leaving Gresham Street, Macpherson and Scholar went on to the offices of HSBC where they had tea and biscuits with its urbane executive chairman Stephen Green. Although technically domiciled in the UK, the engine which drove HSBC was on the other side of the world in Asia. It was therefore in a quite separate category to its UK counterparts. Nevertheless, its support for the Government's overall strategy would be an important seal of approval.

Finally, they visited John Varley at Barclays' headquarters in Canary Wharf, a gleaming 32-story skyscraper with the bank's name and logo emblazoned in blue across the top of the building. Varley preferred to talk to them alone so his chairman Marcus Agius was absent from the meeting. It was a deliberate ploy on the part of the Barclays board which had already assigned specific roles to its leadership team for the duration of the crisis: in addition to Macpherson and Scholar, Varley would man mark Darling and Paul Myners at the Treasury, Sants at the FSA and King and Gieve at the Bank; Agius would take his opposite number Adair Turner at the FSA; Bob Diamond, chief of Barclays Capital, the bank's global investment banking arm, took Paul Tucker, the BoE's Executive Director, Markets.

Varley found Macpherson unreadable and a little enigmatic. But he quickly struck up a rapport with Scholar who, in the absence of Darling, would become his principal interlocutor with the Government. Scholar was unfailingly available, always on the end of the line when he was needed. Macpherson proved a little more elusive, at least for Varley.

The lightening tour of the banks did not tell Macpherson much he did not already know or suspect. All of the banks were fixated with the shortage of liquidity and all of them were reluctant to accept that more capital was needed (although Blank tended towards the pragmatic view that if this was what the Government was intent upon, the banks might as well accommodate it).

But what did become evident to him, and what he told Darling that evening as the two men met over a whisky to discuss the outcome of Macpherson's travels around the City, was that the banks faced a common problem which needed to be owned and addressed collectively. Even strong banks needed to be bound into the solution because if they weren't, each bank would be picked off one by one, starting with the weakest. It also became clear to Macpherson that a number of the banks, RBS in particular, had a very imperfect grasp of the quality of the assets in their portfolios. He had come away from his meeting with Goodwin with a growing concern that no-one inside the bank was aware of quite how worthless a number of its assets were. This prompted the question of whether the Treasury really ought to be devising some kind of US-style TARP scheme to relieve it of its bad assets.

Even at this stage there were some in the Treasury who were still arguing that the UK needed to address the issue of troubled assets by creating a good bank and a bad bank. Darling and Macpherson were less sure and events over the following ten days would harden their conviction that a UK version of TARP was not the answer. They had enough to deal with and couldn't solve everything at once so decided to put TARP to one side.

Macpherson said that, in addition to capital and liquidity, the Government's rescue plan would also need to address the problem of the credit markets which were close to seizing up because few banks were willing any longer to lend to another bank. In order to free up the system, the Government would also need to provide credit guarantees so that banks had the confidence to resume lending to one another and thus be able to lend to their customers.

Whilst Macpherson was interceding before breakfast, lunch and tea, to paraphrase Michael Heseltine, Darling and the rest of the Treasury team was announcing the nationalisation and onward sale of Bradford & Bingley. Because the Government was technically acquiring Bradford & Bingley before offloading the healthy bit of the bank to Santander, it was required to purchase the deposit book. First thing that day, therefore, Nikhil Rathi picked up the phone to Robert Stamen, the head of the Treasury's Debt Management Office. 'We're going to need some cash today,' he said. 'How much?' Stamen asked. 'About £20 billion,' Rathi replied, matter-of-factly. Stamen went into the market that morning and placed £20 billion worth of Treasury bills as if he was selling coffee beans.

Scholar and Baker meanwhile went to meet the Bradford & Bingley board at the bank's London offices in Lamb's Conduit Street. Baker had learnt a few lessons from the nationalisation of Northern Rock and had a brisk way of dealing with the boards of failed banks. 'We're going to keep the CEO and a couple of the non-executives but the rest of you don't need to stay,' she told them. They were in shock but they maintained their dignity and politely told Baker they would do whatever they could to help the Government.

The rescue of Bradford & Bingley ended up being such a text book exercise that Darling even had time that morning to hold a meeting with Rosenfield in his private office to discuss the contents of the annual Mais lecture – a speech that he was due to give the following week at the Cass Business School and named in honour of a former Lord Mayor of the City of London.

From there, he had been due to meet Brown in Downing Street at lunchtime for a wider stocktaking session. An awful lot of meetings were taking place in Number Ten. Quite often they did not have a specific agenda. Rather they were designed to reassure the Prime Minister that things were being done and progress was being made, contrary to what his own shadow team were telling him.

In the event, the meeting was rescheduled to 4pm because Darling was tied up doing a round of media interviews about Bradford & Bingley. As he left Brown to make his way back to the Treasury, Darling received a text from his daughter Anna who was travelling in South America. She was stuck on the border between Bolivia and Peru because Catriona, the girlfriend she was travelling with, had had her passport, money and credit cards stolen. The previous week Anna had telephoned her father to describe a gunfight she was watching from the window of the hostel she was staying in. It was a timely reminder to Darling that he might be engulfed in the biggest banking crisis in a generation, but family still came first

It was also not the only unwelcome news that the Chancellor received from overseas that day. In Europe, Fortis bank had to be rescued with the help of an €11 billion bailout from the Dutch, Belgian and Luxembourg governments whilst the German government stepped in to keep Hypo Real Estate afloat. Iceland's banking system was going into freefall too, forcing the government in Reykjavik to bail out Glitnir, one of the country's big three banks. It was relevant to the UK because Glitnir's largest shareholder Stodi was due to take large shareholdings in Baugur, the owner of the House of Fraser chain of department stores and the toy store Hamleys. It was of even greater significance because it indicated that the two other big Icelandic banks, Kaupthing and Landsbanki, both of which had major operations in the UK, were also teetering. Between them, they owned a host of UK assets ranging from retail parks and football clubs to property developments. The savings of thousands of UK investors, including several large charities and local councils, were also deposited with the two banks.

Worse news was to come from the US, however. Wachovia, America's fourth biggest retail bank, fell over (it was eventually rescued by Wells Fargo) while Congress voted to reject TARP. The decision prompted a global stock market crash. On Wall Street, the S&P500 ended the day 8.5 per cent lower while the Dow Jones closed 7 per cent down, wiping some $1 trillion off the value of US shares. In London, the FTSE100 closed 5.3 per cent down, led by RBS, Lloyds and HBOS, all of which suffered double digit percentage falls in their share price.

Day 5 – Tuesday 30 September

The Irish Bombshell

The news from Dublin was bad. In fact it could not have been much worse. Overnight Ireland had unilaterally decided to guarantee all deposits in every Irish bank, bar one. The decision had been taken in the small hours of the morning by the Taoiseach Brian Cowen without consulting any other member of the European Union including the UK, Ireland's biggest and closest trading partner.

The story had come too late to make any of that morning's newspapers, the front pages of which were dominated by accounts of 'Meltdown Monday' and how US stocks had suffered their worst day since the Great Crash of 1987. Inside, *The FT* carried a full-page analysis of the collapse of Bradford & Bingley accompanied by a rueful picture of Darling announcing the part-nationalisation of the building society turned bank.

Ireland's decision had the effect of darkening his mood further. He cancelled a planned breakfast meeting with Mervyn King and got straight on the telephone to his opposite number in Dublin, the Irish finance minister Brian Lenihan, asking what on earth was going on. But not before Jeremy Heywood in Number Ten had called Darling's private office demanding a similar explanation, only to be told that no-one in the Treasury, FSA or Bank of England knew either because they had been blindsided too.

Darling and Lenihan had what would be described in diplomatic cables as a frank exchange. Although it was not written down in any formal fashion, the two men had had an understanding that they would keep each other informed of what actions they were planning to support their banks.

Lenihan was profusely apologetic, saying that the decision had only been taken at 2am in the morning amid some chaos and confusion in Dublin itself. To the British, it was a classic example of how Ireland was apt to stitch policy together on the hoof by relying on the close, almost incestuous, relationships between its government, central bank and lending banks. It was not even clear that the civil servants in Lenihan's department would have been inside the tent and aware of what was being planned so Macpherson did not bother putting a call into his opposite number in the Irish finance ministry Kevin Cardiff.

The call with Lenihan ended on a slightly lighter note. The two men got on well together and liked each other. Darling said: 'Brian, what happens when people work out that the sum of deposits in Irish banks is somewhat greater than all the money you've got?' Lenihan laughed and said he hoped they didn't find that out too soon.

Darling had put his finger on the fatal flaw in the scheme. Ireland could never have delivered on its promise had that blanket guarantee ever been called upon because the sums involved would have exceeded the nation's entire economic output many times over. In fact, what the move had inadvertently done was to shift the onus from the solvency of Ireland's banks to the solvency of the state. As would become painfully apparent later, the country itself was all but bankrupt.

But at the time that did not matter. What mattered was the effect Ireland's decision would have on the rest of Europe. In London – but also in Paris and Berlin and The Hague – the fear was that it would prompt a run on their own banks as savers withdrew their money and deposited it with Irish banks, ignoring the certain reality that the Irish guarantee was not worth the parliamentary paper it was written on. The fragile mood across Europe was not helped by an erroneous news report in the middle of the morning that Angela Merkel had agreed a similar guarantee for Germany's banks. Darling spent the next hour on the phone to Christine Lagarde, the French Finance Minister, and Wouter Boss, the Dutch Finance Minister, to discuss the implications of the Irish announcement. He tried, in vain, to reach his German counterpart, Peer Steinbrueck, to find out what was going on in Berlin. Eventually he had to ask the Foreign Secretary David Miliband to call his opposite number in Germany to establish the position of the Merkel government.

For the UK, there was a further, more specific concern: the Irish guarantee did not extend to Ulster Bank, which was part of RBS, and the last thing Darling needed was a further headache for RBS. His next phone call was therefore to Neelie Kroes, the EU Competition Commissioner, to flag up the UK's concern that Ireland was discriminating against Ulster Bank and thus acting unlawfully. At the same time as Darling was on the line to Kroes, Brown was speaking to the Taoiseach in Dublin to ask that Ireland extend the deposits guarantee to subsidiaries of foreign-owned banks.

Brown then summoned Vadera to ask whether in her opinion the UK bank recapitalisation plan could be brought forward. Vadera told the Prime Minister she had 'an outline in her head' but still needed to road test it with a handful of bankers whose judgement and views she trusted – Robin Budenberg and David Soanes at UBS and Peter Sands, the chief executive of Standard Chartered. She decided to convene a private meeting of the group. Scholar got wind of it and asked to attend too.

Scholar knew Vadera well from her days as a member of the Treasury's Council of Economic Advisers and the pair of them were ideally placed to act as a bridge between the Treasury and Number Ten. The relationship between Chancellor and Prime Minister is often tricky. In the case of Darling and Brown it was especially so for the simple reason that Brown was not only adjusting to being Prime Minister, he was also adjusting to no longer being Chancellor of the Exchequer.

The two men were also chalk and cheese in terms of style and approach. Brown was the big picture politician who wanted to get things done at a stroke. Darling was the classically cautious Edinburgh lawyer who wanted to get things right and was much more methodical in his thought processes. Brown's approach to problem-solving was lateral: throw it open to as many different, random people as possible and then wait, as if through some strange Darwinian process, for the correct answer to filter back. Darling's style was deductive, sequential, pragmatic and far better suited, so most in the Treasury thought, to the challenge the country's financial system faced. The rescue had to be got right institutionally, financially and also legally. If it went wrong, the Government would pay a very high price.

Darling was not happy with Vadera's involvement. As he would later observe: 'Like many investment bankers I have met, she appears to believe that unless there is blood on the carpet, preferably that of her own colleagues, then she has not done her job.' However, Scholar and Macpherson persuaded him that despite 'the high transactional cost' of working with Vadera, it was something the Treasury should embrace in its own self-interest. First, it would give Darling line of sight on the parallel rescue plan being devised by Brown's circle of advisers. Second, Brown listened to her more than any other minister. If Brown was going to sign off on the Treasury's plan, Darling needed the PM's approval and Vadera was the one person capable of delivering that. In any event, Brown would ultimately need to own the bailout of the banking system owing to the sheer scale of the intervention being planned and because he was the only one who could sell it to the rest of the world.

That day Darling's mind was not on who would claim authorship of the bank rescue. His objective was simply to get through the day without having to guarantee all deposits in all British banks. At the time, the Financial Services Compensation Scheme guaranteed savings up to maximum of £35,000 per investor.

There were two other nagging worries on his mind that day. One was HBOS. The other was the deteriorating condition of the Icelandic banks. Darling was receiving alarming updates from the FSA about what was happening inside their UK subsidiaries. Kaupthing's internet bank Edge had 150,000 UK savers who between them had deposited £3 billion with the bank. Landsbanki's online UK bank Icesave had 300,000 customers who had invested a total of £4.5 billion. Iceland had given undertakings that sufficient funds would be put into Landsbanki to protect its UK depositors. But this had not happened. Moreover, Kaupthing had quietly taken some £600 million of depositors' money out of its UK branches and repatriated the money back to Iceland. If the haemorrhaging of cash continued then Darling would have to either designate them as terrorist organisations and confiscate their UK assets or use the powers the Government had given itself at the time of Northern Rock's nationalisation to transfer their UK operation to another bank.

The HBOS problem concerned its plummeting share price. The markets were recovering some of the ground lost in the previous day's sell-off and Lloyds shares had risen by 4 per cent. HBOS shares, on the other hand, were still in freefall, dropping a further 14 per cent when, in theory, they should have been in lockstep with the Lloyds share price. It suggested the markets were having serious doubts about whether the Lloyds/HBOS merger would actually happen.

Over in Downing Street, Brown had also been alerted to what was happening to HBOS shares. After the market closed, he was obliged to issue a statement re-iterating the Government's support for the merger with Lloyds and his confidence that the deal would complete successfully.

Remarkable as it was at this time of financial crisis, Darling still had to attend to other commitments in his diary. So, having spent the morning dealing with Ireland and Iceland, he had to switch his attention back to more prosaic duties. First up was a meeting with Mike Clasper, the chairman of Her Majesty's Revenue and Customs. It was not a priority and it was the sort of meeting Darling could have done without. But Clasper was not a man to be denied. He had spent most of his career in the private sector in senior business roles, most recently as chief executive of the airports operator BAA, and was used to getting his way in a most un-Whitehall style, and so Darling reluctantly took the meeting.

Clasper appeased, Darling returned to rather more pressing matters. Not only did the unfolding financial crisis leave him facing trial by media, there were also any number of political mantraps to navigate. The Conservatives were up in Birmingham holding their annual party conference. David Cameron was doing plenty of banker bashing and the shadow Chancellor George Osborne was carefully trying to position himself as the man with a plan of his own to fix the banking system.

Darling wanted to keep them sufficiently on board so that when his rescue was unveiled it was not shot down by the Opposition, but equally he wanted to keep most of his powder dry. So he spent the rest of that afternoon giving separate briefings on the Government's broad approach to banking reform to his counterparts in the other three main parties – Osborne, the Liberal Democrat's Treasury spokesman Vince Cable and Stuart Hosie of the Scottish National Party. He also authorised Treasury officials to assist Osborne with their thinking about bank reform.

His cross-party duties done, Darling then sat down to prepare for a much more important encounter that would take place a couple of hours later: the first in a series of set-piece meetings with the heads of all the major UK banks to explain what the Government was proposing to do. King and Turner had arrived early to brief the Chancellor on their latest soundings from the financial sector and agree on their tactics for managing the meeting.

By then a lot of thinking had gone into what Darling was going to say – that a system-wide solution was needed and that greater liquidity and credit guarantees would be part of the package alongside capital. This would be the first time that the Government's broad thinking had been shared with the banks collectively. But it was also designed to get the banks' collective view on what they saw as the problem and the solution.

As the bankers arrived they were guided into the Treasury via the side entrance on King Charles Street to avoid the waiting photographers and then escorted one by one to the second floor where they were crammed into a small and overly warm side room to await the Chancellor. At 6pm the bankers were ushered into Darling's office.

They took their seats on one side of the large oblong table. Goodwin sat in the middle in one of the two high-backed chairs with arms. He was flanked on either side by Varley of Barclays and Daniels of Lloyds. Varley had taken his jacket off to reveal his trademark red braces. Daniels was wearing his own trademark two-tone blue pinstriped shirt with white collar and cuffs. Further along the table sat Horta-Osório of Santander, Sands of Standard Chartered, Beale of the Nationwide and Dyfrig John of HSBC. Neither this meeting nor any subsequent ones were attended by HSBC's chairman Stephen Green or its group chief executive Michael Geoghegan. HSBC wanted to make it crystal clear that as far as this crisis was concerned, it was one that affected only its UK subsidiary and not the whole group.

Opposite Goodwin sat Darling in a similar high-backed chair, flanked by King, Turner, Macpherson, Geoffrey Spence, one of the Chancellor's special advisers, and his PPS Rosenfield. Directly behind Goodwin on the wall of the office hung a huge canvas by the Scottish artist John Bellany entitled 'Death's Head'. The painting would become an unhappy portent of corporate demise – none of the bankers who would sit beneath it survived in their jobs.

Darling opened the meeting by telling the banks that the Tripartite was working 'flat out' on a plan which had three broad elements but that he did not want to announce it prematurely for fear that it would cause confusion and risk falling apart, as appeared to be happening with TARP in the US. The Irish announcement that morning had clearly spooked the banks so Darling explained that the UK had not had any advance warning but this only seemed to unnerve them more, reinforcing their suspicion that governments around Europe were not acting in unison.

Goodwin was in belligerent mood. He wanted the Tripartite's tanks off his lawn but he also wanted massive liquidity support from the Government. He was the first to respond to Darling's opening remarks and he began by asking: 'Why don't you do what the Irish have done?' The look on Darling's face was answer enough. Because it would cost £5 trillion and would bankrupt the country. If Goodwin's fate was not already decided, it was settled then. The sense of entitlement, the expectation that the taxpayer would write a blank cheque to keep the banks afloat, was breathtaking in its audacity.

As the discussion progressed, it became clear that none of the bankers present had any appetite for raising new capital. They mostly argued that liquidity was the key although Varley made the point that loan guarantees were also important to unfreeze the credit markets and enable the banks to lend to one another and to their customers. Daniels made the most eloquent case. The Government believed that forcing the banks to hold more capital would make them bullet proof and restore confidence in the market allowing them to fund themselves properly. But that confused capital and liquidity. When markets were in a panic, no amount of capital was going to solve the liquidity crisis, he argued. How much capital a bank needed was determined by how much risk it took on and, in Lloyds case, the business model was conservative and risk averse. What the banks required was funding and on better terms than the Bank of England's Special Liquidity Scheme which was mandatory in all but name and expensive to access.

Varley was also critical of the Bank's delay in introducing the Special Liquidity Scheme and pointed out that overcapitalised banks could be as problematic as undercapitalised ones and did not make sense economically. Their arguments fell on deaf ears although Darling did gain the impression that Varley took a more realistic approach to what the banks were being asked to agree to than anyone else present. It also helped that Varley was the elder statesman amongst those present and the one banker who seemed able to act as a bridge between the truculence of Goodwin and the determination of the Tripartite. At one point Darling turned to Macpherson and commented: 'He seems to be one of the comparatively few bankers who can see the bigger picture.'

Horta-Osório kept largely quiet – he was there more as an observer than participant – while John, Sands and Beale seemed to take the view that much of what was discussed had only limited application to their banks.

From Darling's point of view, it had not been a particularly satisfactory end to the day. The banks were not united in what they did want but they were all agreed on the one thing they didn't need. As the bankers trooped out, he consoled himself with one thing: at least they had been as good as their word and news of the meeting had not leaked. Fifteen minutes later, the Treasury's Press Secretary Steve Field began to receive the first telephone calls from the BBC and *Financial Times* asking how the meeting had gone and what had been discussed.

Day 6 – Wednesday 1 October

Breakfast at Number Ten

The headlines did not make especially encouraging reading on the morning of Wednesday 1 October. Martin Wolf, *The Financial Times'* esteemed financial commentator, wrote a bleak piece entitled 'We are watching the disintegration of the financial system'. In *The Times* meanwhile the equally revered Anatole Kaletsky was writing that 'punishing greedy bankers does not amount to a rescue plan'. *The Guardian* and *Times* both splashed on the Lloyds/HBOS deal being in jeopardy and Brown's struggle to shore up the rescue of the bank.

Darling and his team were not overly worried by negative press coverage. Politicians complaining about the media were a bit like farmers grumbling over the weather. By this time, they had stopped reading the papers anyway and were focused intensely on where the next timebomb would detonate and trying to defuse it. Events were unfolding at such pace that there was no point in attempting to manage the media. Instead, the watchwords had become: assess the problem; find a solution; explain the action.

By the end of the day it seemed that Brown's action had indeed produced a solution to the problem of the HBOS share price. Buoyed by the Prime Minister's assurance that the Lloyds deal was on course, HBOS shares rose by a record amount to close 21 per cent higher by the end of trading in London. Ship steadied. What neither the media nor the markets were aware of, however, was that Brown and Darling had also authorised the Bank of England to begin providing Emergency Liquidity Assistance to HBOS that afternoon in conditions of utmost secrecy. It would last six weeks and peak at £25.4 billion on 13 November.

Had traders on the London stock market been aware of that piece of news, then sentiment towards the Lloyds takeover of HBOS would almost certainly have been less favourable. The bank was slipping into the sea more quickly than anyone could imagine, kept afloat only by the enormous sums being injected into the business by the Bank of England unbeknown to the outside world.

This secret emergency liquidity differed in some important respects from the Special Liquidity Scheme that had been launched publicly six months earlier and was available to all banks. The Special Liquidity Scheme involved the banks exchanging high-quality mortgage-backed securities for Treasury bills which could then be used as collateral to obtain cash. In order to obtain Emergency Liquidity Assistance, HBOS needed only to post low-quality unsecuritised mortgage and loan assets as collateral. But it did also need to pay a two per cent fee.

Over the next six weeks, HBOS would swap assets with a book value of £66.1 billion – far in excess of the £25.4 billion it received in return. The assets took the form of four pools of mortgages that were in the process of being securitised. The reason for the discrepancy in value was that the HBOS assets would almost certainly not fetch book value. The Government was covering itself in the likely event that HBOS collapsed and it had to realise the value of the assets it had taken in. Alternately, if the taxpayer became a major shareholder in HBOS, then the Emergency Liquidity Assistance effectively became money that the Government was lending to itself.

This Emergency Liquidity Assistance was the same that the Bank had advanced to Northern Rock a year earlier. Northern Rock made the fatal miscalculation that if the outside world was aware of the secret funding it was receiving from the Bank of England, it would reassure the markets that the 'lender of last resort' was standing behind the bank and therefore it was safe. It had the direct opposite effect. It told the world that the bank was going bust so get your money out before it is too late.

Darling and King had yet another breakfast meeting with Brown at Number Ten, not so much to discuss any of the details surrounding the plan but to keep the Prime Minister abreast of the general progress and reassure him that plenty of activity was taking place. The meeting was also attended by the Cabinet Secretary Gus O'Donnell, known colloquially within the Civil Service as GOD.

King dryly noted in his diary: 'Breakfast at Number Ten, it's beginning to be a regular event'. By now he largely restricted his engagement to small meetings with Brown and Darling and their most senior advisers. It was also now plain to the Governor that Number 10 was losing confidence in the ability of Number 11 to make the crisis go away. His had increasingly come to that view during his regular monthly sessions with Brown that had begun in the summer and now he was convinced of it. Darling's preferred modus operandi, or so it appeared to King, was to get the banks in the room, get everyone to agree on what should be done and proceed from there. But the banks would never willingly go down this route because they did not believe the underlying problem was a lack of capital in the banking system.

King felt Brown was instinctively more inclined to share the Governor's view. He wanted the PM to get the big six banks in the room and tell them: 'Look, the Bank of England has advised me you need this many billion pounds of capital in aggregate between you. I want you to sort out between you how much each bank is going to take. None of you can take nothing because everyone has to take part. I'll come back in two hours. Let me know what you've decided. If you can't agree, we'll decide for you.'

Back at the Treasury, Mark Bowman, the department's Budget Director, was waiting patiently for a meeting with Darling to discuss preparations for the Autumn Statement or Pre-Budget Report as it had become known. He had been in to see Rosenfield, the gatekeeper of Darling's diary, pleading for an audience. Along with the Budget itself, this is ordinarily one of the two most important set piece events in the Treasury's calendar. The meeting did not take place. Rosenfield's diary entry read: 'Postponed until further notice'.

Instead Darling took a meeting with Rathi and a couple of other Treasury officials. One of them had come into the office that day wearing a dark pink shirt with white collars and cuffs. 'Why are you dressed like Daniels?', the Chancellor demanded to know. 'Are you trying to tell me something?.' It was mainly said in jest but at the same time it was an indication of how sensitised Darling had become to the bank CEOs he was meeting almost daily. There were two items on the agenda: one was an analysis of how the Lloyds/HBOS merger would affect the overall recapitalisation plan; the other was a further discussion about the impact on UK banks of Ireland's bank deposit guarantee.

As lunchtime approached, Darling just had time to squeeze in a call with Christine Lagarde in Paris. Lagarde had become one of Darling's closest allies on the Continent as the UK strove to hold Europe's governments together and pursue a common approach to their banks. 'In Christine we trust' became the mantra in Darling's private office. They exchanged perspectives on how the Irish bank guarantee was playing out in their respective countries. Lagarde asked Darling how worried he was about the effect on RBS. Darling said it was not exactly helpful but, being the cautious type, he didn't want to be drawn further. After all, information is power and some of France's banks had a vested interest in seeing RBS in trouble. Entente cordiale was all well and good, but there were limits.

Late in the afternoon Darling had an abrupt change of pace and subject: his driver took him across the river to Lambeth Palace where he spent an hour with the Archbishop of Canterbury, Rowan Williams, discussing how best to protect the vulnerable in society. The vulnerable, in this context, did not include the country's banks. Darling was glad of the brief respite it offered from the financial crisis. It was important to him to maintain a balance in his political life and that meant doing the normal business as well as the difficult stuff.

As it happened, the approach of RBS and its chief executive towards the vulnerable in society was one of the small but significant factors that hardened attitudes against the bank in government and specifically in Downing Street. Brown had first encountered Fred Goodwin during the privatisation of Rosyth dockyard, which was next door to his Dunfermline East constituency and one of the biggest employers in the area. Even then he never much liked the cut of this overly-confident businessman. Goodwin was one of the accountants from Touche Ross working on the sale of Rosyth. When Brown became Chancellor, he appointed the philanthropic venture capitalist Sir Ronald Cohen to head up a Commission on Unclaimed Assets. The country's banks and insurance companies had £2 billion of 'orphan assets' on their books – money belonging to customers who had died or had never bothered to claim it. Sir Ronald's job was to persuade the banks to hand over the cash so it could be used to fund community projects, youth centres, literacy programmes and the like. Every bank was prepared, if not overjoyed, to back the scheme. Brown went to see Goodwin in his Edinburgh office and discovered that RBS was the odd man out.

Whilst Darling was on ecclesiastic duties, Vadera was pre-occupied with the more secular. She knew plenty about raising new capital and lubricating the financial system with liquidity, but less about the arcane business of credit guarantees – how to price them, what maturity dates to set and the like. And so she made contact with Peter Sands at Standard Chartered, and suggested they meet for a small informal drinks party that night. Vadera could not hold the event inside the Cabinet Office so she asked if Sands could host it at Standard Chartered's headquarters in Basinghall Avenue, a short walk north from the Bank of England. Sands readily agreed. Vadera arrived at his offices just before 7 pm. She brought with her Scholar, Budenberg and Soanes. Sands was accompanied by his finance director Richard Meddings. This is who Vadera really needed to speak to along with the bank's head of treasury because they were the people with intimate knowledge of how the inter-bank lending market worked. There was no danger of Standard Chartered being enrolled into the Government's recapitalisation scheme itself so there was no conflict of interest. As the drinks party was winding up, Sands agreed that they would write up their portion of the plan overnight and send it across to Vadera.

The day ended with some better news. Wall Street had stabilised after the Senate approved TARP, prompting Geithner at the New York Fed to recite Churchill's famous adage that 'the Americans always do the right thing after trying everything else'. In London there was also relief that TARP had been passed. But it was combined with a conviction that the UK had been correct in pursuing a different remedy for its banking crisis. It had been a huge struggle to get TARP through the Hill and in doing so the Bush administration had used up much of its political capital. There was no such thing as Troubled Assets. There were only Troubled Banks. What the UK needed was a solution to that problem which was simple, low in execution risk and politically acceptable.

Day 7 – Thursday 2 October

Whose Plan is it Anyway?

The 'outline in her head' of how to resolve the banking crisis that Vadera had spoken about to Brown on Tuesday had become words on a page. When she arrived at her office, an email was waiting for her from Sands setting out Standard Chartered's blueprint for how the Government could construct a credit guarantee scheme to encourage the banks to lend to one another. She cut and pasted their contribution into the document she had already created containing the two other elements of the plan – liquidity and recapitalisation – and forwarded it under plain cover to Scholar who in turn submitted it to Darling without explaining where it had come from. Darling approved the plan and that night Vadera presented it to Brown. It was a short note setting out her three-pronged strategy: recapitalisation of the banks; access to enhanced liquidity and government credit guarantees to underpin bank lending. It would be implemented in two stages: first a public announcement of the overarching plan inviting the banking sector to participate; second, bank by bank agreement on the amount of taxpayer's capital they would have to accept.

Brown remarked that it was very similar to the plan that was being worked on by the Tripartite under the supervision of Darling and Macpherson although it appeared to go into greater detail. It also bore a passing resemblance to the menu of options that had been printed in that morning's *Financial Times* in a lengthy analysis by its economics editor Chris Giles. *The FT* article ranked the choices available to the Chancellor on a sliding scale from very likely to not a chance. It concluded that the probable outcome would be an extension of the Special Liquidity Programme, recapitalisation of the banks and the creation of a government-owned 'bad bank'. The prospect of the UK introducing its own version of TARP was deemed unlikely while the UK would only go down the road of an Irish-style guarantee of all bank deposits 'if things get very bad'.

Brown put a call into Darling and King to tell them he had received Vadera's note and that they should convene at Number Ten that evening to discuss it. He acknowledged that it was not too dissimilar to the plan that had been developed within the Treasury but he contended that it was more 'practically worked through' as far as the arrangements for injecting capital into the banks were concerned.

King was sat in his offices in Threadneedle Street. The Bank's headquarters were completed in 1828 to a design by the architect Sir John Soane and substantially remodelled in the 1930s but they had lost none of their opulence. In addition to his dining room and working office, the Governor also enjoyed the use of a sitting room decorated with gold brocade and enjoying a view into the courtyard below which is lined with mulberry trees and reserved for the Governor's use only.

He was writing a terse one-page memo which ended with a three-word exhortation: 'Just do it.' After receiving the call from Brown, he tore up the memo. Perhaps that evening's meeting would be the moment when decisive action was taken at last.

Darling was not entirely clear what the point of the meeting was, other than to reassure the PM that activity was taking place. Nevertheless, he agreed to get together that evening with Brown and King.

The Prime Minister then spent the rest of the day planning the Cabinet reshuffle that he would announce the following day.

Darling, meanwhile, was juggling several other balls. At lunchtime, he called Lagarde again – by this time they were talking on an almost daily basis. He also got through to the

German finance minister Peer Steinbrueck in the afternoon to compare notes. And he squeezed in that Pre-Budget Report meeting after all with his Budget Director Mark Bowman.

The Chancellor had also been due to speak to Iceland's Prime Minister, Geir Haarde. It was not going to be a friendly or easy call and it had already been postponed from earlier in the week. Darling was not quite going to read the riot act. But he was intending to put on record his strong objections to the way funds were being removed from UK subsidiaries of Icelandic banks and repatriated back to Reykjavik. He would explain how the Government planned to stop this. In the event, the call was delayed once again until the following day.

Stock markets were not having a good day on either side of the Atlantic though Lloyds and HBOS shares were continuing to rally for a second consecutive day. But briefly, at least, the media's attention had switched away from the financial crisis and onto a juicier story: the London Mayor Boris Johnson had sacked Sir Ian Blair as Commissioner of the Metropolitan Police after losing confidence in him. Blair's position had been under threat ever since the accidental shooting in 2005 of the Brazilian electrician Jean Charles de Menezes in a botched police anti-terrorism operation. But Johnson had always been lukewarm in his support for the Commissioner and in the run-up to his ousting a series of hostile stories had appeared about Blair in what was seen as a concerted Tory plot to undermine him.

At 7.20pm Darling headed over to Number Ten for the meeting with Brown. He brought Macpherson and Scholar with him. Rosenfield was taking a note of the meeting. King also made his way over from the Bank of England. Brown was accompanied by Vadera and Heywood. By that time, Brown and Darling were broadly in agreement about what the broad shape of the bank rescue would look like. But King was still lobbying for the recapitalisation of the banks to be achieved through a compulsory scheme. It should cover the UK's top eight banks and the Government should be prepared to inject a minimum of £40 billion and more if necessary, he told Brown.

The meeting then went on to discuss the note that Vadera had drawn up, something that clearly irked the Treasury team since they regarded it largely as a re-tread of the work they had already done.

Brown made the case for announcing the bank rescue the following Monday. But Darling was cautious about doing anything that had not been agreed with the banks. Macpherson was still engaged in his shuttle diplomacy around the square mile attempting to get the bank CEOs onside. As the meeting wore on, the atmosphere became increasingly strained. It was the first time that King had seen Darling get genuinely ratty with Brown in the presence of others.

At one point, Macpherson reached into his bag and took out an apple. He then proceeded in his languid old Etonian style to peel it very slowly with the Swiss army penknife he carried with him. The apple-peeling exercise transfixed everyone in the room for a time and that irritated the Prime Minister, even though he knew Macpherson well and had worked with him for a number of years. Darling concluded that Macpherson's actions were not entirely innocent and allowed himself a smile. Macpherson put it down to cathartic distraction.

King left Downing Street and as he was driven back to Threadneedle Street he wrote in his diary: 'Meeting ended as ever without any decision being made. What is lacking is political courage.'

Day 8 – Friday 3 October

The Risky Reshuffle

The Prince of Darkness returns. The Svengali who had engineered three successive Labour election victories was back in Cabinet.

The appointment of Peter Mandelson as Business Secretary was the centrepiece of Gordon Brown's reshuffle. Little did Brown know then, but Mandelson's re-entry into British politics would be mired in controversy before he had even set foot properly inside the Department for Business's Victoria Street headquarters.

However, it was another, less-well reported junior ministerial appointment two days day later that was to prove more significant for the bailout of the UK financial system. Paul Myners, star fund manager and City grandee, would be made Financial Services Secretary to the Treasury – or City Minister for short. Myners came with a reputation as one of the Square Mile's best-known and most feared bruisers. As chairman of Marks & Spencer he had seen off a hostile bid from the equally pugnacious retail entrepreneur Philip Green, no mean feat in itself.

The task of forcing the bankers into line would require plenty of hand-to-hand combat and Myners was the perfect man for the job. And he knew the bankers' language. Myners had had a tough start in life after being adopted at an early age by a Cornish butcher-cum-fisherman and his hairdresser wife and brought up in Truro. After training as a teacher and then trying his hand at financial journalism, he entered the City as a junior portfolio manager, rising to become chief executive of the respected fund management group Gartmore. From there he went on to become chairman of the Guardian Media Group and the property giant Land Securities. So he was a City grandee but also one with what a Labour party insider described to *The Independent* as 'a genuine instinct for social justice' – just what the circumstances demanded.

As neither Mandelson nor Myners were MPs, it was necessary to elevate them to the House of Lords in order that they could take up their ministerial appointments. Vadera was also made a junior minister in the Cabinet Office that weekend. It meant two things: first, no need any longer for subterfuge over her role; second, instant access to the Prime Minister through the ground floor corridor connecting numbers 10, 11 and 12 Downing Street.

Vadera had already asked Myners over to her office in the Business Department on the Friday to brief him ahead of the formal announcement of his appointment. His face went pale as she explained that what the Government was proposing would entail an awful lot of legislation being passed by the Lords and the Prime Minister was looking for someone to shepherd it through. Brown did not want Vadera tied up with those duties – and nor did she – so it would be necessary for the Treasury to have a minister in the second chamber. Myners was the perfect candidate. Moreover, his other skills were exactly what the Government would need when the blood shedding began.

The reshuffle quickly replaced the sacking of Sir Ian Blair as the main political story of the week. Although that morning's front pages were full of headlines about his departure – 'Boris knifes police chief' as *The Independent* put it – there was a more intriguing little story on the inside pages of *The Sun*. George Pascoe-Watson, the paper's respected and well-informed political editor and as it happened another Edinburgh alumni, had filed a piece the day before speculating on the Cabinet reshuffle and stating that Darling's position as Chancellor was 'safe... for now'.

It would have been extraordinary had the Prime Minister replaced his Chancellor at the height of the biggest financial crisis the country had witnessed in a generation. But the mere fact that the story had appeared reflected the animus towards Darling among some in the Brown entourage. There were plenty of courtiers who would not have been unhappy to see the back of him – Brown's special adviser Damian McBride, for one. Ed Balls, Brown's ex-special adviser who had been promoted to Secretary of State for Children, Schools and Families when he became Prime Minister, for another. And then there was Brown's former press spokesman Charlie 'Load of Bollocks' Whelan who was still freelancing for his old boss. Whelan was so-called because when he wanted to confirm something whilst appearing simultaneously to deny it, he would describe the story as 'a load of bollocks'. If a story was 100 per cent copper-bottomed, then it would be 'an absolute load of bollocks'.

Whilst Brown was completing the reshuffle – hiring and firing ministers by mobile phone from the back of the Prime Ministerial limo – Mandelson popped into the Treasury at lunchtime to visit Darling. The Whitehall protocol was that the more junior minister met the more senior minister at the latter's office. Scholar knew Mandelson well and when he introduced the new member of the Cabinet to Darling's private office there was a sharp but discernible intake of collective breath. Normally, Mandelson was beautifully coiffed and perfectly turned out, but when he walked in he was wearing a scruffy jacket and old pair of jeans. Nevertheless, he still had those piercing eyes and way of staring intently at someone that was disarming but unsettling in equal measure.

After Mandelson had left, Darling turned his attention to one of the many timebombs that were lying in wait for him. Written on the casing was the single word 'Iceland' and it was about to detonate. Turner had been in to see the Chancellor at 8.15 that morning to update him on the latest situation concerning the Icelandic banks. The FSA was monitoring them by the hour and Turner reported that they were haemorrhaging cash from their UK operations. The destination of the money was Iceland, putting the interests of Icelandic savers above those of UK depositors. Kaupthing's internet bank the Edge was under the direct supervision of the FSA and so was not a problem. The Treasury had already made provision using the Northern Rock legislation to transfer Kaupthing's UK operations to the Dutch bank ING. But Landsbanki's Icesave division was more problematic. Because Iceland was a member of the European Economic Area, it was able to operate branches in the UK whilst the guarantor of the deposits remained in Iceland. Landsbanki's deposits, including the £4.5 billion owed to British savers, therefore belonged technically to Iceland. Darling sought advice from Charles Randell at Slaughter & May and the Treasury's own legal department. He was told that the only way to prevent Landsbanki's deposits leaving the country was to use anti-terrorism legislation passed in 2001 to freeze the assets on the grounds that Landsbanki's actions were detrimental to the interests of the UK economy.

At 2.30pm Darling picked up the phone and spoke finally to the Icelandic Prime Minister Geir Haarde. Brown had been due to make the call but was on his way to an emergency meeting of European leaders in Paris and so asked the Chancellor to deputise for him. Darling's PPS Rosenfield was on the call. Darling told Haarde that the FSA had been in touch with its counterpart in Iceland warning that it was about to intervene to stop any further cash being transferred from the UK and asking for the return of the money that had already been taken out. Haarde told him that he had not been sighted on the problem and was it possible to negotiate over the sum. Darling replied he was not in the market to negotiate over people's savings.

Haarde sought to reassure him that Iceland intended to pass legislation that weekend which would protect the interests of all Landsbanki's savers. They would be able to take advantage of Iceland's own investor compensation scheme should Landsbanki go under.

It was an inconclusive and unsatisfactory end to the conversation and one which would lead to further claim and counter claim as relations between the UK and Icelandic governments deteriorated over the next seven days. An hour later, Darling called Brown who by now had left Downing Street for Chequers to prepare for a meeting the following day in Paris with President Sarkozy and a number of other European leaders. Darling briefed him on the call that had just taken place.

In Canary Wharf, the FSA announced that the level of depositor protection under the Financial Services Compensation

Scheme, would rise from £35,000 to £50,000 per account from the following Tuesday. It was good news for savers with the two Icelandic banks especially.

On the stock market, meanwhile, HBOS shares had continued to rally, rising a further 18 per cent. Lloyds was well ensconced in HBOS's offices, an army of 200 accountants, lawyers and investment bankers conducting due diligence on the bank it was busy acquiring. As they waded through the bank's loan book they discovered to their horror the full extent of the huge risks that its corporate lending department led by Peter Cummings had been taking, particularly on commercial property. Even so, none of these was sufficient for the leadership of Lloyds to question the wisdom of the deal. With the benefit of hindsight, Daniels and Blank would acknowledge that more due diligence should have been carried out – Lloyds only did one sixth of the amount it would normally undertake in an acquisition. They still felt that the transformative potential of the merger made the risks worthwhile although history would show that they under-estimated two things: the sheer scale of HBOS's liabilities and the extent of the impact that the looming recession would have on the HBOS balance sheet.

Having briefed Brown, Darling set off for Heathrow. He was making a flying visit back to Scotland to attend the Balerno music festival the following day in his Edinburgh South West constituency. The timing was terrible but Darling had missed the festival the year before and had promised its organisers he would make it this time.

Things in London seemed to be under control, in as much as they could be. He could not have been more wrong.

At 7am that morning, a delegation from Her Majesty's Official Opposition had been in to see King for a one-hour meeting at the Bank of England. The delegation consisted of the Conservative leader David Cameron, the shadow Chancellor George Osborne and Osborne's chief of staff, an ambitious and upcoming young politician by the name of Matt Hancock.

Darling could not control the Governor's diary and he was free to see whomever he wanted. The Governor had three meetings a year with the Opposition and each one of them was approved by the Treasury. There was one simple ground rule: the Governor would not reveal anything to the Opposition about the Government's intentions or policies which was not in the public domain; and equally, he would not divulge the details of conversations he had with Opposition leaders to the Government.

It was obvious by now that the country was facing a national crisis and that the banks sat at the epicentre of that crisis. King spelled out to his guests some of the paths that could be pursued to extricate the country from the bad place that it was in. One was to carry on as usual, providing liquidity support to the banking system and hope that things improved; a second was to instruct the FSA to use its regulatory powers to require the banks to raise new capital; a third was a comprehensive recapitalisation programme.

After the Tory trio had left, King sat down and wrote another note to the Prime Minister and Chancellor suggesting a way to implement his plan. And this time he did send it. Impose a compulsory scheme, extend it to the top eight banks and ensure that all of them participated otherwise they would try to peel off one by one. To his surprise, it did not prompt another meeting at Number Ten: Brown was too busy with his Cabinet reshuffle.

There has since been much dispute since about what exactly was said at that meeting with Cameron, Osborne and Hancock in the Governor's office. King insists that he was speaking at a level of generality and at no point discussed what the Government was inclined to do although he did voice his opinion that it had to make a decision and soon.

Whatever was said, inferred or concluded, Osborne came away with enough material to use that weekend to his advantage and to the acute discomfort of the Chancellor.

Tackled a few months later by Darling on where he had got his intelligence from, Osborne airily replied: 'Oh, Mervyn was very expansive.'

Day 9 – Saturday 4 October

HBOS on the Brink

The consensus, at least in the Press, was that the return of Mandelson to Brown's 'economic war Cabinet' represented a considerable gamble. *The Financial Times* published a sceptical leading article on his appointment whilst the Sun's front page carried a picture of the two men with Brown in the front of shot under the headline: 'I'm behind you: Mandy's pledge to old enemy'. A snide reference to Mandelson's homosexuality? A warning that Brown had better watch his back? Or perhaps a bit of both.

Brown had stayed overnight in Chequers en route to Paris for the G4 summit on the banking crisis with the leaders of France, Germany and Italy. He had bigger fish to fry than worrying whether it would be third time lucky for Mandelson in his new Cabinet job (he had been forced to resign in disgrace from the Government on two previous occasions: first over a home loan from his ministerial colleague and friend Geoffrey Robinson; the second time over a passport application by a member of the wealthy Indian family the Hindujas). Before he left for the Elysée Palace, however, Brown had a potentially explosive domestic crisis to sort out.

As he was preparing to depart, Brown received a call from Sir Victor Blank at Lloyds. Blank had travelled down from the family home in Hampstead Garden Suburb the previous evening and was staying at their weekend home in the country, an old Elizabethan manor house in Stadhampton, just south of Oxford.

Blank had woken early and was finishing breakfast when the phone rang. It was Daniels on the line. Daniels told him that he had just taken a call from Hornby at HBOS, who was in a state of some distress. Hornby told him that the Bank of England was not cooperating as agreed and he did not know whether HBOS could open on Monday morning because it had very nearly run out of money. It was trying to obtain emergency liquidity from the Bank but the Governor was putting his foot down and demanding assets in return as collateral for the loan which the bank could not provide in time. The Bank was operating to the letter of the law and telling HBOS that it had to go through the formal procedures but it was taking time to submit the necessary collateral in a form acceptable to the Bank. The Governor seemed to have formed the view that if HBOS was short of money, then 'damn it, let the future owners have skin in the game' and help it out.

Lloyds had already lent HBOS £10 billion by this time and was not in the market to advance any more. In any event, the two banks were still technically competitors at this point although they were in merger talks which meant Lloyds had to step very carefully and get the approval of its lawyers to ensure any transactions with HBOS were correct and in order.

HBOS was caught in a perfect storm: a large chunk of deposits with the bank were reaching maturity and it had no chance of rolling them over, business customers were withdrawing their balances and the bank was struggling to get its hands on overnight money from other banks and counterparties for repayment the following day. 'Andy's wondering if there's anything we can do,' Daniels told Blank.

The two men were not certain whether HBOS wasn't making a large drama out of a small crisis. It would not have been the first time. Hornby and his chairman Dennis Stevenson were constantly fretting about whether they had the cash to open the bank and fill its ATMs when they were not complaining about the form filling and bureaucratic hoops the Bank was making them jump through.

But they had to take Hornby's words on trust. Blank came off the phone and told his wife Sylvia he had just had some 'horrifying news'. It was another sunny day and so he went for a walk in the garden wondering 'what the hell to do'. If HBOS couldn't open its doors on Monday, then other banks would quickly find themselves in trouble too and Britain really would have a banking crisis on its hands. If HBOS did not open on Monday, then there would be no bank left for Lloyds to buy. He came back in and told Sylvia he would have to ring the Prime Minister, not something Blank normally did on a Saturday morning. The Lloyds chairman was not sure what else he could do. But if the Prime Minister was unsighted on the situation – as he might well be having spent the previous day pre-occupied with his Cabinet reshuffle – then he needed to know.

The Downing Street switchboard recognised his number and put Blank through to Chequers. Brown came to the phone and asked what the problem was. Blank told him the situation at HBOS was critical. Brown said: 'Leave it to me, I'll call you back.' He then briefed Vadera on HBOS's little local difficulty and asked if she could help.

An hour later the phone rang again in Stadhampton. It was Brown with a short message: 'Crisis averted'. Number Ten had spoken to some people, Blank didn't know precisely who, and the problem was sorted. HBOS would get the money it needed. Whoever Downing Street had connected with, however, it was not the Governor.

King was at home where he spent most of the morning on the telephone, first to his opposite number in Iceland's central bank, and then to Turner at the FSA discussing the UK's plan of action for when the Icelandic banks went belly up.

But the Governor's reluctance to provide liquidity to the banks was well-known. It was one step short of the 'moral hazard' that was such anathema to him – the idea that if bank knew it would always be rescued then it would feel free to take undue risks in pursuit of short-term returns. It was on a par with his mistrust of the markets and those who worked in them. Number Ten thought it odd that in the almost daily meetings that were taking place between the Tripartite and Prime Minister, King almost always showed up alone, not even choosing to bring his director of markets, Paul Tucker, with him.

When Darling heard about the near-disaster that had been narrowly averted, he was his usual pragmatic self. He knew there was a high probability that the taxpayer was about to end up owning a large slug of HBOS. 'Let's look upon it as an investment,' he said. 'At least it guarantees we'll inherit a warm body and not a dead corpse.'

HBOS lived to fight another day, but Hornby would not be long for the world of banking, which was something that Daniels regretted on a personal level. Hornby had been one of the golden boys of his business generation – top of his class at Harvard Business School followed by a phenomenally successful stint at the supermarket group Asda after which he was lured to HBOS with an enormous golden hello and made the youngest ever CEO of a FTSE100 company.

Hornby had all the business jargon, a young and sparky management team and he was tremendously popular with the bank's staff who warmed to his ethos, leadership style and mission to break up the oligopoly of the Big Four banks. In the good times when the credit markets were open for business, he was a hero and could afford to run a thinly capitalised bank with huge liquidity risks. But he was a retailer and not a banker (and nor was his chairman Dennis Stevenson) and did not understand what the head of HBOS's commercial lending division Peter Cummings was doing. After Lloyds completed the takeover it admitted, with a somewhat curious use of language, that 40 per cent of HBOS's £432 billion loan book was 'outside Lloyds' appetite'. Of the £116 billion of corporate loans on its books, two-thirds should never have been written.

HBOS sorted, Brown flew to Paris in the afternoon to attend the mini summit. Vadera was making the trip with him. Even though Fortis and Dexia had just been rescued by the Belgian, Dutch and Luxembourg governments, Dresdner had been forced into a merger with its fellow German bank Commerzbank and Germany's Hypo Real Estate was teetering on the brink, there was still a feeling in Europe that the financial crisis was Anglo-Saxon at heart and therefore really affected only the US and the UK.

Merkel in particular could not comprehend that European banks were generally more highly leveraged and exposed than their US counterparts and did not appreciate just how much US sub-prime debt German banks had on their books.

Brown's task was to convince his counterparts otherwise. President Sarkozy, who was hosting the meeting in the Elysée Palace, was of a similar mind to Brown and was unhappy at Europe's inability to put together a common plan. But could they convince the other leaders present that day – Merkel of Germany and Silvio Berlusconi of Italy? Also in attendance were Jose Manuel Barroso, President of the European Commission, and the head of the European Central Bank Jean-Claude Trichet. Each of the four leaders was allowed one other representative in the room. Vadera sat with Brown, Sarkozy was supported by the French Prime Minister François Fillon. Merkel was accompanied by Jens Weidmann, her chief economic adviser, who simultaneously explained what was being said at the same time as translating for the German Chancellor, even though her English was quite good.

Brown and Trichet did most of the talking. If other European governments weren't yet prepared to make the leap and agree to recapitalise their banks, then some form of concerted action was necessary. What about a European-wide bank deposit guarantee scheme with a ceiling of €100,000, Brown suggested? There had been much criticism all week of Ireland's unilateral decision to guarantee all deposits in Irish banks. This had prompted a flight of deposits from other European banks because everyone suddenly thought their money was safer in Ireland. But it had also painted Ireland's Eurozone allies into a corner. Merkel refused to entertain the idea of a Europe-wide scheme to which Brown replied that each country could retain its own as long as there was a common limit. The discussion was spirited but it produced no consensus. Sarkozy struggled to understand the technicalities of what was being discussed but trusted what was being said by Brown. Berlusconi said virtually nothing complaining that most of the time had been taken up with a discussion about Europe's banks when there were other companies to worry about. He was referring to the share price of the media corporations he owned. But at least the Italian Prime Minister did provide one moment of light relief. As the meeting was about to conclude, he could be heard muttering to his aides 'they are all amateurs, they are all amateurs'. Brown wondered whether Berlusconi was referring to the lack of agreement on a unified action plan when he realised that he was in fact commenting on the failure of his fellow leaders to bring make-up artists with them when there was a press conference in front of the cameras in less than 30 minutes. The four leaders had agreed in advance that there would be no press conference but waiting outside for them were a bunch of Italian broadcast networks.

As they were departing, Brown and Merkel agreed to talk again by telephone but Brown said he could not guarantee that in the meantime the UK would not take some unilateral action of its own to resolve the banking crisis.

Meanwhile, the Sherpas from the respective G4 countries were in a huddle composing the communique that would be issued from Paris. King took a call from Cunliffe who was in attendance. Apparently, they were agonising over the wordsmithing and could not agree on whether to refer to the 'continuity' or the 'soundness' of their respective banking systems. King wondered whether they didn't have slightly more substantive matters on which to focus.

The Paris meeting ended inconclusively, as far as Brown was concerned. When the communique was issued two days later, it stated that the leaders of the G4 stood ready to take 'whatever measures are necessary to maintain financial stability' including increased liquidity support and protection for depositors. There was no explicit mention of recapitalisation.

While Brown was struggling to make headway in Paris, Darling was enjoying the unseasonably pleasant Edinburgh weather and listening to the mix of classical music, recitals and folk that make up the Balerno festival. It was the kind of constituency engagement that even Chancellors need to fulfil and the first time in several weeks that Darling had been able to unwind and enjoy a brief respite from the remorseless, unremitting demands of the financial crisis.

The next day would not be so relaxing for the Chancellor.

Day 10 – Sunday 5 October

The Osborne Ambush

Peter Mandelson had been back in Cabinet for just two days but already he was at the centre of another huge political furore. That morning the front page of *The Sunday Times* carried the banner headline: 'Mandelson damned PM to top Tory'. The story recounted how the newly-appointed Business Secretary had 'dripped pure poison' about Brown into the ear of a senior but unnamed Conservative politician whilst the two men were guests of the Russian oligarch Oleg Deripaska on board his £80 million superyacht Queen K in Corfu the previous August. The following day the unnamed Tory was revealed to be the shadow Chancellor George Osborne.

The story could not have been worse timed for Mandelson. He was due to join a meeting that evening with Brown and other ministers at Number Ten to discuss the bank bailout plan. The Press was already driving a wedge between him and his Prime Minister.

Mandelson sought to brush off *The Sunday Times*'s account of his conversation on board the Queen K as little more than media tittle tattle. Osborne too claimed that light-hearted remarks he had made to the newspaper's journalist had been blown out of all proportion. But the scandal refused to die down. Instead it escalated until it had earned its very own moniker: 'Corfugate'. If the initial story had been a deliberate attempt to sow division within Labour's senior ranks, it backfired badly. Nat Rothschild, scion of the eponymous banking dynasty and the man who had invited his two friends Mandelson and Osborne on board the yacht in the first place, subsequently disclosed that Osborne had brought with him Andrew Feldman, the Tories' top fund raiser. This prompted allegations, vigorously denied, that he had been trying to solicit a donation from the Russian businessman, something which was banned under UK law. The Conservatives' spin doctors struck back, encouraging the Press to ask what Mandelson, who at the time had been the European Union's Trade Commissioner, was doing on board a yacht with a billionaire owner of an aluminium company that had benefited from a reduction in EU tariffs on aluminium imports under his watch.

To critics of Brown, all this jousting between the rival camps was both a distraction from the bigger crisis facing the country and evidence of the serious political miscalculation the Prime Minister had made in bringing his arch enemy back into government when the nation was facing financial Armageddon.

Up in Edinburgh, meanwhile, Alistair Darling was preparing to deal with the fallout from another encounter involving George Osborne – the shadow Chancellor's meeting two days earlier with Mervyn King.

Darling, Osborne and Vince Cable were all due to be grilled on live television by the BBC's Andrew Marr that morning. Osborne and Cable were both being interviewed in the studio. Darling was doing it 'down the line' from the front room of his house in Morningside, baby grand piano and saxophone in the background. It was not the optimal arrangement for an interview as important as this one at such a critical juncture in the country's fortunes. Darling knew he would be staring into the lens of a camera, unable to see the interviewer, pick up visual clues or read his body language.

Osborne went first and as he talked Darling listened with growing incredulity. The shadow Chancellor told Marr how he had discussed banking reforms with Darling and Treasury officials the week before and had then gone on to have a discussion with the Governor about the possibility of recapitalising Britain's banks.

Darling concluded that Osborne knew about the Tripartite's plans and also realised therefore that he was playing with fire. His comments risked alarming the markets and potentially destabilising the rescue plan or making it even more expensive.

Down in London, Darling's aides were listening to the Osborne interview in equal horror. Rosenfield was in his office in the Treasury. Early that the day he had been joking with Darling that he really ought to have got the hedge trimmed because Darling's front garden would look a little unkempt if it were to creep into shot. Now his brain was whirring as he went through the permutations in an attempt to piece together how Osborne could possibly have reached the conclusion that the Government was going to recapitalise the banks. Treasury officials had spoken to Osborne about banking reforms but only in general terms. Osborne had spoken to King but the Governor insisted he did not disclose what the Government was planning. But Osborne's chief of staff was Matt Hancock and Matt Hancock's previous job had been as private secretary to Paul Tucker, the Bank's executive director for financial markets. Degrees of separation. Wheels within wheels.

'Oh, fuck,' Rosenfield said to one of the Treasury officials sat with him after Marr had finished questioning Osborne. Although there was plenty of speculation about what a rescue plan might look like, everyone had been disciplined up until that point. Now the wheels were in danger of coming off.

His boss, Macpherson was even less impressed. It was not the role of the Opposition to make the Government's job any easier, even at times of national crisis. But it was a bit rum and not terribly helpful if the Governor of the Bank of England felt he had carte blanche to brief the Tory high command about what the Government was up to.

The reaction in Downing Street was similar. What on earth had the Governor been saying and what was Osborne's game?

It was then Darling's turn to be interviewed. Rosenfield could see in Darling's eyes that he was wondering 'what the hell' had just happened. By now the Chancellor was in damage-limitation mode. So he talked at length about the difficult situation facing the banks while saying as little as he possibly could, other than that the issue of bank capital was clearly one of many factors that needed to be taken into account. The cat, however, was out of the bag.

Darling spent the next two hours trying to calm down as he worked on the non-statement he would give the House of Commons the following afternoon, its first proper sitting since returning from the summer recess. It would amount to a holding statement because he had nothing of substance to say. Sometimes, they are the trickiest to write.

Meanwhile, another unhelpful development had taken place in Germany. Berlin had stepped in to rescue one of its biggest banks, Hypo Real Estate. But in announcing the news, Angela Merkel had somehow created the erroneous impression that Germany had agreed to guarantee all bank deposits in all German banks, in a similar manner to the Irish. When asked whether German citizens were in danger of losing their money, she had replied: 'No, I can guarantee that.'

Merkel's comments were being televised. One of the private secretaries in Downing Street ran into the horseshoe where Vadera, Heywood and various other officials were gathered and said: 'You've got to listen to this'. Her words were not as tight as they normally were or should have been. In fact what she was seeking to communicate was that the German government had given a political guarantee that it would stand by its banking sector, not that specific undertakings had been given to underwrite savings in its banks up to a set level, much less to guarantee them in totality.

As soon as the story began to run on the newswires from Germany, Sarkozy was on the phone to Brown to tell him that Merkel had been misquoted. Merkel herself called Brown later in the day to provide him with her personal assurance that she had not sought to undermine her counterparts elsewhere in Europe, nor had she intended to steal his thunder.

Darling still needed to do more work on the statement he would make the following day but he also had important business back in London that evening so he headed for the airport to catch the BA shuttle to Heathrow. He arrived at the Treasury at 4pm where he continued to work on his statement. The Osborne interview had intensified the feeding frenzy and increased the anticipation that the Chancellor had something big to announce. But he didn't. He was in the business of expectation management and expectations were running far ahead of themselves. All he was intending to do was report back in the broadest of terms on the work that had been going on during the recess.

The statement finally completed, Darling headed out of the Treasury and made the short walk up Whitehall to Downing Street for his evening meeting with Brown in Number Ten. The meeting took place in the Cabinet room. Although it is the most famed and photographed room in Downing Street, it is one of the more cramped spaces. Also present around the large oval table that evening were Vadera, Heywood from the Cabinet Office, O'Donnell and Macpherson, Scholar, Rosenfield and Khan from the Treasury. And one other new face – the newly appointed City Minister Paul Myners who had only taken up his job that morning.

There was one notable absentee from the meeting in Number Ten – Peter Mandelson. After undertaking a round of Sunday morning television interviews himself, he had been taken ill and gone home in 'unbelievable pain'. He telephoned Brown to say he would not be able to attend that evening because of his condition but did not want to go to hospital. Brown thought his new Business Secretary might have appendicitis so he said he would ask the Health Minister Lord Ara Darzi to pay a home visit. Mandelson thanked him for the offer but said through gritted teeth that it was a doctor, not a politician, he needed. Brown replied: 'He IS a doctor!' Darzi duly called at Mandelson's home, diagnosed kidney stones and packed him off to the Royal Free Hospital for treatment.

The meeting reviewed the events of the day. Politics is like being in permanent campaign mode. If you are not on top of the story, and preferably ahead of it, you are nowhere. Europe was disunited, the banks were in denial, the Press were hunting in packs and it would be a rumbustious House of Commons that Brown and Darling would return to the next day. Brown was frustrated that the Government was not in a position to announce its bailout of the banks the following morning. The near-death experience of HBOS the previous day had heightened his alarm that the bank was on the brink and if HBOS went then RBS,

Lloyds and perhaps Barclays might not be far behind. But others counselled that more time was needed. If the plan came out of the oven half-baked it would make matters even worse, not better.

Brown reluctantly accepted the advice he was being given. He had to console himself with the schadenfreude he felt at the discomfort of his opposite number in Germany. Merkel was still digging herself out of the hole created by her unguarded remarks about standing behind Germany's banks whilst simultaneously being forced to come to the rescue of one of them, Hypo Real Estate.

Khan had prepared a briefing note for Brown to bring him up to speed on the stage the Tripartite had reached in its preparations. Scholar then talked about the plight of the Icelandic banks, highlighting the startling statistic that Iceland's banking system was nine times the size of the country's economy. Whilst the failure of its banks would be catastrophic for Iceland, Brown and Darling agree that it would not be systemic to the UK banking sector.

The meeting ended with an agreement between Brown and Darling that the rescue recapitalisation of the banks would have to be announced at the latest by the following Wednesday. Although there had been a series of meetings with the Governor and the FSA, the precise terms of what the Government was preparing to announce had not been tied down. Nor had the numbers. King was being fantastically rude about the Treasury, Macpherson was at his wits end with the Governor and the FSA had not got the figures together. There was still a lot of work to be done and the Tripartite was fraying at the edges.

As the participants trooped out of the Cabinet room into the reception area, Vadera took Myners and Scholar aside and guided them into Heywood's office just off to the right. In essence, the Government was about to embark on a market operation and that meant it had to command the confidence of the market. Who better to road test it on than the City of London's most respected practitioner: David Mayhew, chairman of JP Morgan Cazenove? Vadera had already brought Budenberg on board but the plan needed a fresh pair of eyes and she could think of no-one more suitable or authoritative than the legendary adviser and dealmaker. Vadera had Mayhew's number in her Blackberry so she rang it, put the phone on speaker, handed it to Myners and suggested he appoint Mayhew there and then. Mayhew accepted the mandate without question. The three-page plan presented to Brown two days earlier was then faxed over to him at home and a meeting with Mayhew and Budenberg was fixed for the following morning.

In Reykjavik, meanwhile, the Icelandic parliament was passing the legislation that would bring its financial compensation scheme into effect, guaranteeing the first €20,887 of savings in every account. But Darling was of the view that Iceland would not stand by the 300,000 British savers in Icesave and that if the UK Government had to pick up the entire bill it could cost the taxpayer as much as £4.5 billion. Darling updated the meeting on his phone call with Iceland's Prime Minister on the previous Friday and Brown said he would put a further call into him later that evening.

Over at the Treasury, Baker and her team were working overtime to prepare for the collapse of Kaupthing and Landsbanki, calculating how many UK savers would be affected and how much it would cost. Officials were engaged in a similar exercise at the FSA's offices in Canary Wharf. Turner was there too, overseeing activities. It was his fifty-third birthday but he did not have any time to celebrate it.

Day 11 – Monday 6 October

Stock Market Meltdown

Darling's attempts at expectation management during his Sunday morning television appearance had failed miserably. He had hoped to buy himself at least 24 hours by dead-batting Marr's volley of questions about what the Government was going to do and when it was going to do it. But he would not be allowed even that slender amount of breathing space.

Monday morning's front pages, bar none, all confidently predicted that the Chancellor was poised for a dramatic state-funded rescue of Britain's banks and speculated with varying degrees of confidence and accuracy as to the size of the stake the Government would take and the cost of the exercise.

The Independent's splash headline was simple enough: 'The £2 trillion question' – a reference to the size of the RBS balance sheet that the taxpayer was about to take on should the part-nationalisation of the bank go ahead. *The Times* and *Guardian* led off on Merkel's apparent decision to guarantee the savings of all German depositors, noting that Germany's 'every man for himself' approach had angered the Treasury whilst raising the stakes for Brown. But the majority of their coverage was devoted to Darling's plans to take shareholdings in the UK's banks.

The Financial Times devoted a further nine pages to the crisis, including one headlined: 'Momentous week for Darling', analysing the challenge facing the Chancellor and how he would navigate his way through the next seven days. As if the politics were not bad enough on their own, the front page of the FT's Companies and Markets section led with a gloomy forecast from the insolvency specialists Begbies Traynor warning of an impending glut of failures in the retail sector.

Darling knew he would not be in a position to deliver what the media and the markets were expecting when he stood up in the House of Commons that afternoon. There were still far too many moving parts and a key one of those was the attitude of the banks themselves. To establish that once and for all, Darling had invited the CEOs of the eight leading banks to a crucial meeting that evening in the Treasury at which the Tripartite would set out its plan and the bankers would respond.

At least there was one small piece of good news: HBOS had managed to open its branches that morning. The cashpoints were full and it was business as usual. The outside world was blissfully unaware of how close the bank had come to collapsing over the weekend.

After rising at 6am and ordering a light breakfast from the kitchen in the basement of Number 11, Darling digested the crop of headlines and then settled down for a 15-minute conference call with his counterparts in France, Germany and Italy – Lagarde, Steinbrueck and Giulio Tremonti, the Italian Finance Minister. The top item on the agenda was Merkel's savings guarantee. Darling pictured Steinbrueck squirming in his seat as he tried to explain how the confusion had arisen. The two men had not seen eye to eye ever since Steinbrueck had accused Darling of being an 'arch-Keynesian'. Steinbrueck meant it as a term of abuse. Darling thought it a bit rich coming from a politician who had spent his life in the Social Democratic Party.

It was left to Lagarde to call the discussion to order and stress the importance of Europe presenting a united front in the face of the financial crisis. If they didn't hang together, they would hang separately. Lagarde was very much the 'shop steward' for Europe's finance ministers. She was also the ideal interlocutor between Europe and America. Among her fellow finance ministers, she was the one who knew the US Treasury Secretary Hank Paulson by far the best. Lagarde had got to know him well when she worked in America as a partner in the law firm Baker McKenzie and he ran the US investment bank Goldman Sachs, one of its biggest clients. Indeed it was not unusual for executives to criss-cross between the law firm and the bank.

In the City, Mayhew and Budenberg met early meanwhile to discuss the plan that Vadera had sent over the previous evening. They then headed for the Cabinet Office where they were met by Vadera and Heywood. Mayhew brought with him Bill Winters, co-head of investment banking at JP Morgan Cazenove, and another of its senior bankers Naguib Kheraj. Budenberg was accompanied by Soanes. The meeting discussed how the capital would be injected into the banking system and the terms of the credit guarantee scheme. Would the capital take the form of ordinary shares, which carried voting rights, or preference shares, which did not but were more expensive to service? Announcing that the banks were getting fresh equity would remove the threat to their solvency that was hanging over them but it would not necessarily unlock the sluice gates and allow liquidity to flood back into the system. It would take months for the funding markets to re-open so the banks would continue to be heavily dependent on the Government's Special Liquidity Scheme.

Whilst these and other abstruse issues were being debated, Darling had ended his finance ministers call and gone next door for a catch-up meeting with Brown. Macpherson and Heywood were also in attendance. Then it was on to the very first meeting of the National Economic Council in Millbank. The launch of the Council had been announced the previous Friday by the Prime Minister alongside his Cabinet reshuffle. In some respects it was a re-incarnation of the NEDC which Harold Wilson's Labour government had created in the 1970s except that its membership was limited to government ministers – representatives of the unions, big business and academia could attend but only by invitation. The body quickly became known as Brown's 'economic war council'.

Darling and the Treasury were suspicious of it from the outset. At best they thought of it as an exercise in displacement activity whereby the Prime Minister would go around the room asking for ideas. At worst, they viewed it as his attempt to cut across the Treasury and give Number Ten a platform for making economic policy announcements of its own – something Brown would never have countenanced when he had been Chancellor.

Alongside Darling at that first meeting were the Foreign Secretary, David Miliband, the new Science Minister Lord Drayson, the new City Minister Paul Myners and eight other Cabinet ministers including Mandelson who had dragged himself from his hospital bed to attend. There was one other new face – the former telecoms regulator Stephen Carter. He had quit his latest job as chief executive of the City's biggest and most prestigious corporate advice and financial communications firm Brunswick to become Brown's head of strategy.

According to its mission statement, the NEC would coordinate "efforts to help families deal with higher food and energy prices" and "provide the forum on how to equip the country for the future by making the right investments in education, skills, science and infrastructure". The Council would also have responsibilities to promote the development of sustainable and secure energy supplies; to tackle barriers to entrepreneurship and small business growth; and to address the UK's housing and planning needs.

Alongside the NEC, Brown had also appointed a bevy of City grandees as business ambassadors with a remit to promote the UK overseas. Among the ambassadors were the chairmen of Barclays and Lloyds – Marcus Agius and Sir Victor Blank – the former chairman of HSBC Sir John Bond and the Sainsbury's chairman Sir Philip Hampton, who would shortly become the new chairman of RBS. They were joined by a clutch of industrialists including Dick Olver of BAE Systems, Sir Kevin Smith of GKN and Paul Skinner of Rio Tinto.

Whilst Darling and his fellow Cabinet members were stuck in the NEC's talking shop, Blank was chairing a meeting of the Lloyds board on the top floor of its nine-storey headquarters. The chairman had been meticulous in keeping the rest of his board abreast of what the bank was doing and what options were open to it. So much so that some members had begun to complain to him about being overworked owing to the sheer number of meetings they were being asked to attend. The going rate for being a non-executive board member of a FTSE100 company was around £40,000 a year. For that, they would be expected to attend ten board meetings a year. In 2008, the Lloyds board met on three dozen occasions. Together with all the preparation they had to undertake in advance and the volume of board papers that had to be read, one board member calculated that he was earning the equivalent of the national minimum wage.

The meeting opened with Daniels giving an update on the progress of the HBOS deal. Due diligence was progressing satisfactorily and, although the HBOS balance sheet was a challenging one, there had been no massive surprises so far. The meeting then went on to discuss two scenarios. In the first, HBOS and RBS both went bust and were nationalised and Barclays followed suit. The economy collapsed and there was a 20-30 per cent slump in house prices. In the second scenario, Paulson's TARP scheme succeeded in saving America's banks, the Bank of England turned the liquidity tap fully on in the UK and the Treasury stepped in with credit guarantees to help revive bank lending. The result was a steep but short recession followed by a strong economic recovery in the second half of 2009. On this basis, Lloyds was still expecting to make an underlying profit of £7 billion the following year.

After mulling over these two possible outcomes, the board concluded by discussing whether Lloyds had the ability, if it so wished, to utilise the Material Adverse Change clause in its merger agreement with HBOS and pull out of the deal. If HBOS then collapsed, would Lloyds be allowed to pick over the carcass of the dead bank by taking over just its mortgage and savings portfolios? Blank and Daniels were firmly of the view that Lloyds had to take the whole thing or nothing.

Daniels reminded his fellow board members that when he took over as chief executive in 2003, Lloyds had run out of growth and needed to regain momentum so it could restore market confidence. It was over-reliant on the UK market, having decided to jettison many of its overseas operations in the last downturn, whilst its insurance business Scottish Widows was still something of a basket case. The bank was, in his words, in a strategic straitjacket. By 2008, Scottish Widows had been turned around and Lloyds had grown revenues and earnings, but it still faced the conundrum of how to build on this success and map out a strategy for the future. It could continue with organic growth in the existing businesses, or it could buy something else.

Blank concluded the meeting by emphasising the huge prize that awaited Lloyds if it could hold its nerve and pull off the deal. It would take the bank from number five to number one in the UK retail banking and mortgage market. HBOS was a once in a generation opportunity to reshape the bank's future. The board unanimously backed the vision of its chairman and CEO.

Darling was pleased though privately mystified by how resolute the Lloyds board was in its determination to proceed. Because of the weekend panic, it would by now have known that HBOS was in receipt of Emergency Liquidity Assistance from the Bank of England. When it opened HBOS's books it would also surely know that it would find itself wading through, in his words, 'a pile of shite'. It subsequently emerged that the due diligence Lloyds carried out on HBOS amounted to one large lever arch file and a crate of supporting documents. Daniels would go on to tell the Commons Treasury Select Committee that it had carried out approximately 5,000 man days of due diligence on HBOS but had it been given more time it would have performed three to five times that amount.

One further meeting took place that day. The new City Minister Myners and Scholar were invited over to Vadera's office around the corner in Victoria Street just beyond Westminster Abbey to hear about a novel and markedly different solution to the banking crisis. Scholar thought Shriti was the only person with the capacity to put together an alternative scheme to that which the Treasury was preparing. But that still required a large team of people and that was not a luxury the Prime Minister's office had.

When he and Myners arrived at Vadera's office they were patched into a teleconference with Michael Klein, an ex-Citigroup banker who was acting as one of the Prime Minister's advisers. Klein was part of a small circle of investment bankers with good connections in the Gulf. Another member of the circle was Amanda Staveley. Whilst still at Citigroup, Klein had helped negotiate a $7.5 billion capital injection into his ailing employer from Sheikh Mansour bin Zayed Al Nahyan, a member of Abu Dhabi's ruling family. Staveley would also tap into the same source of funding when she brokered Abu Dhabi's purchase of the Premiership football club Manchester City. Both Klein and Staveley also advised Barclays separately on capital raising and takeover deals.

Klein had promised the Prime Minister that he could raise a lot of money from the Gulf to help fund the recapitalisation of the UK's banks. And so Brown had told the Treasury that he was someone they should listen to. The idea forming inside Number Ten was that Gulf money could be combined with UK government funding to create a giant pot which Brown could then spray around buying shareholdings in the banks, thereby reducing the UK taxpayer's financial exposure. But there was concern about how reliable Klein's connections really were.

Scholar reported back to Darling and Macpherson on his teleconference discussion. They quickly agreed that the Klein plan would not stack up. Just nailing down the legal structure of a fund which included Gulf sovereign wealth funds would have been fiendishly difficult. There was no time to allow them to carry out due diligence and they would not have agreed to invest based on nothing more than trust or some vague verbal agreement with the UK government. The clock was simply moving too fast. Time was becoming the Treasury's most precious commodity and it wasn't going to waste a minute of it on an idea that had no chance of getting over the line. It was one more 'distraction' that Treasury officials could do without. It was also another example of the two neighbours in Downing Street working in less than perfect harmony.

In Paris, meanwhile, the text of the communique from the weekend's G4 meeting had finally been agreed after much agonising over the wording. The statement said that the leaders of the four countries would take 'whatever measures are necessary to maintain the financial stability of the financial system – whether through liquidity support from central banks, action to deal with individual banks or enhanced depositor protection schemes'. It went on to stress that no depositors had yet lost any money and that the G4 would continue to take 'the necessary measures to protect both the system and individual depositors'. There was no explicit mention of recapitalisation.

Separately, Brown spoke to the Spanish Prime Minister, José Louis Rodriguez Zapatero, at lunchtime to say that Europe's leaders had agreed to coordinate any further announcements about bank guarantees by any one country.

After chairing a couple of internal Treasury meetings, Darling got ready to head over to the House of Commons to give his much-anticipated statement. Just before he left his office he received news that the Icelandic parliament had passed new deposit guarantee legislation and that the country's Prime Minister was sending a letter to the UK government pledging to honour its obligations to all UK depositors. It was a pledge that Darling was inclined to take with a large pinch of sodium chloride.

Darling arrived in the Chamber just after 3pm and stood up to make his holding statement at 3.30pm. Neither the House nor the packed Press gallery were sure quite how the Chancellor was going to play the occasion. His Treasury officials knew he was not yet in a position to announce the Government's rescue plan but would there be enough meat in his statement to keep the critics at bay at least for another couple of days? What he did say – or rather did not say – singularly failed to satisfy one audience: the financial markets.

As Darling spoke shares on the London market began to drop like a stone with banking stocks leading the way. By the time he had finished speaking, the FTSE100 Index had fallen by a record 7.85 per cent – at the time the third biggest one-day decline in its history. RBS and HBOS shares both ended the day 20 per cent lower, Lloyds fell by almost 11 per cent and Barclays was 15 per cent off.

It was not an encouraging backdrop for the meeting with the bankers that would take place later that evening. At 6pm, King and Turner arrived at the Treasury and went up to Darling's office for a private meeting lasting 30 minutes, leaving their officials from the Bank and FSA to set up shop further along the corridor. The three men discussed how they would run the session with the bank CEOs. Darling asked King if he would open the meeting by setting out the position as the Tripartite saw it and then outlining what they proposed to do. King gladly agreed.

Darling had one other duty to perform that night before the big meeting. By an awkward and unfortunate coincidence of timing, he had agreed some weeks ago to host a reception for City Editors and financial commentators in the State dining room on the ground floor of Number 11. The long oak-panelled room with its skylights running the full width between the vaulted ceiling and walls was devised by Sir John Soane, the architect who designed the Bank of England, and is one of the most architecturally significant in Downing Street. It is also decorated with some of the finest examples from the government art collection, as befits a room often used for entertaining heads of state as well as business leaders.

It was the last place Darling wanted to be, but he reasoned that if the reception was cancelled at short notice it would simply reinforce the impression that the Government was in turmoil following that afternoon's market rout. At the same time, he did not want to drop any hints about who he was meeting later that evening.

As the invited journalists made their way in past the gallery of political cartoons, caricatures and engravings of past Chancellors that decorate the staircase leading up to the first floor, amongst their number was the Daily Mail's City Editor Alex Brummer. Apart from being one of the most acerbic commentators on Fleet Street, he also happened to be the father-in-law of Dan Rosenfield, Darling's PPS. Luckily, Rosenfield was good at keeping politics out of family discussions.

The media reception safely navigated, Darling made his way around to the Treasury for the meeting in his office with the bankers. It began at 8pm. Seated on one side of the table were Goodwin of RBS, Varley of Barclays, Daniels of Lloyds, Hornby of HBOS, Horta Osório of Santander, Sands of Standard Chartered, Beale from the Nationwide and Douglas Flint, HSBC's finance director. Seated alongside the Chancellor were King, Turner and Macpherson.

The mood in the room was tense, but not combative or hostile – at least not initially. King opened the meeting by setting out the position as the Tripartite saw it. The banks needed more liquidity and loan guarantees because it was clear that confidence was draining from the market at an alarming rate. They no longer trusted one another to settle their daily interbank trades. But that was not the crux of the problem. In order to resolve their underlying weakness, they needed to raise significantly more capital. Turner, whose job it would be to work out precisely how much more capital, then spelt out how the FSA wanted the banks to help them with the details. The meeting did not go well from then on. The Tripartite were as one but most of the bankers were in markedly differing places. Flint and Beale were relatively relaxed because both knew that they did not need to raise any capital. Indeed Nationwide had more depositors than it knew what to do with which probably explained the Cheshire Cat grin on the face of its chief executive. Horta-Osório was effectively there as an observer – Santander was well-capitalised and, anyway, he had only been running the bank for a short while. Likewise, Standard Chartered was largely an overseas bank which was not in need of capital. Its chief executive Sands, unbeknown to his counterparts, had also been advising the Prime Minister on the bank rescue and was therefore both running with the hare and hunting with the hounds. Hornby simply looked exhausted and dejected.

That left the three key players: Goodwin, Varley and Daniels. Goodwin was once again centrally positioned, the Death's Head gazing down at him from above. Outwardly confident, he opened in reply for the banks, talking at length about how they needed access to liquidity and on more favourable terms. Darling sensed, however, that inwardly he was beginning to panic and crumble.

Daniels was of a similar view to Goodwin but inwardly he was furious at what he saw as the Government's attempt to shanghai the banks and its inability to control the Bank Governor. Moreover, the idea that the recapitalisation scheme was in some way voluntary was both specious and disingenuous. The banks were effectively being told that if they wanted access to liquidity they would have to accept the Government as a shareholder. There was a pistol to their heads. King objected strongly to this line of argument, pointing out that if the Bank did withhold liquidity support then it would very quickly have a full-blown banking crisis on its hands.

Daniels finally said that he would go along with the Government's plans. At this point he felt that the recapitalisation would amount largely to window-dressing: Lloyds ran a conservative, low-risk business model, it had not entered the sub-prime market and mortgages required very little capital because historically they held up very well even in economic downturns. Daniels said he did not think the plan was very good or one that addressed the issue but Lloyds could live with it.

It was left to Varley to try to establish some common, middle ground and bridge the gulf that lay between the two sides of the table. Privately, he felt that the die had already been cast and that the Tripartite were beyond the point where they were prepared to take on board the views of the banks. The purpose of the meeting was to warm the banks up and get a handle on where they would be coming from when the grand recapitalisation plan was presented to them.

Nevertheless, he reasoned that there was little to be gained by the banks remaining at daggers drawn with the Tripartite. It was a time for cool heads and constructive engagement. Unlike Lloyds, Barclays had not convened a board meeting that day to discuss tactics in advance. But Varley had spoken that afternoon to his treasury team to ascertain the bank's exact liquidity position. He had also spoken to a small number of people within the bank whose views were important, notably Bob Diamond the head of its global investment banking arm, Barclays Capital. Finally, he had been in constant touch with his chairman Marcus Agius and they had come to a common view that the bank would require significant amounts of new capital.

So Varley told Darling that alongside day to day liquidity needs, new capital would also be necessary. What he avoided mentioning was that Barclays had already decided where its capital would come from – and it would not be the taxpayer. On 18 September Barclays had announced a £750 million share placing alongside its purchase of Lehman's North American investment banking business. Later that day, Varley and Agius were contacted directly by Sheikh Hamad bin Jassim bin Jabr Al-Thani, the Prime Minister of Qatar and chairman of its sovereign wealth fund Qatar Holding. He had participated in Barclays's fund-raising over the summer and made it clear that if the bank needed to raise significantly more capital then Qatar stood ready to support it. From that moment on, Barclays knew that it would not be a participant in any arrangements which involved the British state taking a shareholding in the company.

The bankers advising the Government – Goldman Sachs, Morgan Stanley, Cazenove and Peter Sands at Standard Chartered – might all be keen for Barclays to take taxpayers' money and end up with a government representative on the board, looking over the shoulder of its management. But they would, wouldn't they? After all, each one of them was a competitor to Barclays and there was little love lost, particularly with Standard Chartered which Barclays had twice tried to buy in the past. It was another of those odd conflicts of interest that added one more layer of complexity to the great banking crisis of 2008.

The meeting came to an end just before 9.30pm. Despite Varley's attempts at emollience, it had not gone well. As Goodwin stood up he snagged his suit jacket on a nail sticking out of his chair. It did not improve his mood. As the bankers filed out promising to keep the discussion they had just had confidential, Darling turned to King, his face a picture of exasperation. It was the first time that the Governor had seen the Chancellor utterly frustrated with the banks. He had sought to make common cause and bring them on board with the Government in a spirit of joint enterprise but they had not responded. Now it was time to get more muscular.

Darling told Macpherson that the Treasury needed to be ready to go in the next 36 hours as it no longer had the luxury of time. He got back to his flat in Downing Street just in time to hear the BBC's Robert Peston giving an incomplete account on the Ten O'clock News of the meeting he had just left. When ministers leaked, they had to do it in private. When bankers did likewise, he concluded, they simply pressed speed dial on their mobile phones as they were walking out of the room.

Day 12 – Tuesday 7 October

The Balti Bailout

A heavy drizzle was falling as London woke up to the morning after the night before. In the wake of Monday's mayhem on the UK stock market, Wall Street had also closed sharply down and Asian stocks had followed suit overnight. But the air was filled with more than just precipitation. It was pregnant with expectation. There was a palpable sense that something quite cataclysmic might be about to happen.

Darling was awake earlier than most. It was still pitch dark and he was being driven to RAF Northolt to board a private jet to Luxembourg where European finance ministers were gathering to discuss, of all things, the insurance industry's insolvency requirements. It was hardly the burning issue of the day. The bathos of it was not lost on the Chancellor. He was being accompanied on the trip by his PPS Rosenfield and Geoffrey Spence, one of his two special advisers. Darling's other special adviser, the former *Glasgow Herald* political editor Catherine MacLeod, had stayed back at base to keep a weather eye on the increasingly febrile atmosphere in Westminster.

Darling wanted to be anywhere but Luxembourg exploring the arcane byways of insurance insolvency but he feared that if he failed to materialise it would send a signal to the rest of Europe that the UK's banks were in even worse shape than previously thought. Ordinarily, Darling travelled to ministerial meetings by scheduled airline but on this occasion he could not afford to be stranded on the Continent if he was needed urgently back in London.

As Darling's jet was touching down in Luxembourg, King was sitting down to breakfast with Sir John Parker, chairman of the Court of the Bank of England, in one of the three private dining rooms in Threadneedle Street. The court is a little-known body but it is central to the Bank's activities because the Governor requires its formal approval for any operations he wishes to carry out. King had needed its authority to begin providing Emergency Liquidity Assistance to HBOS six days earlier and he would need similar approval to do the same for RBS.

King's fellow regulator, the FSA chairman Adair Turner, was also on the way into work. Turner's chauffeur had picked him up from his home in Kensington at 6.45am to make the eight-mile journey to the FSA's Canary Wharf headquarters.

Three miles across the capital, meanwhile, the chief executive of RBS Fred Goodwin was being collected from the Ritz in his chauffeur-driven Mercedes S-Class and taken to the Landmark Hotel in Marylebone where he was addressing the annual Merrill Lynch banking and finance conference. Goodwin knew Merrill Lynch well from the £21 billion takeover of NatWest in 2000 when he was advised by one of the US firm's star investment bankers Matthew Greenburgh.

Darling, King, Turner, Goodwin. Four men whose paths would align dramatically later that day.

As he was being driven to Northolt, Darling scanned the newspaper front pages. He had become inured to bad press coverage but that morning's crop of headlines was of a particularly poor vintage. 'Markets slump as Darling fails to calm investor fears' screamed *The Guardian*. The story recounted how the Chancellor had pledged to do 'whatever it takes' to end the banking crisis but had disappointed the City by omitting to explain what that might be. Accompanying the text was a share price graphic super-imposed over a giant pixelated image of Darling's head showing how the FTSE100 Index had crashed by almost 8 per cent in the ten minutes it took the Chancellor to deliver his non-statement to the Commons. The paper's leading article was scarcely any more forgiving, commenting that, faced with a banking crisis of enormous proportions, the Chancellor had simply opted to 'clasp his hands and pray'.

On the BBC News, Robert Peston twisted the knife in deeper. His blog and radio report ran at 7am. It stated that bankers were concerned Darling did not have a plan for rescuing the banks and did not know what he was doing. As he listened to this account of the meeting on his car radio, Turner's eyes widened and his head began to rock gently from side to side. It was as if Peston had been a fly on the wall inside the Treasury, so specific was the detail. Turner was just waiting for him to describe the biscuits they had taken with their tea. It was clear then to the FSA chairman that a rescue plan could be delayed no longer: it would need to be agreed that day and announced the following morning.

Darling had been around long enough to know that politics was a rough and tumble game and its participants needed to have a tough skin. But this really was a travesty of what had taken place the previous evening. As their jet took off, Rosenfield asked him what he had made of the coverage. Through gritted teeth, Darling uttered a one-word reply: 'Disingenuous.' It was restrained in the circumstances.

As their plane came in to land at around 8.30 am CET Spence looked out of the window and remarked dryly that two Icelandic jumbo jets were parked up on the apron. They really should have been named Landsbanki and Kaupthing. It served as a mental note that whatever else the day held, Darling was due a call with that country's finance minister before he left Luxembourg.

The European Commission's Luxembourg headquarters is a grim shed of a building looking out onto an industrial wasteland. Darling and his aides reached the venue at 9am CET. It was an hour earlier in London and the stock market had just opened. Rosenfield had forgotten his pass and so had to race through security at the Chancellor's side with uniformed guards in pursuit.

They made themselves comfortable in the room set aside for the UK delegation and Darling made his way down to join his fellow finance ministers, leaving instructions with Spence and Rosenfield that they were to watch the markets like hawks and alert him if anything happened that he needed to know about.

Around the same time as Darling was taking his place in the conference chamber in Luxembourg, Goodwin was striding onto the stage in the Landmark Hotel's Empire Room to address the Merrill Lynch conference in London. The Barclays CEO John Varley had been first to speak. Goodwin was second up. At 8.45am he launched into his PowerPoint presentation. It was a canter through RBS's 'diversified and high-quality portfolio' of businesses that would see the bank survive and prosper despite the 'challenging times'.

As he spoke, murmurings could be heard from his audience of bankers, financiers and fund managers as they began to check the alerts on their Blackberries and iPhones and read Paul Murphy's live description of what was happening to bank stocks in his *FT* Alphaville column. RBS shares were tanking, forcing the London Stock Exchange to suspend them twice. By the time Goodwin had finished speaking 30 minutes later they were down by almost 30 per cent. By the end of the day they would have fallen by 39 per cent to 900p amid the heaviest trading in RBS shares witnessed in a single day, wiping £6 billion from the company's stock market value. During the short Q&A that followed Goodwin's presentation, he was asked if he was aware what was happening to his share price. Goodwin looked a little startled but flat-batted the question as best he could. He took a couple more questions before being hurried off stage in the direction of his S-Class.

It was now 9.15am in London and 10.15am in Luxembourg. In the Treasury, Baker and Rathi had been monitoring the RBS share price on the Reuters terminal which sits outside the Chancellor's office. Spence was doing likewise in Luxembourg and gave the Chancellor the bleak news which Darling digested before heading back into the chamber. Christine Lagarde appeared at his shoulder and said: 'It looks bad, doesn't it? What are you going to do?' Darling replied that he would deal with it and hoped Lagarde would not mind if he had to leave early.

By this time Goodwin had left the Landmark, his chauffeur weaving a route through the heavy traffic towards RBS's London offices at 280 Bishopsgate, an imposing glass and steel structure on the north-east side of the City. Goodwin phoned his chairman Sir Tom McKillop from the car. McKillop was already ensconced in the RBS 'war room' on the 12th floor. Sandwiched between the chairman's and chief executive's offices it was the same room from which RBS had masterminded its takeover of NatWest eight years earlier. McKillop had already tried phoning King at the Bank only to be told he was at breakfast. He had then tried to reach Darling and Brown, again without success. Goodwin computed the information and then called the bank's finance director Guy Whittaker to ask whether RBS could survive the day. The answer: no, not without Bank of England support.

Breakfast with Sir John Parker over, King got back to this office and immediately returned the call to McKillop. The RBS chairman did most of the talking, telling the Governor in the starkest terms that the bank would not be able to get through to the end of the day. King replaced the receiver and gazed out of his office window down onto the garden court below with its arbour of mulberry trees. The court was the Governor's private space for his use only, a tranquil oasis amid the hustle and bustle and deal-making of the nearby City trading rooms where King could walk and think. There was no time for strolling today. He picked up the phone to Turner and told him that the Bank would need to put Emergency Liquidity Assistance in place for RBS forthwith. The two men agreed that it was now essential the recapitalisation of the banking system was announced as soon as possible. King called Andrew Bailey, the Bank's Executive Director for Banking, and Paul Tucker, Executive Director for Markets, into his office and told them it was essential that the Bank got RBS safely through the day. He then opened his diary and wrote: 'The crisis is coming to a head.'

By now it was approaching 11.30am in Luxembourg and McKillop was finally about to get through to Darling. Spence was frantically gesticulating in an attempt to extricate Darling from the conference chamber but Rosenfield was determined that his boss was not going to appear panicked in front of the UK's 'competitors'. Part of the charade was always to appear to be in control so he casually ushered the Chancellor upstairs and back up to the UK delegation office. Spence entered ahead of him and ordered everyone to clear the room. At the time it was being occupied by Kim Darroch, the UK's senior EU diplomat. (Darroch would go on to become British Ambassador to Washington where he served with distinction until he was forced out by President Trump over leaked diplomatic cables in which Darroch criticised the 'dysfunctional state' of the Trump administration).

McKillop was patched into the call with Darling through the Chancellor's private office in the Treasury. They were taking notes in London. Rosenfield and Spence were listening on the speaker phone. The call lasted no more than five minutes. McKillop told the Chancellor: 'We are haemorrhaging money and something has to be done. We going to go bust this afternoon. What are you going to do about it?' Darling asked him how long the bank could keep going. McKillop replied: 'A couple of hours maybe'. Darling put the phone down and stared out onto the miserable industrial estate that the room overlooked. His officials were stunned. There was silence in the room. It was finally broken by Spence who looked up and said: 'That's it, it's over.'

It wasn't over. In fact, the atmosphere in the room was remarkably calm. Darling was used to existential crises and events which you knew could happen even if you didn't know when they would occur. He likened the call to the moment on the morning of 7 July 2005 when he asked his private secretary to check out reports that three power outages appeared to have hit the London Underground in quick succession. Darling was Transport Secretary at the time and it quickly became apparent that those electrical failures were in fact bombs exploding on the Tube system. Darling had a plan then. And he had a plan now.

Unlike a year earlier when Northern Rock collapsed, the Government had passed legislation enabling it to nationalise failing financial institutions, not that Darling wanted to go down this route with what was now the world's biggest bank. It had also drawn up a set of arrangements for taking insolvent banks into 'resolution' as it had done with Bradford & Bingley, but this would be a sub-optimal way of dealing with RBS. Finally, it was also on the point of announcing its broader plan to recapitalise the banking sector and secure its long-term future but this had yet to be finalised. So the Government could act quickly in a way it had been hamstrung from doing 12 months previously. But first it had to resolve RBS's immediate crisis. If RBS were to collapse, it would eclipse entirely the failure of Northern Rock and even Lehman Brothers. It would send shock waves reverberating around the world. The failure of the bank would be seismic. Branches would not open, its cash machines would stop dispensing money, business customers would not be able to transact their day-to-day business and RBS would not be able to fulfil its commitments to other banks who had lent it overnight money. In short, a financial meltdown of almost incalculable proportions beckoned.

Darling consulted Brown in Downing Street and the two men agreed that emergency liquidity had to be pumped into RBS immediately to keep the bank in business for the rest of the day. Darling then called Macpherson in London and told him to ring the Bank of England and instruct it to make the necessary arrangements. Macpherson picked up the phone and got through to Sir John Gieve, the Deputy Governor responsible for financial stability. Gieve told him that the situation was under control.

Brown called King at 1pm to ascertain that RBS was getting the support it needed and impress upon him, if further instruction was needed, that the bank must not be allowed to fail that day. By now the Governor was beginning to feel as if he was drinking from a fire hydrant, such were the volume of calls coming into his office telling the Bank that RBS had to be kept alive.

King re-assured the Prime Minister that he had already briefed Bailey and Tucker to set up a bilateral facility to prop up RBS for the remainder of the day and overnight in the US because the bank would need both sterling and dollars to keep going. Bailey would look after RBS's sterling needs. Tucker would deal with the Federal Reserve in New York. There was no pre-arranged limit on the amount RBS could draw upon.

Brown also wanted to know what the Bank of England was proposing to do about the Special Liquidity Scheme which had been operating publicly since the previous April. King suggested they announce a doubling of the facility from £100 billion to £200 billion.

By now, Goodwin was back in the Bishopsgate war room and taking calls on the speaker phone from non-executive directors as they called in. He was also his calm, quiet and undemonstrative self, even though he knew by then that the game was almost certainly up. At midday, he convened a meeting of the bank's Executive Management Committee to assess exactly how much money was in its branches, how much more it would need to see the day through and what internal message the leadership of the bank should be communicating to its worried staff. In an effort to make sure its ATMs were full and avoid the danger of queues building up outside its branches, the head of RBS's UK banking operations, Alan Dickinson, had doubled the amount of cash they were allowed to hold a fortnight earlier. He had also begun reporting daily to Goodwin on how well its supply of bank notes was holding up.

Goodwin also passed a message to Bill Winters of JP Morgan Chase, the biggest bank in the United States, asking it to continue transacting with RBS as its counter-party. This would demonstrate that RBS was not in imminent danger of becoming insolvent which in turn would give the Bank of England the legal cover to extend Emergency Liquidity Assistance. As with Bradford & Bingley, the Bank would not have been allowed to inject more money into RBS if it knew the bank was insolvent or about to become so. John Cummins, RBS's group treasurer, was then despatched to the Bank of England. When Cummins arrived he went straight up to Bailey's office and asked if RBS could borrow £25 billion. 'Of course,' Bailey replied, 'are you certain that's enough?' There was just one problem: RBS was running out of assets that it could package up and offer the Bank as collateral. After looking down the banking equivalent of its sofa, RBS managed to scrape the collateral together in the shape of four pools of mortgages and a selection of loans to retail customers, large corporates and small and medium sized enterprises (SMEs).

Meanwhile Tucker picked up the phone to his opposite number in the Fed. The voice on the other end of the line said RBS could have as much money as it needed. The Bank of England's credit was good and so he didn't even need to get authorisation from his boss. That day two facilities were set up, one for £29.4 billion, the other for $25 billion. Ten days later support for RBS peaked at £36.4 billion. Between them, RBS and HBOS received a total of £61.8 billion in Bank of England support.

By now Treasury officials were frenetically working on the rescue plan that would be announced the following day. Myners was supervising the team. The plan had three elements: a doubling in the size of the Special Liquidity Scheme to £200 billion as King had outlined to Brown earlier; the creation of a £250 billion credit guarantee scheme underwritten by the Government to provide the commercial banks with the confidence to begin lending to one another again; and a recapitalisation of the banks using taxpayers' money. The exact amount of capital was, however, a moveable feast. The FSA seemed to believe that £25 billion would do it. By now the Bank of England put the figure closer to £100 billion.

Despite the enormous amount of activity taking place inside the Treasury, King was still not convinced that it would bring forth a fully-fledged plan capable of being announced. He had been there too many times before in the past two weeks. Every time he thought a decision was about to be taken it was deferred to another day. He therefore asked three of his officials – de Weymarn, Miles and Haldane – to pop down to the Treasury to see what was going on. When they returned de Weymarn told his boss: 'There are 30 people in one room endlessly debating issues but not making decisions. Myners and Vadera are coming in, asking questions and then leaving again but no-one is obviously in charge.' It neither improved King's mood nor eased his concerns that he was about to witness yet another false dawn.

Whilst Darling was on the phone to the Treasury from Luxembourg, Rosenfield was contacting the pilot of their private jet, telling him to have the engines running. By now it was lunchtime and Darling urgently needed to get back to London. But he had one more call he needed to make before he could leave. Rosenfield patched him through to the Icelandic finance minister Arni Mathiesen. Iceland's financial regulator the FME had taken control of Landsbanki that morning and placed it in receivership. Darling wanted assurances that Iceland would compensate the 300,000 British investors who had £4.5 billion deposited with Landsbanki's UK arm, Icesave. Iceland's newly-enacted depositor protection scheme would safeguard the first £16,500 in each savings account.

The contents of that call have since been hotly disputed. A transcript of the call showed that Mathiesen did indeed give Darling such an assurance. However, the Chancellor came off the phone and told his officials: 'They won't stand behind it'. He repeated the assertion on radio the following morning.

The Icelandic call dealt with, Darling and his officials then made to leave. As the Chancellor's party hurried from the building they were spotted by a passing film crew. At least we've provided them with some footage for the early afternoon news bulletins, he thought. At the last minute, the Treasury's Director General of International Finance, Stephen Pickford, decided to hitch a ride home with them. He had arrived in Luxembourg the day before to prepare for the Chancellor's arrival. He just made the plane.

The weather was still squally as they took off from Luxembourg. Their small private jet endured a buffeting all the way back home which left Spence feeling especially queasy. As the aircraft made its final approach to the runway at Northolt, it began to sway violently prompting all four men to wonder briefly if they were actually going to land.

Safely inside the commercial air terminal at Northolt, Darling and his officials were picked up by a waiting government car and taken back to the Treasury. They arrived at 4pm and the Chancellor went almost immediately into emergency session, convening a meeting with Myners, Vadera, the Economic Secretary to the Treasury Yvette Cooper, Macpherson and Scholar. There was one other new face in the room – John Kingman, Second Permanent Secretary to the Treasury and the civil servant who had been in charge of the rescue, attempted auction and subsequent nationalisation of Northern Rock a year earlier.

Kingman was another high-octane operator. His father, also called John Kingman, was a celebrated British mathematician and inventor of coalescent theory. His son had dabbled for a while in financial journalism on the *Financial Times's* Lex column and also worked for John Browne in the CEO's office at BP and for the investment bank Rothschild before joining the Treasury.

The bespectacled Kingman was an expert in execution and he would take responsibility for negotiating the recapitalisation of RBS and Lloyds/HBOS whilst Scholar handled Barclays. After all the talking, theorising and scenario-planning, the Tripartite was now at the business end of the process and it needed senior officials with hands on experience of saving failed banks. They would be dealing with institutions facing massive liquidity problems and individuals who were functioning under conditions of extreme distress and still unwilling to accept how badly they had failed. Kingman was familiar with both. His job was not to spend time worrying about how much capital they needed, but rather to get them to take the money and accept the consequences which would flow from that for their reputations and careers.

Macpherson, technically the Treasury's accounting officer, recalled the meeting vividly: 'There wasn't any panic but there was an awareness that the situation was getting more serious and the need to intervene was becoming more urgent but it was important to get it right and not throw good money after bad. There was also a very strong camaraderie within the Treasury. We'd been preparing for this scenario for a year, we'd dealt with B&B professionally and so we had a degree of self-confidence that we could save the banking system and, if we couldn't, we'd have a good try at doing it in a reasonably professional and effective way.'

There was one other skill set that the Treasury was short of: expertise to help it establish just how much capital each bank would need and therefore what the ask on the taxpayer would be. Neither Darling nor King had confidence that the FSA was sufficiently equipped to handle the task on its own. That afternoon, therefore, a handful of investment banks were contacted by the Treasury's director of financial markets Mridul Hedge and invited to tender for the business. It was what is known in the City as a 'beauty parade' for what would prove a beast of a job.

There was only a small number of unconflicted investment banks that the Treasury could approach for this mandate – most of the best known names in the City were either already working for the Government, giving private ad hoc advice to Brown and Vadera or else acting as brokers and advisers to one of the commercial banks that the state was busy rescuing. One of those who did get the call was James Leigh-Pemberton. He had an unimpeachable pedigree: not only was he the highly-rated chief executive of Credit Suisse's UK operations but his father, Robin

Leigh-Pemberton, happened to have been a Governor of the Bank of England himself. Another product of the Eton and Oxford assembly line, Leigh-Pemberton also possessed a financial acumen as wide as his mischievous grin.

Leigh-Pemberton thought long and hard about the phone call from Hedge. Credit Suisse already had rather a lot on its own plate. Its entire corporate customer base was being affected by the financial crisis in one way or another. Every institutional client with any leverage was worrying about whether and how they could refinance their borrowings or reduce them. And the debt and equity markets were extremely volatile. It was difficult to get any other bank to quote terms for lending money even on a one week basis but at least it was still possible to buy and sell shares – market makers were still quoting prices and banks could transact. But Credit Suisse had one important advantage: unlike its Swiss competitor UBS it had not been necessary for Credit Suisse to go cap in hand to the Swiss government for capital because it did not have any exposure to US residential mortgage-backed securities.

After weighing all of this up, Leigh-Pemberton decided he would go along to the beauty parade the following afternoon. He immediately called over two of his senior colleagues – Ewen Stevenson, the head of the investment bank's financial institutions group, and Sebastian Grigg, head of UK investment banking. They had an afternoon to work on their pitch.

Whilst the immediate problem of saving RBS from the scrap heap was being addressed by Cooper, Macpherson and the Bank, Myners was busy elsewhere in the Treasury doing what he enjoyed best – roughing up bankers. Darling noted that he was taking to his new role as City Minister with some gusto. Vadera accompanied him to most of the meetings.

A meeting with all the bank CEOs had been convened for 7.30pm that evening at which they would be told exactly what the Government proposed to do and effectively ordered to fall into line if they did not want to end up as dead meat in the morning. But first Myners wanted to do a bit of tenderising and so two of the banks were summoned to attend the Treasury that afternoon.

First in was Fred Goodwin of RBS who had left the 12th floor of 280 Bishopsgate for his encounter with Myners. After slipping into the Treasury by the now-familiar side entrance, he was escorted up to Myners's office on the second floor, down the corridor from the Chancellor's room. When he entered he was greeted not just by Myners. Also present were Kingman and Mayhew of JP Morgan Cazenove. Although the chain-smoking Mayhew had been brought onto the bench of government advisers to add his weight and influence to the final negotiations because he was of the most respected corporate advisers in the City, in another incarnation he was also, of course, a fierce rival of RBS's corporate banking arm. It was yet another of those conflicts of interest with which the bank bailout was awash.

After a bruising meeting, Goodwin left the Treasury, reportedly having told Myners: 'No business ever dies because it has run out of capital. They die because they run out of cash.' Next for the Myners treatment were Daniels and Blank from Lloyds. By now Scholar had joined the interrogation panel. Myners was acutely aware that the successful completion of the Lloyds/HBOS deal was crucial to the entire recapitalisation plan. If Lloyds pulled out of the takeover, then HBOS would almost certainly collapse, forcing the Government to nationalise it as well as RBS and if that happened then the contagion could spread to the remaining banks putting their future in doubt. Daniels calculated, therefore that he had a certain amount of bargaining power. There were a dozen issues that he had concerns about ranging from the ability of Lloyds to determine its own dividend policy and executive remuneration to the extent of ministerial interference in the management of the bank if it became a significant shareholder. He did not relish Lloyds being used by the Government as an instrument of its political will. Above all, he was worried about Lloyds being pigeon-holed as a 'problem bank' and wanted assurances that every other bank would be taking part in the government bailout.

Daniels had just begun to run through his shopping list of concerns when Myners cut across him, saying he was not there to negotiate and that the price of accepting government capital would be much less management freedom. He also demanded that Lloyds remove the Material Adverse Change clause from its merger agreement with HBOS. Daniels' anger boiled over and he stormed out of the room, telling Myners that he could not possibly get his board to recommend what was being proposed unless his concerns were satisfactorily addressed. It was left to his chairman to use all his skills of diplomacy to calm his chief executive down. Daniels eventually agreed to come back into the room after Myners promised him that there was nothing to be alarmed about. 'Don't worry your pretty little heads,' he told Blank and Daniels. 'We will have time afterwards to sort out the details. I can assure you we are going to address your concerns.' Daniels had to make a call as to whether he was going to take the minister's promises on trust. He reflected later that it was not the smartest move he had ever made in his long business career.

In Downing Street, meanwhile, the idea that the Gulf states might be persuaded to use some of their vast oil wealth to help bankroll the Government's bank rescue plan was refusing to lie down and die, despite having been rejected out of hand by the Treasury only the day before. Unbeknown to Darling, Brown decided to call the Prime Minister of Qatar, Sheikh Hamad bin Jassim, to urge him to consider supporting the recapitalisation of Britain's banks. Brown knew that the Qataris were interested in investing in the UK's banks and he was not theologically wedded to the idea that all the capital must come from the UK taxpayer.

The Prime Minister's great strength all along had been his ability to persuade, cajole and sometimes browbeat other governments into accepting that the same fundamental fault line ran through their banking systems. That demanded a unified and uniform response because one country could not succeed on its own given the global, integrated nature of the finance industry. Brown had used his Rolodex to great effect, calling his fellow world leaders night and day to make the case. But the call to Qatar was one that Darling had not seen coming.

He only found out about it subsequently when Macpherson asked him whether he had been aware of the conversation between Brown and the Sheikh. When a Prime Minister makes a call of that nature, a note is taken and circulated to a very restricted list of senior civil servants in other departments. The note had passed under Macpherson's nose but not that of his boss.

With the benefit of hindsight, Brown's decision to reach out to the Sheikh seemed all the more peculiar given how badly he reacted when Barclays chose not to take part in the Government's recapitalisation scheme and instead raise the new capital it needed from... the Qataris. Brown later bitterly criticised the way in which deal had been engineered and lubricated with commission payments.

Barclays itself was not hauled before the headmaster that afternoon. Instead, Agius convened a board meeting so the bank's leadership could discuss and agree tactics before Varley went into battle that night. Those who were in Barclays tower in Canary Wharf made their way up to the 31st floor. The remaining board members dialled in. It was one of 27 board meetings that the bank held in 2008. In a normal year it would meet nine times.

By now it was clear to the Barclays board that they would not be taking the Government's money. Further contact had been made with the Qataris and Barclays was confident they would provide a substantial proportion of the capital that the bank would need.

It had also become clear to Varley that when the banks gathered that evening at the Treasury they would be separated into sheep and goats. There would be some that had no option but to take government capital. There would be some who would be capable of raising the capital elsewhere. And there would be some such as HSBC who didn't really need to raise any new capital at all. Varley knew where Barclays would sit on that spectrum. He also mused that Lloyds would have been In the same advantageous position as Barclays, had it not made the strange strategic error of buying HBOS.

At 5pm King arrived at the Treasury and was shown up to Darling's office. A short while later Turner arrived and joined them. They spent the next hour discussing the plan, the core elements of which were now in place. There was still one glaring exception: exactly how much capital would they force the banks to take?

At 6pm, Darling, King and Turner headed around to Downing Street to meet Brown. Vadera was already there when they arrived. They gathered in the small office that Brown occasionally used off the open plan private office in No 12. Before the meeting began,

Vadera was thanked for all the hard work she and her small team of investment bank advisers had put in to develop the rescue plan and bring it to the point of fruition.

They then got onto the primary purpose of the gathering – to agree what the division of labour would be that night between the Chancellor and the Prime Minister. Darling would deal with the bankers. Brown would use his international clout and connections to brief other world leaders on what the UK intended to do and seek to get their buy-in for similar action. That night he would make one last call to Bush and Paulson in the White House to see whether they were in a position to make a simultaneous and coordinated announcement the following day that America's banks were being recapitalised in similar fashion. They would thank Brown for the heads-up but caution that the US could not yet give that commitment.

Turner and King departed, leaving Brown and Darling to discuss the Prime Minister's two other pre-requisites for the rescue plan: there would have to be specific restraints on the ability of the banks to take excessive risks in future and there would have to be a wholesale clear-out in their boardrooms.

As they strolled out of Downing Street, Turner took King aside and volunteered that he had been in a great many meetings over the previous two weeks to plan and prepare for the bank rescue and yet he could not recall a single investment banker having been present at any of them. Had he missed something or was the Governor similarly confused? King turned to him with a smile and said: 'One good idea is worth a thousand investment bankers.'

At the same time as the Prime Minister and Chancellor were agreeing tactics, the CEOs of the big eight banks were also putting their heads together. At 6pm they dialled into a joint conference call to discuss how they would handle the impending meeting with Darling, King and Turner. It was not something they had done before but the meeting the previous evening had gone so badly that the realised they needed to present a united front. If they did not achieve that, then the Tripartite would steamroller them.

The call quickly turned rancorous. Goodwin had been humiliated twice already that day: first seeing his share price disintegrate as he boasted of the bank's core strengths to a room of his peers; second being forced to go cap in hand to the Bank of England to stay afloat. But he remained unrepentant or else in denial, prompting several of those on the line to gang up on him, accusing RBS of having tainted the entire financial sector and bringing a plague down upon all their houses. The sentiment was not helped by what had happened to banking stocks on the London market that afternoon. RBS shares had closed 39 per cent lower but it had also dragged the rest of the sector down with it. Lloyds was off 13 per cent, Barclays shares had fallen by almost 9 per cent and HBOS was down by a whopping 41 per cent. RBS had pulled the other banks under and made the market question once again whether HBOS could survive. Goodwin, who was a fan of neither HBOS nor Barclays having battled with them in contested takeover bids before, hit back. He argued that HBOS was the real villain of the piece and questioned whether Lloyds could be its saviour. It was not a good dress rehearsal for the meeting with the Chancellor that would begin 90 minutes later.

At 7.30pm the executive limousines arrive at the Treasury and the bankers are escorted up to the second floor – surroundings with which they are now becoming very familiar. They are all in attendance – Goodwin, Varley, Daniels, Hornby, Beale, Horta-Osório, Sands and Dyfrig John of HSBC. Darling speaks for only 15 minutes and tells them that in the morning the Government will announce that it is recapitalising the banks, injecting more liquidity into the system and introducing the credit guarantee scheme.

There is no specific mention of the amount of capital they will have to take but the figure ranges from £25 billion to £100 billion, depending on how many of the banks ended up participating in the scheme. A place holder has been reserved for Barclays in anticipation that it might yet be dragooned into taking part.

The bankers reply that they will accept the offer of liquidity and loan guarantees but they are still not interested in the Government's capital. Daniels re-iterates that Lloyds runs a very conservative balance sheet and needs little additional capital. Varley intimates that it is unlikely to need government capital at all as it has other options available to it. But he adds that £25 billion sounds like an extremely large number. Goodwin repeats yet again that his problem is one of liquidity and warns that if the Government insists on tens of billions of pounds in new equity being issued it will spook the markets even further and make the crisis worse. Dyfrig John says HSBC is in no need of capital from the Government and will not therefore be participating in the scheme. King replies if that is the case, then it needed to understand for the avoidance of any doubt that the Bank would not act as it traditionally did as 'lender of last resort'. HSBC would receive no special liquidity support. If it ran into trouble, then it was on its own.

By now Darling's patience is finally at an end. He tells the assembled bankers that the deal on the table is the only one in town and that if they don't accept capital they can't have liquidity or guarantees either. For the first time during the crisis, Darling is genuinely worried that he will wake up in the morning to a terrible body count – a row of dead banks. Finally, one of the bankers asks him what will happen if there is no agreement. Darling replies: 'We either do something or we don't. If we don't I have nothing else and God help all of us.' Alistair Darling is neither religious nor taken to overstatement. For that reason, Rosenfield writes the reply down verbatim in his notebook.

With that, the bankers were dismissed and told to regroup in the Permanent Secretary's meeting room next to the Chancellor's office. As they got up to leave, Goodwin looked like he was strolling off for a round of golf for all the trauma he had been through during the day. Varley had his sleeves rolled up, fingers tucked into his trademark braces. Hornby looked for all the world as if he might spontaneously combust.

Myners, Kingman and Scholar joined King and Turner back in the Chancellor's office. They had a further discussion and agreed to start work on the announcement of the recapitalisation.

For the next two hours the second and third floors of the Treasury became a mine of activity. Each of the bankers moved into a separate room to decide whether they would accept Government's terms. Every nook and cranny of the building was crammed with officials, bankers, lawyers and advisers arguing over the last dot and comma of the proposal. At one point Darling emerged from his office to witness a grey-haired banker being lectured to by what looked like a teenager. 'I've just been through your books and, yes, you do need that much capital,' the banker was being told.

Rathi, one of the Chancellor's key officials who had responsibility for overseeing the recapitalisation of HBOS, remembers being startled at how little insight the CEOs and CFOs of the individual banks had into the quality of the assets on their balance sheets. That night, therefore, he and his fellow officials were having to make some broad and quite sweeping assumptions about the quality of their loan books. The lesson he would learn from that night was that when you thought you had reached a big enough number you needed to double it.

At 9pm the Treasury team sent out for curry from Darling's favourite Indian restaurant – Gandhi's in Kennington close to the old flat he occupied before becoming Chancellor. It was the reason that next day the bank rescue would be christened 'the Balti bailout'. Darling ordered his usual chicken tandoori. The bankers and their advisers were invited to tuck in to but decided to demur. Mayhew was especially sniffy about the Indian – not his favourite cuisine. Either they had lost their appetites or were too nervous to eat.

The bill came to £350 and was paid for using Rosenfield's credit card. Darling's messenger Kevin Whelan, who had worked for successive Chancellors all the way back to Norman Lamont, was despatched to collect the food. The Treasury accounts department subsequently queried Rosenfield's expenses claim. Even though it was about to spend close to £500 billion bailing out the banking system, it still needed a list of everyone who had eaten that evening.

Whilst Goodwin was still arm-wrestling with Darling's team in the Treasury, the RBS chairman McKillop finally got through to Brown. His refrain was similar to the one his chief executive had been arguing all evening. Despite the bank's near-death experience, McKillop still seemed to be in denial, saying that all RBS needed was overnight finance. Brown did not believe him any more than Darling had done earlier in the day. The Prime Minister concluded that RBS was not a temporary victim of a credit crunch that would unwind sooner or later. Its problems were structural, not circumstantial. The bank owned assets of unimaginable toxicity, the extent of which it was unaware, and had too little capital to cover its losses.

McKillop, a fellow Scot, also wanted Brown to make an immediate announcement to the markets that Emergency Liquidity Assistance was being provided to RBS by the Bank of England. And he wanted the announcement to be made in time to catch the Ten O'clock News because he was concerned otherwise that queues would start forming at RBS branches in the morning. Had the bankers not learned their lesson? This was exactly the message that Northern Rock had allowed to slip out 12 months earlier. Far from buttressing the bank and reassuring the markets, it had the opposite effect. It drove a run on the business from which the bank never recovered. It merely served to underline how out of their depth were some of the men at the helm of Britain's biggest banks. McKillop was a chemist who had run the pharmaceutical giant AstraZeneca very successfully until 2006 when he retired and, somewhat reluctantly, took on the chairmanship of RBS. He was no banker – but then nor were Andy Hornby and Dennis Stevenson, respectively chief executive and chairman of HBOS. McKillop could by now see his illustrious business career ending in the car crash to end all car crashes as he presided over the demise of the world's biggest bank. He was desperate to avoid that fate and the footnote in history which would go with it.

By 10.30pm it was apparent that some of the bankers were still attempting to hold out against the recapitalisation element of the plan, even though Myners had been taking them individually into his office and, with the help of Vadera, explaining why they didn't have any other option. Darling called them back into his office for once final session and said that whilst they could finesse the detail, they had to accept the principle and key elements of the rescue.

With that he told Macpherson and the assembled bankers that it was now 11pm and he was going to bed. 'I have to be up at the crack of dawn and I have got to be ready to perform word perfectly to the world's media and then the House,' he told them. 'If I make the slightest slip it could be disastrous. I don't know about you lot but I can't do that without a proper night's sleep.'

The bankers and their advisers looked at Darling somewhat agog. In the world of high finance, it was a badge of honour to stay up all night negotiating a deal. If you weren't still awake at 4am, you hadn't struck a good bargain. Luckily, Darling was a sound sleeper. But he also wanted to communicate a clear message to the banks that they had reached the end of the road. The bankers returned to the Permanent Secretary's meeting room where they had congregated earlier.

Macpherson left it to Kingman and Scholar to 'finesse the detail' as the Chancellor had put it. The two of them relocated to Myners's room at the end of the corridor on the second floor to discuss what would constitute an appropriate amount of capital. Myners, like Darling, was close to the end of his tether and said the bankers would never agree to a figure because they were like rabbits caught in the headlights.

Scholar finally said they had to fix on a number. 'Why not make it £50 billion? If it's not enough, we can always add to it.' He and Kingman then returned to the room housing the bankers and told them: 'The figure is £50 billion, and we'll announce it at 7am.' At which point the meeting ended and the Treasury team got on with drafting the Chancellor's statement.

Scholar communicated the figure to Darling, who was by now back in his flat in Number 11. Darling updated Brown next door who said they should hold one last call with Turner and King to finalise the statement to be issued the following day to ensure it was clear on the amount of capital being made available and the conditions attached to it, in particular as regards to executive remuneration.

Vadera was despatched to speak to Green of HSBC to gain reassurance that although it would not take part in the scheme, it would support the plan by agreeing to raise a token amount of capital. She felt she needed Brown's support for what she was about to ask, so Vadera went back to Number Ten. Together they telephoned Green. Urbane as ever, Green politely said the Government did not need to worry.

With that, Brown then put in one last call to Washington to let Bush know that the announcement would be coming in the morning.

It was now midnight but there would be more drama to come before the great Balti bailout was properly cooked and ready to serve up to the waiting world.

Day 13 – Wednesday 8 October

Prepare to Pack your Bags

The Prime Minister and the Chancellor may have both retired to bed but there was still a great deal more work to be done to produce the text of a final announcement that could be put before the two men for their approval and signature. So for the next few hours, the teams of officials, lawyers, bankers and advisers scattered around the Treasury beavered away on the precise wording of the statement that would be released on the Stock Exchange's Regulatory News Service before the financial markets opened in London that morning.

It was 2.30am before agreement was finally reached between the Treasury and the bankers on the terms of the government bailout. Myners, Kingman and Scholar called the bankers back into the meeting room adjacent to Darling's office and got them to sign up to the recapitalisation plan. As the bankers finally began to depart for their homes, Myners took Goodwin aside and told him he was 'in a bit of trouble'. Goodwin knew at that moment that his card was marked and he had only a handful of days left in charge of the world's biggest bank

Macpherson had gone home to Earls Court to grab an hour's sleep. He had not been in long when Rosenfield called and said he needed to come back. It was 4am. Some last-minute changes to the statement were being demanded by the banks and he needed to see them. As senior accounting officer in the Treasury he was at the apex of the organisation and responsible for any spending commitments the department made. If there were changes to any documentation then he would need to be there to oversee. He dressed and headed for Earls Court Underground station hoping to catch one of the first tube trains of the day. On the platform, he bumped into the Treasury's director of communications Steve Field. There was no sign of a train arriving so the two men shared a taxi into the Treasury instead. Sod the expense.

At 5am the phone rang in Darling's bedroom. It was Rosenfield on the line and he gave Darling the same information he had relayed to Macpherson. He was downstairs in the lobby of Number 10. Although most of the bankers had left the Treasury by 3am, he had been up all night wordsmithing the statement with the help, and sometimes the interference, of the lawyers and advisers working for the banks. Although the banks had signed off on the statement that the Government was due to issue in two hours' time, they were now having second thoughts. Rosenfield told Darling that the banks, led by RBS, were concerned that an announcement stating baldly that they needed £50 billion in capital would spook the markets and destabilise even the sounder institutions amongst them. Could the statement not be re-jigged to say that £25 billion in new equity was being injected into the banks now with a further £25 billion available if they needed it? Darling agreed to the minor presentational change, well aware that the banks were not fooling anyone: the markets, and more particularly the media, would add the two figures together anyway and come up with the biggest number they possibly could.

He dressed quickly, took the lift down to the ground floor and crossed through the passage connecting Numbers 10 and 11. Gathered in the half-light of dawn in the sitting room of Number 11 were Macpherson, Scholar, Rosenfield, Rathi and Baker, looking haggard after their all-nighter in the Treasury.

Brown had woken early too and while he dressed he spoke to his wife Sarah. He told her that the family might need to get ready to pack their belongings and leave Downing Street. The Prime Minister was not asking his wife to predict the outcome of the global financial crisis but there were important domestic considerations to take into account. The Browns had two very young sons, John and Fraser, and they might shortly find themselves homeless too.

Brown knew that if the plan failed and confidence continued to ebb away then he would have no choice but to resign as Prime Minister. Perhaps Brown had in mind a conversation which had taken place the previous evening with Damian McBride, his special adviser. McBride, not a man given to understatement, had told the Prime Minister in graphic terms that if the rescue plan failed then banks would shut their doors, cash points would dry up, debit cards would not be accepted in shops and restaurants. If people could not buy food and medicines then they would start smashing windows and helping themselves. In that case, the army might need to be called onto the streets and night-time curfews imposed.

In fact, the reality was a little less lurid and somewhat more prosaic. Discussions had indeed taken place with the Ministry of Defence about what would happen if the bank rescue failed. But those conversations were focused more on how the cash network would be physically stocked and how the bank notes would get into the system. The army would indeed be on the street but it would be for the purpose of ferrying cash, not carrying arms and apprehending looters. Ministers also looked briefly at the possibility of co-opting Post Office branches to keep cash flowing into the economy but soon realised that the only viable network was the one owned by the banks.

Brown joined the ghostly gathering in the sitting room. Scholar told him that one of the questions that still had to be settled was whether to guarantee all deposits in all British banks, not just the first £50,0000 in each account. The previous evening the Treasury had come under renewed pressure from the bank CEOs to follow the example set a week earlier by the Irish and do just that. The Prime Minister and Chancellor would need to clarify the Government's position before any announcement was made to the market and certainly before there was any engagement with the media or MPs in the Commons chamber. Scholar's view was that it would mean taking on an enormous and unwarranted liability and should be resisted. His view prevailed. Except in one respect – the Icelandic banks. Later that day, Darling would announce that he had decided to guarantee every last penny that every British saver had deposited with Landsbanki's Icesave and Kaupthing, amounting to some £4.5 billion.

At 5.28am Brown and Darling signed off the rescue plan. It ran to 30 pages and had three main elements: A £50 billion injection of capital into the banking system by the taxpayer in return for which the state would become a major shareholder in several banks; a doubling in the Special Liquidity Scheme to make £200 billion of cash available to the banks; and a £250 billion credit guarantee scheme underwritten by the Government to encourage the banks to start lending again to one another and the wider economy.

Half an hour later Darling was in his office working on the statement that he would make to the Commons later that day and perusing the morning papers. The coverage was merciless. Whoever had been briefing on behalf of the banks the night before had cleverly turned the story around. It was now the banks that were demanding action and calling for an injection of public funds and the Chancellor who had lost control and was being forced to act as events began to spiral out of his control. His hurried departure from Luxembourg had been prompted by the leak of the rescue deal.

Darling reflected that he could have given the media an even bigger and entirely accurate story to report – that the world's biggest bank would have gone bust overnight had it not been for emergency funding from the Bank of England. The one figure all the newspapers got correct was the amount of new capital the Government would be offering to inject into the banking system. 'Taxpayers on hook for £50bn bailout' was *The Times's* front page headline. 'But will it be enough to save us?' added *The Independent*. The paper's Business and City Editor, Jeremy Warner, delivered a particularly caustic verdict on the Chancellor's performance, even musing that the collapse in the RBS share price might have been the result of 'cack-handed' government briefing. 'Certainly, it conforms to the Treasury's inept handling of this crisis,' Warner went on, 'where kite-flying and leaks over what course of action the Government might or might not adopt have only succeeded in making a bad situation infinitely worse.'

The Daily Telegraph also splashed with the bank bailout but its other front page story by editor-at-large Jeff Randall, himself a former *Sunday Times* and BBC Business Editor, told how Goodwin and McKillop would both have to 'walk the plank' as the price of RBS being rescued.

At 6.30am Brown called the Governor to brief him on the announcement that would be made 30 minutes later and to ensure that the Bank was ready to extend the necessary funds under the expanded Special Liquidity Scheme.

By 7am calls from the broadcasters were beginning to pour into the Treasury's press office where they were being fielded by Darling's Press Secretary and Catherine MacLeod. Ordinarily, they would have briefed the media the night before and pre-arranged a series of interviews. But they were not able to on this occasion because of the market sensitive nature of the statement that was about to be made. BBC Radio 4's Today programme wanted the Chancellor for its 7.10am slot but the announcement had still not appeared on the RNS system. Last minute wordsmithing and formatting was taking place. At 7.08am it appeared on the screens and Darling switched into media mode, conducting a series of radio and television interviews from the broadcast studios close to the Houses of Parliament on Millbank. Radio 4's *Today* programme would be the toughest test of the morning. Darling didn't expect to get a deferential reception but nor was it hostile. The programme was more interested in getting its head around what had been announced and conveying the news to its audience in a comprehensible way rather than 'kebabbing' its interviewee in Neil Kinnock's memorable phrase.

Darling was also quizzed about the fate of British investors in Icelandic banks. He again said that Iceland's government had no intention of honouring its obligations to UK savers. In Reykjavik, the government was busy nationalising the country's three main banks, Kaupthing, Landsbanki and Glitnir.

Whilst Darling was doing the rounds of the media, Rosenfield was busy cancelling various engagements in his diary. The Chancellor had been scheduled to deliver the annual Cass Business School lecture than evening but he was going to have to pull out. Rosenfield apologised for the short notice but explained that had he telephoned them the previous day and the news had got out then it would merely have stoked yet more media speculation about what the Chancellor was doing.

Media interviews over, Darling was preparing to return to the Treasury when Brown called him to say that he thought there needed to be a news conference in Downing Street so they could expand on the rescue plan that had just been announced. Darling disagreed but Brown was insistent. Darling's maxim was 'Quit while you're ahead'. He had survived the early morning media round and the statement itself was comprehensive. The more he and the Prime Minister were invited to explain what they had done, the greater the chance of one of them slipping on a banana skin.

But Brown argued that the sheer scale of what they were announcing required the Prime Minister to be front and centre of the announcement. Darling conferred with Macpherson whose view was that the magnitude of what the Government was doing was such that the PM had to own it and sell it to the nation as much as the Chancellor, a bit like a Budget. Brown also needed to sell it to rest of the world. As long as the Prime Minister and Chancellor were aligned, the rest did not matter.

By now it was 8.30am and Darling was on his way back to Number 11 where he needed to call George Osborne and Vince Cable to walk them through the announcement that had just been made. Darling was still feeling bruised over the way that Osborne had ambushed him on television two days earlier. But he reasoned that if he was going to get through his Commons statement later that day with the minimum of political flak then it was better for the shadow Chancellor to feel the love and think that he had been brought inside the tent.

Downing Street, meanwhile, was bustling with activity as the media began to arrive. The press conference was scheduled for 9am but it was nearer to 9.30am before it finally got underway in the State Dining room. Again designed by Sir John Soane, this is the largest room in Downing Street. Its vaulted, arched ceiling occupies the floor above and a huge portrait of George II painted by John Shackleton gazes down from the oak-panelled walls above the fireplace onto a giant horse-shoe shaped table seating 65.

Darling ordered a round of bacon rolls from the basement cafeteria in Downing Street and then took a call from his office in the Treasury telling him that the Icelandic government would indeed not be compensating British savers in its failed banks. Having digested this news along with his breakfast, he made his way downstairs bumping into his flat keeper Connie on route. She looked him up and down as she frequently did to ensure that the Chancellor was properly turned out.

Brown was also making his way to the press conference, flanked by Vadera. Even at this stage, he did not know whether the solution they had come up with would stand the test of time. The UK's banks were having to be dragged kicking and screaming into the scheme, the US had still not committed to injecting capital into its banks and many of Europe's capitals remained in denial that they had a banking problem at all. There was still a huge risk that the Brown would find himself alone and isolated.

He turned to Vadera and asked whether she thought he would still be Prime Minister at the end of the day, let alone the end of the week. In typically direct style, Vadera replied: 'It doesn't matter. What matters is that we are doing the right thing.'

The press conference lasted one hour and went surprisingly well considering how hostile that morning's newspapers had been. Rosenfield and Michael Ellam, the Downing Street Press Secretary, were at the back of the room keeping an eye on their respective charges. There had been concern that the competition between the Treasury and Number 10 over who should claim authorship of the rescue plan might spill over into public view. In the event, the news conference passed off in an 'orderly, constructive and co-ordinated' fashion, as one observer put it. The one man who could arguably lay claim to being the father of the bank recapitalisation, Mervyn King, was not present.

Brown repeated the claim made earlier by Darling that Iceland was acting illegally by refusing to compensate British investors in its banks. But he did not get the kind of detailed, forensic questioning he and Darling had been expecting. The one awkward moment came when Newsnight's Paul Mason stood up, television cameras trained on Brown, and asked whether he would apologise to the British people 'for the fear, the panic of forty-eight hours in the financial markets, for the silent bank run. You are the ultimate stewards of the financial system so don't you owe them an apology?'

Darling returned to the Treasury at 10am and checked in with his diary secretary Marilyne to ensure everything was in place for his planned trip that coming weekend to the G7 and IMF meetings in Washington. His messenger Kevin, who had spent the previous evening collecting curries from Gandhi's, brought Darling a cup of coffee. In accordance with an obscure Treasury custom, he got paid for every cup he served and as Kevin had worked for six Chancellors over two decades he had managed to tuck away a tidy sum. Refreshed and re-caffeinated, Darling then began work putting the finishing touches to the statement he would deliver at midday to the Commons.

Meanwhile Brown had headed back to his office in Number 12 to begin bashing the phone, calling Europe's leaders to urge them to follow the blueprint that the UK had laid out for them. He spoke to Merkel in Germany and Berlusconi in Italy but could not get through to Sarkozy at the Elysée in Paris. It was important that Brown spoke to Sarkozy. Although the French President was not on top of the details, he was the most supportive of all Europe's leaders and he trusted Brown. Brown finally got through to Sarkozy on his mobile with Fletcher, his private secretary for foreign affairs, acting as translator as the call progressed. The conversation ended with Sarkozy inviting Brown to attend a formal meeting of Eurozone leaders the following Sunday in Paris – the first time such a gathering had ever admitted anyone from outside the single currency, let alone agreed to be addressed by them.

Brown also found time to put a call into the Finnish Prime Minister Matti Vanhanen who was about to visit London. In advance of the trip, Brown wanted to extend his condolences for a shooting at a university campus in the west of Finland the two weeks earlier that had claimed the lives of ten young people. The act of kindness was typical of Brown and a reminder that, however bleak the financial outlook may have been, there are some things which transcend politics and the dull science of economics.

After the news conference, Vadera returned to the Cabinet Office where she relaxed by kicking off her shoes and lying back in her stocking feet on the sofa. Her reverie was interrupted by a call from Goodwin at RBS who said he hoped Vadera was sitting down. She didn't bother telling him she was fully prone but asked what was on his mind. Goodwin replied that he had not yet had the opportunity to brief his board. Despite this, and not withstanding his insistence the previous evening that RBS did not require capital from the Government, it might on reflection need £5 billion, perhaps as much as £10 billion. Vadera knew the RBS board had been sounded out because she had spoken directly that morning to a few of its members. She thought about what Goodwin had just admitted and said that she was shocked – not by how much he reckoned RBS would need, but how little. In the event, it would be forced to take £20 billion in exchange for the taxpayer taking a 58 per cent stake in the bank. A further recapitalisation three months later would see the amount put in by the Government increase to £45.5 billion and its stake in the bank increase briefly to 84.4 per cent.

At 11.40am as Brown was making his way to the chamber to listen to Darling deliver his noon statement, King phoned him with a 20-minute warning: at noon, just as the Chancellor stood up, the Bank would announce a half-point reduction in interest rates as part of a co-ordinated move by central banks across the world to cut the cost of borrowing. The US Federal Reserve, the European Central Bank as well as the central banks of Japan and Switzerland would be joining in the action. King prided himself on the fact that, unlike Brown's recapitalisation of the banks, plans for this co-ordinated rate cut had not leaked, even though he had been discussing it for ten days with Ben Bernanke of the Fed. Unlike finance ministers and even prime ministers who had a habit of changing, sometimes unexpectedly, central bankers were in it for the long haul and were much more joined at the hip, meeting six times a year in Basel to discuss monetary policy and the financial outlook. They could keep a confidence. 'The rate cut didn't leak because we didn't tell the politicians,' King commented.

In contrast to the high drama of the preceding two days, the Chancellor's statement to the Commons passed off without too many fireworks. Conservative members on the Opposition benches greeted the bailout with grudging acceptance. Vince

Cable, the Liberal Democrat Treasury spokesman, even supported Darling. Perhaps not surprising as he was one of the very first British politicians to have identified lack of bank capital as being at the root of the financial system's difficulties.

The judgement of the markets was less enthusiastic. The FTSE100 Index had been in negative territory for most of the day and ended the session 5.2 per cent down. Lloyds and Barclays shares both fell by a similar amount. But at least the announcement appeared to have stopped the rot in the two most exposed banks: RBS shares rose fractionally after the previous day's record collapse whilst HBOS stock ended the day 24 per cent higher. However, at this stage share traders were still blissfully unaware that the two banks were in receipt of emergency liquidity support to allow them to remain open. This secret liquidity support would peak at £61.4 billion. In return the two banks would deposit collateral with the Government worth in excess of £100 billion.

Whilst Brown and Darling were waiting to see whether their plan would succeed, the boards of both Barclays and Lloyds were meeting yet again to digest the Government's announcement and review where they stood. Opening the meeting of the Lloyds board in Gresham Street, Daniels told his fellow directors that irrespective of whether the HBOS deal went ahead the bank would still need to raise new capital, if not from the Government then from another source. However, at that stage it was confident that the amount would not exceed £2 billion, based on the indications it had received from its regulator the FSA.

Some directors questioned whether Lloyds could acquire only HBOS's branch network and deposits in much the same way that Santander had cherry-picked Bradford & Bingley. They were told that was not an option because it would first require the Government to nationalise HBOS and then break it up into a bad bank and a good bank which Darling was not keen to do. In any event, the process would probably have taken months and the Government would be obliged to hold an open auction in which Lloyds could outflanked by a rival such as Standard Chartered which had mooted the idea of paying £1 for the HBOS branch network.

There was one thing Lloyds could do – and that was renegotiate the amount it was paying for HBOS in light of the fast-deteriorating condition of the bank. Matthew Greenburgh, Daniels's adviser at Merrill Lynch, was already on the case and running the numbers to see how big a price reduction he could squeeze out of Simon Robey – his opposite number at Morgan Stanley, advisers to HBOS.

Others were worried that taking capital from the Government might fall foul of EU competition law but Daniels reassured them that it came under the heading of special emergency provisions and would not be blocked by Brussels, especially if a host of other European governments ended up taking similar action.

The meeting then went on to consider whether it could get the new capital it needed from the Middle East since it was known that the Gulf states of Qatar and Abu Dhabi were in the market to invest in UK banks. Blank and Daniels had indeed received at least one approach from an intermediary in the Gulf but they had dismissed it. It appeared to them that the intermediary was mainly concerned about the commission that they could earn on any such fund-raising. The idea that Lloyds might lend a very large sum of money to a Middle East investor who would then buy shares in the bank did not seem a very good idea to Blank. He'd spent enough time as a lawyer to know that it was quite probably unlawful as well as unlikely.

At the end of the board meeting, Lloyds issued a short, bland statement welcoming the Government's determination 'to bring stability and certainty to the UK banking industry', adding that its acquisition of HBOS was progressing.

Over in Canary Wharf, the board was also meeting on the 31st floor of the Barclays building. The bank did have a plan for raising the capital it would need from the Gulf and that plan was nearing fruition. Varley had been due to fly out to Qatar that day with Roger Jenkins, the chairman of Barclays's Middle East investment banking division, to discuss the terms of the capital raising with Sheikh Hamad bin Jassim. The announcement of the Government rescue plan had forced the Barclays CEO to delay his trip to Doha until Saturday. The rest of the Barclays board meeting that day was devoted to a discussion about how the bank would execute its dramatic dash for cash to the Gulf.

The Commons statement successfully negotiated, Darling and his core Treasury team turned their full attention to Iceland. Using powers available to it under a piece of 2001 anti-terrorism legislation, the Government had frozen Landsbanki's UK assets earlier in the day. The FSA simultaneously declared Landsbanki's UK division Icesave to be in default. Meanwhile Darling used the Northern Rock legislation, the Banking (Special Provisions) Act, 2008 to transfer all the retail deposits held in Kaupthing's UK subsidiary Kaupthing Singer Friedlander over to the Dutch bank ING. Later that day, the Icelandic government nationalised Kaupthing, its biggest bank, saying the UK government's actions had left it with no alternative.

For a brief moment, Iceland's financial crisis threatened to provoke a diplomatic crisis to rival the Cod Wars of the mid-1970s. Asked how he felt about his country being treated as if it were a terrorist organisation, Iceland's Prime Minister Geir Haarde responded with commendable understatement, saying that it was not very pleasant. 'I'm afraid not many governments would have taken that very kindly, to be put in that category,' he said.

There had been no strict financial imperative for guaranteeing all British deposits in the Icelandic banks. The two banks might have been systemic to Iceland but they weren't systemic to the financial stability of the UK. There was, however, a political imperative. Many of Icesave's biggest depositors were local authorities and charities, ranging from children's hospices to a donkey sanctuary in Yorkshire. With no fewer than 108 councils in England, Wales and Scotland at risk of losing £800 million deposited with the Icelandic banks, Darling sensed the electoral damage that would be done unless the Government stepped in to protect that money. Fifteen police forces and Transport for London were also among the potential victims.

With his finely-tuned political antennae, Turner, could also understand Darling's motivation. However, the Bank Governor Mervyn King could not understand why the Government was expending so much of its energy and political capital on a couple of banks that were not systemic to the UK's financial wellbeing in a far-away country 'the size of Wolverhampton' when it had bigger fish still to fry that week. Then again, the Bank was not required to see the wider political ramifications or take account of the uncertainty that would be engendered if Icesave collapsed with no proper safety net for its British depositors.

Macpherson, the Treasury's most senior civil servant, agreed with King. And for that reason he was obliged to advise Darling that there was no case for intervening on value for money grounds and guaranteeing all UK deposits in the Icelandic banks. As the Treasury's accounting officer, Macpherson was responsible for ensuring that government money was spent legally and with propriety. Bailing out Icesave's depositors breached those principles. That in turn required Darling to issue a formal direction to Macpherson – making it clear that he had instructed the Permanent Secretary to adopt a course of action which he had advised the Chancellor against. It was the first and only time that Darling had to give Macpherson such a direction. In true Whitehall style, it was done in a perfectly good-natured fashion. Nevertheless, it would take the UK government eight years to recover the £4.5 billion it paid out to depositors in Icesave from the liquidators of Landsbanki.

Meanwhile the beauty parade to select an investment bank to help Darling work out the exact capital requirements of each of the UK's banks had begun. The Credit Suisse team lead by Leigh-Pemberton arrived at the Treasury just after lunch. They were taken up to a modest little room on the second floor, sat down at a small circular table and interrogated for 45 minutes by a panel consisting of Kingman, Scholar and Hedge.

When investment banks pitch for new business their presentations typically run to several dozen PowerPoint slides supplemented by a large tome of densely-written analysis. On this occasion, Leigh-Pemberton produced just four slides from his briefcase. There was no point spending an age burnishing his credentials for the mandate or endlessly rehearsing how the banks had gotten into trouble. Everyone around the table was 'laser focused on what the problem was, what's its scale, what is the solution and can we work with these people', according to Leigh Pemberton.

He and his colleagues, Ewen Stevenson and Sebastian Grigg, had only had 24 hours to assemble their thoughts. They based their estimate of how much capital the Government would need to inject by looking at the experiences of other banks and then calculating how much less various baskets of assets – commercial real estate, mortgage-backed securities and leveraged loans – would actually be worth when they were 'marked to market'. On this basis, they calculated that Lloyds and HBOS would need about £20 billion between them while RBS would require nearer £40 billion. Although there was a placeholder in the Government's scheme for Barclays, Credit Suisse was prevented from advising the Treasury because, wearing another hat, it was already acting as broker to the bank.

Leigh-Pemberton then said he thought it would take three or four weeks to crunch all the numbers and line up the recapitalisation. He was in the ballpark as far as the quantum of capital was concerned but a long way out on the timetable. 'We have three or four days, not three or four weeks,' Scholar told him. 'We need to announce this next Monday.'

With that the Credit Suisse team left to return to their offices in Canary Wharf. Four hours later, Hedge rang back to say they had got the job but she also wanted to know how much Credit Suisse would charge. Leigh-Pemberton said it would depend on how long the mandate lasted and how much more support the Treasury needed but £5 million would be a good starting point.

He then called Zurich and spoke to his boss – a straight-talking American called Brady Dougan who had taken over as chief executive of Credit Suisse the year before. Leigh-Pemberton wanted to know whether Dougan was comfortable with him taking on the mandate because it would consume an enormous amount of resource and would result in Credit Suisse having a higher media profile that it would ordinarily be happy with. And the firm would inevitably lose money on it.

Dougan was unequivocal. If the Government wanted to work with Credit Suisse and Credit Suisse had the capability and knowhow to help, then it should allocate all necessary resources to the task regardless of whether the numbers added up to a profitable mandate. In the event, Credit Suisse would end up earning £15.4 million from the Government. It was hired on a retainer of £200,000 a month for one year with the promise of a

£1.5 million bonus and then subsequently asked to advise on the Government's Asset Protection Scheme, which was a way of insuring the bank's against future losses, on £300,000 a month plus a £3 million success fee. Even so, its fees were still only half those charged by the lawyers Slaughter & May.

Two hours later, Leigh-Pemberton was back in Scholar's office ready to begin work that same night. He was accompanied by Stevenson and Grigg and two further colleagues – George Maddison who would head up the team reviewing the Lloyds/HBOS balance sheet and Jerome Henrion who would lead the team carrying out the same job at RBS. Scholar greeted them wearing suit trousers, a pair of very battered black brogues and a bright red T-shirt. The Credit Suisse team were dressed in their City best and briefly wondered what they had let themselves in for but they quickly realised that no-one had time to stand on ceremony. This was about execution and getting the job done, not sucking up to the client and keeping the chairman onside. Or worrying unduly about attire.

Leigh-Pemberton had met Darling before and was impressed by the Chancellor's determination as he saw it to do the right thing and what was practicable but also fair to the public even though ideologically the most attractive option would have been simply to nationalise everything. Myners he knew from his previous incarnation in the City and he was well aware of the hard-driving minister's appetite for 3am meetings and, of course, his take-no-prisoners approach. What he hadn't bargained for was the civil service. He was immediately struck by the ability of the team the Treasury had assembled for the bailout. Rathi, for instance, had worked in anti-terrorism before joining the Treasury so it was reasonable to wonder what he knew about capital ratios and shareholder dilution. But he had grasped the issues immediately.

The feeling was mutual. Rathi said: 'Jamie Leigh-Pemberton was a class act. He was able to speak our language, he presented very effectively, had a good team, wasn't conflicted and wasn't charging too much. And he got it. He was one of the few bankers who understood the public policy and political dimensions of what we were doing.'

Twenty-four hours after that first working session with Scholar, Credit Suisse would have a team of 80 people working on the project, equal to around 10 per cent of its entire London-based investment banking division. Many of them had been taken off other mandates with corporate clients. The team was based at Credit Suisse's offices at 45 Pall Mall where a floor had been cleared for the purpose. It was a short walk across St James Park to the rear entrance of the Treasury. Handily, it was also within striking distance of Leigh-Pemberton's flat in Marsham Street. He would be working long hours with little sleep.

Day 14 – Thursday 9 October

Thunderbirds Are Go

Unlike the Prime Minister, who had awoken on Wednesday morning not knowing whether he would still be in Downing Street come Wednesday night, Darling never had what he calls 'a Gordon Brown moment'. He was confident the Government could weather the crisis because it had a coherent plan which it could finance from its own balance sheet. That plan had been put into effect and now it was time to move into the execution phase.

Though he professed not to take any notice of the media, Thursday morning's headlines must surely have done wonders for Darling's confidence and resolve in that respect. The coverage could not have been more different from the battering he had taken only 24 hours earlier. It was best summed up by the front page of *The Sun* which took its cue from Darling's saturnine looks and thick black eyebrows by picturing him as Scott Tracy, the hero commander from the Thunderbirds. The banner headline read 'International Rescue' and the paper christened his plan FAB. The acronym stood for Flippin' Astronomical Bailout. The Chancellor's private office loved *The Sun* front page and had it framed. Darling's daughter Anna, safely back from her gap year in South America, loved it too and texted her father to tell him so.

Inside, the paper's editorial said: 'After days of dithering, the Government finally looks like it has a plan. But is it the right plan?'

The rest of the media certainly thought so. *The Times* described it as an 'intelligent' strategy to shore up the banks, despite their own recklessness, whilst the *Financial Times* leader commented: 'It comes to something when creating a national fiscal problem is the right answer. Yet that is the case in the UK.' In his front-page commentary in *The Guardian*, Nils Pratley, the paper's chief financial columnist, noted presciently that whilst the amount of money going into the banks was enormous, the taxpayers' shareholdings in the banks might have to rise even further. On the inside pages, Will 'The State We're In' Hutton wrote a commentary stating: 'Incredibly, it may have fallen to Gordon Brown to show the world how to avoid a slump'.

That was indeed the next task to hand, which was why Darling was preparing to fly over to Washington that evening for the annual meeting of the G7 group of industrial nations and the International Monetary Fund. If the Brown/Darling rescue plan was to succeed, it was vital that other nations around the world followed the UK's lead. The financial crisis was a global one and it demanded a coordinated, international response.

Even at this late stage, 24 hours after the Government's recapitalisation fund had been announced, there were still those around Brown clinging to the idea that some grand Middle East-funded rescue of the British banking system could be pulled out of the hat. Leigh-Pemberton was taken aside by Myners and Scholar and asked what he thought of the Michael Klein plan. Leigh-Pemberton made a rude one-handed gesture. The most important thing was to stick to the plan as announced because there was no longer any time left to consider other options. There were a lot of big cheeses floating around the edges of the crisis and demanding that their views be listened to. That kind of extraneous input had to be shut down, politely but firmly. Credit Suisse had a mandate from the Treasury and it had just three days left to complete it otherwise the banks might not open on Monday morning.

Before he left for the United States, Darling wondered if he could pour some oil on the troubled waters of the UK's relationship with Iceland. The Government's actions in freezing or confiscating the assets of Icesave and Kaupthing Edge, the apparent labelling of the country as a terrorist organisation and the hotly disputed call with the Icelandic finance minister had strained relations to breaking point. And so Darling rang Reykjavik and offered to send a team of Treasury officials over to see what could be salvaged from the wreckage and set out the UK's plans to protect depositors' money. The two governments would need to work together if the problems were to be resolved. Kirstin Baker was the official deputed to lead the UK delegation. Scholar asked her to pack her bags and get ready to fly to the Icelandic capital the following afternoon.

Scholar himself was preparing to fly to Washington that lunchtime – an advance party to prepare the ground for the arrival of the Chancellor later. His cab had just reached the A4 Chiswick flyover on its way to Heathrow and Scholar was absent-mindedly gazing out of the window wondering where the famous old neon sign advertising the wonders of Lucozade had gone when his phone rang. It was a very worried sounding Rathi on the other end of the line. The Treasury was receiving hourly reports from the FSA and the Bank of England about what was happening at RBS. The bank was slipping into the sea at an alarming rate. Billions of pounds in emergency liquidity were being pumped secretly into the bank but it was not obvious that even this would be enough to keep it going until the end of the week. And yet, despite all of this, its shares were still defying gravity, climbing a further 6 per cent whilst the FTSE100 and other banking stocks were in retreat once again. It bore all the hallmarks of a disorderly market. Should RBS shares be suspended? Did the Government need to step in and take the bank over?

Rathi was concerned that it might not be the best moment for Scholar to fly to Washington. He politely enquired whether his boss wouldn't be better advised to abandon the trip and return to base. Scholar briefly thought about asking his driver to take the first slip road he could find and turn around. But then he decided to press ahead. Macpherson had remained in London and Kingman had come on board. He couldn't think of two safer pair of hands. In any event, Scholar could add real and purposeful value to the Chancellor's trip to Washington. He was well-connected inside the Beltway from the time he had spent there in the embassy and IMF. That would enable him to short-circuit the usual bureaucratic channels to make sure Darling made the most of his short time in the US capital and got to see the people he needed to see. There were also various people Scholar needed to connect with and various things he needed to do when he got to Washington. He was expected at a meeting of the Financial Stability Forum, a wider gathering of finance ministers, central banks and regulators from the G20. However acute the condition was of RBS, the bigger picture was this: the global financial system had to be stabilised if Britain's banks were to be saved.

Whilst Darling and his Treasury officials were preparing for the G7/IMF meetings in Washington, Leigh-Pemberton's team was getting down to work. Leigh-Pemberton himself decided he needed to stick limpet-like to the client so from that Thursday until the following Monday he did not leave the Treasury building except to grab a few hours' sleep at his flat around the corner in Westminster. He was locked into a constant cycle of meetings and discussions with Kingman and Macpherson reviewing the work streams that had been completed and deciding what needed to happen next.

It also gave Leigh-Pemberton the chance to see up close and at first-hand, how competent the Treasury team was. As the work progressed, he kept making a note of all those officials he would like to have poached for Credit Suisse. There were at least four of them, starting with Ruth Curtice, who worked on the RBS team. She was the daughter of the political scientist Sir John Curtice and had graduated as an astrophysicist. Like him, she had an extraordinary ability to absorb information.

A core team made up of 10-12 Credit Suisse staff was based at 45 Pall Mall co-ordinating everything under the supervision of an ex-Australian special forces operative called Tom Ng. Most of the manpower was concentrated in the teams carrying out the detailed analysis of balance sheets inside the headquarters of RBS, Lloyds and HBOS.

Maddison and his Credit Suisse colleagues received a polite welcome when they arrived at Lloyds headquarters in Gresham Street at 9am that morning to begin poring over its loan books. A similar greeting awaited the team that Leigh-Pemberton had despatched to the London offices of HBOS. Daniels and Blank were confident Lloyds would get a reasonably clean bill of health and both were adamant that it was not going to be classified as a 'troubled bank'. But they accepted that Credit Suisse had a job to do.

The leadership of Lloyds also had a huge amount of respect for Leigh-Pemberton personally and so had no intention of being unhelpful and obstructive, much less confrontational. What gave them grounds for concern, however, was that Lloyds was essentially a retail bank and the Credit Suisse team might not really understand retail banking. Lloyds prided itself on its low-risk mortgage portfolio, conservative loan to value ratios and the tough employment and residency tests borrowers had to pass. Would Maddison's team be capable of differentiating between that and Northern Rock-style mortgage portfolios with much higher loan to value ratios and much less stringent credit checks on borrowers? In other words, could they separate sheep from goats, prime from non-prime? The same applied to Lloyds's personal loans, credit card and corporate lending portfolios.

When Henrion and his team arrived at RBS's Bishopsgate headquarters, the reception could not have been more different from the one accorded to Maddison. Thomas Huertes, a senior official from the FSA, was already there and ready to assist them. The RBS executives were not so well disposed. 'Where's your search warrant?' was the unspoken question they felt they were being asked at every turn. 'Why are you here? This is our bank and there's nothing wrong with it. You are not welcome so prove to me you need to be here.' Leigh-Pemberton resisted the temptation to ring Goodwin and tell him to call off his dogs but a quiet word was had by Treasury officials, making it clear that RBS must give Credit Suisse all the assistance and access it needed.

It was a relatively easy task for the two teams to assess and quantify the liabilities of the three banks which principally consisted of their deposit books. The problem lay on the asset side of the balance sheet, especially with HBOS. In the case of Northern Rock a year earlier, the problem was largely that the bank had relied upon a funding model that was massively over-dependent on the wholesale financial markets for liquidity. With

HBOS and RBS, the Credit Suisse team discovered hundreds upon hundreds of 'crap' loans, written on the wrong terms to businesses with lousy credit ratings that were not worth anything.

Although the two banks had resolutely maintained that what they were suffering from was a lack of liquidity, it was clear their fundamental problem was one of solvency. The poor quality of their assets meant that when they were marked to market it would become obvious that the two banks did not have big enough capital bases to support their lending, irrespective of whether they could gain access to liquidity, which they couldn't because banks with toxic assets find it difficult to borrow money from anyone.

Whilst Credit Suisse was crawling all over Lloyds, HBOS and RBS, the chief executive of Barclays was having a quite different conversation with his regulator. Varley called Hector Sants that morning as the FSA's chief executive was being driven into work from his Oxfordshire home to tell him that Barclays would not need to issue shares to the Government because it was confident it could raise the necessary capital from the Gulf. Sants responded that when the Treasury had announced its £50 billion recapitalisation plan the previous day, it had calculated Barclays would require £13 billion of that. Could Barclays really raise that kind of money on its own? It was a big number intended to shock the bank and indeed it did cause a frisson to run around the Barclays boardroom when Varley's fellow directors learnt what was in the Government's planning assumptions.

If Sants thought that Barclays would buckle at that point and agree to take part, he was wrong. Varley said Barclays thought that its capital requirement was nearer to £7 billion and the bank had received 'very warm indications' from Qatar that it was prepared to put up the necessary capital. Sants replied that the FSA would be undertaking a 48-hour 'stress test' of Barclays capital requirements starting the following day and they would then see who was right.

Varley was also left in no doubt that the Prime Minister would be very unhappy if it turned out that Barclays was not taking part in his grand scheme. Brown and Darling suspected that Barclays's main motivation for not wanting the Government as a significant shareholder was to protect the fabulous executive bonuses being paid out to Bob Diamond and his colleagues in the investment banking arm of the business. If ministers were looking over the bank's shoulder and had a representative on the board, then they would put a stop to that, along with overly-generous dividend payments to shareholders.

Barclays regarded that as a facile, politically convenient argument. The board certainly placed a high degree of importance on its ability to pay market rates and attract the best talent and also determine future dividend policy. But the overwhelming reason it did not want to be part-owned by the Government was that it would throw a giant spanner into the bank's strategic planning process.

In 2003, 75 per cent of its earnings had come from the UK, mostly from retail and commercial banking. Varley and his colleagues set a course to reduce that to 25 per cent and instead make investment banking and management the growth engines of the business by targeting overseas markets in Asia, the US and Middle East. By 2008 it had largely achieved that objective with 65-70 per cent of revenues generated outside the UK. It had also doubled its pre-tax profits. Barclays was reverting to the kind of bank it had been in the 1960s when it was a hugely international business with a major presence in lucrative but also controversial markets such as apartheid-era South Africa.

It knew that if it became a creature of government, then that strategy would be killed stone dead because it was irrelevant to the needs of the UK economy. Partial government ownership would have completely distorted its lending policy and required the bank to prioritise loans to UK businesses. Barclays had therefore taken a strategic decision that unless the cost of taking taxpayers' money was vastly lower than raising it elsewhere, it would avoid having to issue shares to the Government if at all possible. The board was unanimous in support of Varley, some more enthusiastically so than others. The most vocal supporter was the non-executive director Sir Nigel Rudd, the City buccaneer who had founded the Williams Holdings conglomerate. But Varley reassured him he was pushing at an open door.

Brown's attitude towards Barclays was ambivalent. He would later describe the manner in which the bank raised its capital from

Qatar and Abu Dhabi as 'unconscionable'. Rebuffing the Government had been a way of denouncing its state recapitalisation of the banking system and scoring a cheap political point. Worse, Barclays had made it more difficult for Brown to persuade the British public that this was a crisis that affected the whole banking system and undermined his ability to persuade legislators in other countries that far-reaching banking reforms were urgently needed. It was Barclays and not the Government that was taking an ideological stand on the issue – and a hypocritical one to boot, by proclaiming to the world that it was not in need of support from the UK taxpayer whilst simultaneously taking state money from the Gulf. Brown later softened his criticism, saying that Barclays had been lucky that sovereign wealth funds were ready to bankroll its capital raising, arguing that it was actually a good result for the UK taxpayer because as far as he was concerned 'the less government money used, the better'.

Darling, as ever, was more pragmatic. He was not much bothered where Barclays got its capital from as long as it could raise enough money. His main concern was whether it could do that without having to fall back on the Government's fund. Macpherson was of a similar mind. He could understand the irritation others felt that Barclays appeared to be freeloading on the back of the government's scheme whilst still not being part of it: benefiting from the stability it created whilst not becoming part state-owned. But for him, the longer any bank stayed in state hands, the more value would be destroyed so it would be counter-productive to insist that Barclays took money from the taxpayer purely on a point of principle.

Whatever Brown's true feelings, there is no doubt that there was an animus towards Barclays in Downing Street which may well have been fed by King. Varley had a good personal relationship with the Bank Governor but it was clear that King had little time for Barclays, viewing it as a poster child for the kind of 'casino banking' that he so detested and mistrusted. He was concerned about the size of its investment banking balance sheet and nervous about the propensity for Barclays to bring the whole system down by taking on too much risk. In particular, King disliked Diamond, the head of Barclays Capital, who had never been sufficiently deferential to the Governor. As an American, Diamond had difficulty navigating British etiquette rules, memorably discombobulating MPs on the Treasury Select Committee on one occasion by insisting on calling them all by their first names while giving evidence. Diamond would go on to succeed Varley as chief executive but King, in turn, would exact his revenge, forcing Barclays to sack him over the bank's involvement in the Libor interest rate rigging scandal in 2012.

Darling left Downing Street late on the Thursday afternoon to catch his Virgin Atlantic flight to Washington, accompanied by Rosenfield, Pickford and his two special advisers, Spence and MacLeod. He was looking forward to the seven-hour flight. It would give him time to take stock of the last few days, catch up on the other papers that were still languishing unread at the bottom of his ministerial red box and think about how to approach the Washington meeting because it could not be another routine G7 meeting followed by a bland communique.

Little did he know that he was also flying into another Wall Street maelstrom. By the time Darling's flight touched down, the Dow Jones had fallen by 7.4 per cent and the S&P500 by almost 8 per cent, spooked by fears that the US was about to follow Britain's lead and nationalise its banking system. It was the biggest fall in the US stock market since Black Monday in 1987.

Rosenfield had called ahead to the British Embassy to ask whether its kitchen could lay on a steak and chips dinner when they arrived. The Treasury team had been working 20 hours days non-stop for two weeks and they wanted to relax just a little and let their hair down for one evening before the grind began of the G7 and IMF meetings.

The embassy compound at 3100 Massachusetts Avenue NW consists of three buildings: the Ambassador's residence, designed by Sir Edward Lutyens to resemble an English country manor, the old chancery and the new chancery, built in the 1950s when the diplomatic service was running out of space. Darling and his entourage got there early that evening. No sooner had they arrived than a car pulled up alongside the statue of Sir Winston Churchill that stands outside the embassy grounds, one foot planted in

British territory, the other in the District of Columbia. Out stepped Tom Scholar. He had been driven there in his brother's bright red vintage VW Beetle. At least it matched the colour of Scholar's T-shirt.

Day 15 – Friday 10 October

Waiting on the World

The leaders of the world's most developed nations could not have been playing for higher stakes. And the financial markets knew it. Darling woke at 6am Washington time after an unsettled night – unusually for him – to learn that shares were also in freefall in London following the previous day's dramatic sell-off on Wall Street. In the space of just seven minutes, some £90 billion had been wiped off the value of the value of Britain's leading companies. The FTSE100 was down by more than 5 per cent and by the end of the day it would have fallen by almost 9 per cent – its biggest one-day decline in more than two decades, steeper even than the sell-offs after 9/11 in 2001 and the bursting of the dot.com bubble in 2000. It was far from clear to the Chancellor that the rescue plan had worked – or would work. The banks were leading the market downwards. Barclays shares had halved since the start of the year and Lloyds's stock was languishing at its lowest level in two decades. Even the safe havens of HSBC and Standard Chartered – two banks with relatively small exposure to the UK – were under water.

If the markets were going to regain their composure and if the contagion was to be confined to the financial sector and not infect the real economy, then it was essential that the Group of Seven meeting was more than a talking shop. Its leaders had to step up, unite and confront the malaise at the heart of their banking systems in the same way that the UK had. The splash headline in that morning's *Times* summed it up: 'World must follow my example, says Brown'.

Darling began the day by having breakfast at the Ambassador's residence with Scholar to talk through their plan of action. If this was going to be the G7 that agreed on a global strategy to resolve the banking crisis then it would have to be orchestrated with military efficiency.

There was also the nagging worry that, whatever programmes the G7 finance ministers might announce that weekend, it could take many months for them to begin to directly affect the way global financial transactions took place and to fix the world's banking systems. As John Silvia, chief economist with the US bank Wachovia, observed: 'Do you think this is Yul Brynner and the Magnificent Seven? No.'

Before he set off from his quarters in the embassy to the IMF's offices in Pennsylvania Avenue a couple of miles south where the G7 meeting was taking place, the Chancellor had more parochial matters to attend to back home. Darling joined a conference call with Brown in London. Kingman and Heywood were also sat with the Prime Minister. The main item on the agenda was the leadership of RBS and HBOS. It was a relatively short discussion because the four men quickly agreed that Goodwin had to be removed as chief executive of RBS. McKillop had asked to stay on as chairman until the bank's AGM the following year but that was not tenable, either. Hornby and Stevenson would also have to leave HBOS. Stevenson would have gone anyway once the Lloyds takeover was complete because there was no need for two chairmen, but Hornby had hoped to stay on with the merged bank in some senior role.

They also agreed that Stephen Hester, then still the chief executive of the property group British Land, would be parachuted in as chief executive of RBS. He had been sounded out a few days earlier and had agreed to take on the job. The task of finding a new chairman would have to wait a little longer. It took until the following January to fill the post when Sir Philip Hampton was appointed. At the time he was chairman of the supermarket group

J Sainsbury and chairman of UK Financial Investments, the body set up to look after the Government's ownership of assets in failed banks such as Northern Rock and Bradford & Bingley.

The board of RBS had reached the same conclusion, at least in respect of its chief executive. Whilst the fate of Goodwin was being decided in Downing Street, the bank's non-executive directors (NEDs), led by McKillop and the senior non-executive director Bob Scott, were holding two conference calls of their own. The first, at 10am, was attended by all 14 NEDs. The bank's star-studded board included Peter Sutherland, the former European Competition Commissioner, and the former Treasury mandarin Sir Steve Robson. Along with the other NEDs, they agreed that Goodwin should go and that Johnny Cameron, the head of RBS's investment banking arm and a close confidante of the chief executive, should also be asked to resign. But the board expressed its strong support for McKillop remaining as chairman until the following year's annual meeting. The second call at 1pm was limited to the four members of the board's nominations committee – McKillop, Scott, Sutherland and Archie Hunter – and RBS's general counsel and group secretary Miller McLean. They agreed the basis on which Goodwin should depart. Rather than being dismissed he would leave 'at the request of the company' – a small but important distinction which would have a major bearing on his pension entitlement. McKillop and Scott were delegated to negotiate the precise terms of his departure. The nominations committee also discussed the option of Goodwin being replaced by an interim CEO whilst a full search was launched for a permanent successor. They decided there was no time for that and recommended that Hester be given the job.

The Downing Street conference call over, Darling then moved into G7 mode. Arriving at the IMF's headquarters he made straight for Paulson and Lagarde. The three finance ministers agreed that the G7 meeting needed to be short and focused and it should come up with a five-point plan for tackling the banking crisis capable of being communicated on one side of A4. Darling then went into a series of bilateral meetings with the chairman of the Federal Reserve Bernanke, Italy's finance minister Tremonti, Russia's finance minister Alexei Kudrin and Dominic Strauss-

Kahn, then managing director of the IMF – a position he would hold until his downfall and disgrace three years later. DSK, as he liked to be known, seemed to be preoccupied mainly with Iceland, which was also a subject close to Darling's heart but not his central focus over that particular weekend. He finished the round of one-to-one meetings confident for the first time that his fellow finance ministers were in broad agreement on the need to take shareholdings in their own banks.

King and Turner had by now also reached Washington. King would spend the next two days making the case for recapitalisation with his fellow central bankers. Turner, when he wasn't in contact with his CEO Sants back in London, would do much the same with his counterparts overseeing financial regulation in other countries. King did not detect a collective view among other central bankers that recapitalisation was the way to proceed with the exception of the US. He could see in their body language and their eyes that a large chunk of money set aside for TARP was going to be redirected into buying bank shares.

King did not make any secret of his view that the £50 billion recapitalisation fund announced three days earlier might not be enough. In private briefings with UK journalists, he mused on whether it might be necessary for the Government to take the banks fully into public ownership. *The Times* reported the Governor's thoughts, sparking fresh panic in the markets, until the story was taken down at the request of the Bank.

Brown, meanwhile, was taking a rare break from the crisis. Whilst the fate of the world's financial sector hung in the balance and stock markets were once again in freefall, the Prime Minister had found the time to make a two-hour trip to the Cheltenham Literature Festival. Accompanying him was the veteran anti-nuclear arms campaigner and Labour MP Joan Ruddock who had just been made junior Energy and Climate Change Minister in the reshuffle. On the way there, he spoke constantly on the telephone – to the European President Barroso twice, to President Sarkozy and Chancellor Merkel and, finally, to Darling once again in Washington.

On route, Brown stopped off in Swindon to honour a long-standing diary commitment. He arrived in Cheltenham early in the afternoon and made his way to its imposing Victorian town hall where the Prime Minister had agreed to be interviewed by *The Times* columnist and author Ben Macintyre about a book he had written on unsung, everyday war heroes. Brown, like Darling, took the view that it was important sometimes to stick to a schedule and not allow yourself to be consumed by permanent crisis.

The audience of A-Level politics students, local dignitaries and book lovers let out a collective gasp when Brown took to the stage, reasoning that a literary festival was an unlikely place to encounter a prime minister in the thick of a global financial crisis. Macintyre attempted to keep the focus on literary matters, but Brown quickly turned the event into a tutorial on global financial crises and how to resolve them. And why he was the man best placed to lead the country and the world to economic safety.

Brown appeared physically exhausted and yet also in expansive, amusing and animated mood. His book about ordinary people finding courage in extraordinary circumstances, about inner resources and moral strength, and about leadership could not have been more apposite to the circumstances the country was facing.

As the interview progressed, Macintyre quoted the French general Marshal Foch who famously sent a report back to headquarters during the Battle of the Marne in 1914 which read 'My centre is giving way. My right is retreating. Situation excellent. I shall attack.' He then asked: 'Do you feel like that Prime Minister?

Brown paused and then addressed his audience directly: 'I just hope the experience I've gained over the last ten years is going to be of use to people in dealing with this particular set of problems now,' he said. 'I can't predict what's going to happen in the next few months. I know we have taken decisive action and I want other countries to follow us.'

Back in London, the Credit Suisse team were racing against the clock to complete their assessments of how much capital each bank would need. Maddison and his team spent most of the morning at the FSA's offices in Canary Wharf, comparing its estimates of Lloyds's and HBOS's requirements with their own. They concluded that the regulator had not lifted the bonnet sufficiently and discovered the true horror of how bad HBOS's asset portfolio really was. They reconvened at 45 Pall Mall and then headed over to the Treasury. Hornby was there. They left him with a long list of additional material they needed from the bank and arranged to meet him again the following morning.

Leigh-Pemberton was in Myners's office in the Treasury in discussion with the minister and Kingman. Although strictly speaking his job was confined to working out how the Government's £50 billion pot of capital should be divided between the three banks, he had quickly found himself being asked for his advice on a much wider range of matters. The Government was intent on getting its money's worth, after all. They wanted to know what he thought was the best course of action to take with RBS: keep it as an independent, listed bank with its own management and outside shareholders; or nationalise it and put ministers in direct control? Either way, it was going to be the most enormous task to defuse the bomb that RBS had become and return it to commercial viability. Leigh-Pemberton's view was unequivocal – if the business was fully-nationalised, the Government would struggle to attract and retain the calibre of management required to achieve that goal. To operate as a commercial entity, there needed to be good, strong professionals running the bank and it had to have a board with its own sense of independence.

It was helpful advice for Myners as he turned his attention to the series of crucial encounters with bank CEOs which were about to start that afternoon and run through into Saturday and Sunday. The running order was Lloyds, HBOS and lastly RBS.

Barclays could wait until later. Scholar had been deputed to negotiate with the bank and a placeholder had been left open for it to join the Government's scheme. But because Credit Suisse's brief was limited to the other three banks, the Treasury did not have a good line of sight into the state of Barclays's balance sheet. The FSA was in the driving seat as far as negotiations with Barclays were concerned and Sants was telling Scholar that the bank was not being very co-operative. Scholar's own view was that Varley himself had been a helpful, constructive and creative contributor to the Treasury's thinking. But the bank itself was in a fight for its survival as an independent institution which probably explained why it was trying to keep its regulator at arm's length.

The most that Scholar could do was speak to Varley by phone. He rang him from Washington around mid-morning and the two men had a friendly though inconclusive conversation. Scholar came off the phone thinking there was still a possibility that Barclays would participate because he was unsure whether the bank had the ability to raise the required amount of capital elsewhere. Varley knew otherwise.

Daniels and Blank had been asked to get to the Treasury for 3.30pm for the meeting with Myners. The minister would be accompanied by what Blank referred to as the Treasury Quartet – Kingman, Sants, Gieve and Leigh-Pemberton: the banking industry's very own version of the four horsemen of the apocalypse. The mood was extraordinarily fragile. The markets were in meltdown once again and Lloyds and HBOS shares were in freefall. They would end the day 10 per cent and 19 per cent lower respectively. Apart from the general market mayhem, two specific worries were gnawing away at Daniels – first that Lloyds would be forced to raise much more capital than it thought necessary; second that it would end up being stigmatised on Monday as a 'bad bank'. The indications coming from Credit Suisse did nothing to assuage his fears – they were now suggesting that Lloyds might need as much as £4 billion from the Government. At the beginning of the week the FSA had put the figure at £1.5 billion. What the hell, Daniels wondered, was going on?

Daniels decided it was important therefore that the bank's finance director Tim Tookey also attended the meeting. He rang him at 11am. Tookey was in Edinburgh at the time chairing the group's monthly finance meeting in the offices of its life insurance business Scottish Widows. He apologised to Daniels and said he thought it was too short notice to make a 3.30pm meeting in London. Daniels told him to get to the airport and get on the first plane and if there wasn't a commercial flight available then he should hire a private jet.

Tookey made it to the Treasury at 3.15pm. He, Daniels and Blank were shown up to one of the tired-looking meeting rooms on the second floor overlooking Horse Guards Parade. Lloyds shares were standing at 189p – their lowest in two decades – and would fall further to 123p by close of trading. Daniels still had a long list of issues to resolve in relation to its takeover of HBOS including assurances on government interference, executive remuneration, dividend policy and lending to small businesses. It was not as incendiary as his meeting with Myners three days earlier which had ended with Daniels storming out of the room.

For the 'Quartet', the only real issue was the amount of capital that would need to be injected into Lloyds, the terms on which the money went in and the degree of dilution it would result in for the banks existing shareholders who would find themselves owning less of the bank than they had the day before. Leigh-Pemberton had decided to operate on the basis of what he called 'the David Mayhew principle' (so named after the legendary Cazenove banker). The principle was simple: if they were going into the market to raise capital, they needed to go big. They could not leave a scintilla of doubt afterwards in anyone's mind that the banks were now anything other than properly capitalised. If the Government had subsequently to inject even more capital then the impact of the initial equity raising would be diluted. It was a sensible principle and in normal circumstances it would have worked. But RBS was anything but normal and so the following February the Government would need to subscribe for a further £13 billion in RBS shares. Ultimately, the taxpayer would end up owning 84 per cent of RBS, costing a total of £45.5 billion

Daniels was still exercised by one other concern. It was the same worry that had been nagging at him since it became clear that the Government was intent on recapitalising the British banking system: were ALL of the banks being made to participate? Would ALL of their CEOs be in the Treasury that weekend negotiating with the Treasury over the amount of capital they would be taking? Kingman assured him that HSBC and Standard Chartered would be covered by the announcement the Treasury intended to make on Monday. What about Barclays? Daniels asked. 'Everyone is taking the Queen's shilling' Gieve reassured him.

The Quartet had one more bank meeting to attend later that evening with Goodwin and McKillop of RBS. But first they needed some final political guidance. At 5pm London time, noon on the eastern seaboard, Darling, Scholar, Spence and Rosenfield gathered in the UK office at the IMF's Washington headquarters on Pennsylvania Avenue, opposite the World Bank and a short stroll from the White House. They called Downing Street and were patched through to the conferencing facility in Brown's office. Sat with the Prime Minister were Macpherson, Kingman and Rathi from the Treasury and Heywood from Number Ten. By this time the Bank Governor was no longer involved. King had lost the argument that the recapitalisation should be compulsory and cover all eight top banks and the Treasury had taken a firm grasp of the reins. They were also about to determine the size of the individual capital injections that would be announced on the Monday morning, subject to some final haggling over the weekend.

Kingman opened the discussion by saying he had been told McKillop was angling to remain with RBS until next year's AGM. Brown cut in, saying: 'In my view he is not the right person to chair the board going forward.' Kingman said he had sounded out Hester's views on the matter and the incoming CEO had offered no support for McKillop to stay. So the chairman was definitely out. Darling noted that Hester would be the first non-Scottish CEO of RBS in its 280-year history. The politics and employment implications of that would be interesting. The Chancellor was thinking ahead and mentally rehearsing his lines for Monday morning. Kingman said if it was any help, none of RBS's global markets division, the part of the bank that would bear the brunt of cutbacks, was based in Edinburgh.

Kingman went on to caution that the Lloyds/HBOS merger could yet fall apart and if it did how should HBOS be dealt with as a standalone bank? The options were not attractive and boiled down realistically to just one: nationalisation. Darling said that, on balance, he remained keen for the merger to go ahead but that Lloyds could not expect any special treatment to persuade it to go through with the deal. The discussion then turned to the logistics of how Monday's announcement would be managed: who would take responsibility for the Stock Exchange statement and where the press conference would take place. There were two outstanding issues: Goodwin's pension and Hester's remuneration, neither of which had yet been settled.

It was 8pm and therefore dark by the time Goodwin's Mercedes S-Class glided down King Charles Street and into the side entrance to the Treasury, depositing him and McKillop in the circular courtyard that divides the two halves of the building. Even banks have investment banks to advise them. RBS's adviser was UBS and it was also in attendance. McKillop and Goodwin were not the first visitors to find it odd that, once beyond the security gates, it was possible to wander freely around the complex without let or hindrance. Myners and the Quartet were waiting for them on the ground floor. They had been joined by Charles Randell from Slaughter & May and James Leigh-Pemberton from Credit Suisse. It was not going to be an easy meeting and the discussion would be mostly one way. Goodwin and McKillop were told in broad outline what the terms of the recapitalisation would be and what conditions would be attached to it. By then, they knew the game was up although the coup de grace would not take place until the weekend.

While a glum-faced Goodwin and McKillop were exiting the building, Kirstin Baker was sat in her third-floor office in the Treasury, weekend bag packed and waiting to head for the airport to fly to Reykjavik. The phone went. It was Scholar to tell her that the trip was cancelled because there was going to be far too much work to do in London that weekend.

There was one piece of good news, however, for the ranks of exhausted Treasury officials. Louise Tullet, the Treasury's head of operations, had been down to see Rathi earlier in the day. Up until then, the team working on the bank rescue had been left largely to their own devices – ordering in food, sleeping on sofas when they did not have time to get home to their beds, typing and printing their own documents. Everything would change that weekend. 'Tell us what you need and we'll organise it,' Tullet told him. 'Hotel rooms, food and drink, extra secretarial support. Just let me know.' If Tuesday night had been the Balti Bailout, Saturday and Sunday would become Pizza Weekend.

Late into the evening, the G7 came out with its communique. It was as good as Darling and Brown could have hoped. It had committed to take 'urgent and exceptional action' to bail out the world's financial system. 'All necessary steps' would be taken to achieve this, including the part-nationalisation of banks.

The communique was short and consisted of a five-point plan as Darling, Paulson and Lagarde had agreed. The key pledge was to 'ensure that our banks and other financial intermediaries, as needed, can raise capital from public as well as private sources in sufficient amounts to re-establish confidence and permit them to continue lending to households and businesses'. Significantly, Paulson confirmed that the Bush administration would use some of the $700 billion earmarked for its TARP scheme to buy stakes directly in US banks.

All in all, a good day's work. Scholar left for the airport to catch the red eye back to London. It was going to be a busy weekend.

Day 16 – Saturday 11 October

Nice Day for a Drive-By Shooting

Scholar landed back at Heathrow just before 7am and took a cab to his flat in Russell Square where he showered and put on a change of clothes. He decided to walk into work to get some fresh air and so took the short-cut through Covent Garden market, already bustling with shoppers and tourists, arriving in his office at lunchtime. This would be a busy day inside the Treasury too. By now the team working on the bailout had swollen to more than 200, made up of Treasury, Bank of England and FSA officials supplemented by an army of investment bankers, lawyers and accountants temporarily added to the government payroll at a cost which would exceed £100 million.

Up until then, they had been surviving on cake and biscuits and whatever else they could lay their hands on as they turned up for work – thin rations for a team working at the very limits of its capacity and occasionally prone to make mistakes or simply forget to complete tasks through sheer fatigue and stress. Now, finally, the Treasury's catering machine had kicked into action. Pizzas all round.

A series of meetings had been lined up with the chairman and CEO of each bank at which they would be given the terms and conditions on which they were being recapitalised. They would each be dealt with on separate floors to minimise the possibility of bumping into one another on the way in or out. Myners and

Kingman were handling RBS and Lloyds/HBOS. Scholar would be responsible for talking to Barclays. They were all braced for some difficult discussions. Myners was relishing the encounters, which is more than can be said for the bankers who found his approach to them bullying and intimidating. 'He behaved like a butcher's boy,' said one aggrieved banker.

In Washington, Darling had risen early. He called Rosenfield to check on his schedule for the day and was told his first meeting of the morning would be with Paulson. By now Darling and the US Treasury Secretary had built up a good rapport – as had Rosenfield with his opposite number in Washington, a bluff Texan called Jim Wilkinson who served as Paulson's chief of staff. As he always did when Rosenfield was in town, Wilkinson treated him to breakfast that morning at Washington's oldest restaurant, the Old Ebbitt Grill on 15th street, a favourite watering hole for Congressmen and the White House Press corps alike. It was important that the two aides understood the political landscape in each other's home territory so they spent time exchanging notes.

Darling and Paulson reviewed the overnight reaction to the communique that the G7 had issued late the previous evening. *The Guardian* headline captured the essence of what had been decided: 'G7 agrees global rescue plan'. The accompanying story also quoted Darling as saying: 'If international cooperation is to mean anything, it means governments have to move on from simply agreeing a general approach, and doing something to resolve the problems we are facing today.'

In a foretaste of the tough talking that lay ahead in London, the Chancellor also made it plain that the Government would exact a heavy price from UK bank chiefs deemed to have been at fault for creating the crisis. He said taxpayers 'won't accept people taking large risks that have had hugely damaging effects, not just on individual institutions, but on the wider economic system. Agreements will be negotiated.'

Darling told Paulson that the struggle he had encountered getting TARP through the US Congress had persuaded the UK not to attempt to push through a similar scheme but to seek cross-party support instead for recapitalisation of its banks. Paulson replied that the UK's determination to insist on recapitalising its banks rather than buying up their toxic assets had helped smooth the way for the US to do likewise and re-direct a large chunk of its TARP budget into the purchase of bank shares. 'You drafted behind us and we'll draft behind you,' he said in his Texan drawl.

Back in London, Lloyds had already been into the Treasury to learn its fate by the time Scholar reached his desk. Blank, Daniels and Tookey had seen Myners and Kingman mid-morning in a ground floor office of the Treasury. The meeting with the Lloyds trio opened with a nasty surprise. The £4 billion figure they had been given the previous day for the amount of capital the bank would need to raise was already out of date. Furthermore, the amount that HBOS required was roughly double the amount that Lloyds would need. Myners could not give them precise figures, nor could he explain why the numbers had moved northwards in the space of 24 hours. They would need to ask Sants at the FSA. There was worse news to come. If Lloyds did not go through with the takeover of HBOS then it would need to raise even more capital as a standalone business. It was, as Sants would later bluntly state, a stick with which to beat them into going through with the merger.

Blank and Daniels reacted with a mixture of anger and incredulity and asked Myners if they could go back to the FSA and discuss the numbers. They were told that they could not and, even if they did, it would make no difference to the outcome. Kingman did not have any sympathy for RBS and Goodwin. But he did feel a little bit of Lloyds's pain. Daniels did not want to be in the Treasury, nor did he believe he needed to be. The only reason Daniels was there at all was because Lloyds had done the Government a favour by agreeing to rescue HBOS, which everyone accepted needed to be recapitalised. But now here he was being told that he would have to accept billions more in taxpayers' support for his own bank even if the deal did not go ahead.

Lloyds was being asked to accept a whole range of conditions and restrictions on its future behaviour without knowing what the consequences would be or what its precise capital requirement was. Daniels and Blank knew at that point that they were being railroaded but what other choice did they have? It was going to be difficult for a bank that was still largely dependent on the UK retail banking, mortgage and savings market to raise capital elsewhere – and certainly not from foreign sovereign wealth funds – and the only source of liquidity was the Bank of England. Its regulator was going to determine what its capital needs were and it was going to have to accept it or it might not be able to open its doors on Monday either. At least Barclays was in the same boat, wasn't it? Barclays was indeed in the building and being dealt with, he was assured.

Blank, Daniels and Tookey left the Treasury as frustrated as they were furious. When they arrived back in Gresham Street, Tookey called the FSA to ask where its new numbers had come from and how they had been calculated. He was told they were not the FSA's numbers but the Treasury's, courtesy of Credit Suisse.

This merely served to rub salt into the wounds. The leadership of Lloyds was sceptical anyway of the ability of the FSA and Credit Suisse to understand the distinction between its business model and that of HBOS. The conversation that had just taken place reinforced this concern. HBOS was exposed to a high-risk portfolio of assets largely made up of tenuous property loans that would rapidly become loss-making if there was the slightest downturn in the economy. Lloyds was a model of conservative probity by comparison so how come there wasn't a much bigger delta between the amounts of capital the two banks would need to raise?

Kingman aside, there wasn't much sympathy for Lloyds's arguments elsewhere in the Treasury. Daniels' posture and attitude were seen by other officials as arrogant and misplaced. They also questioned why the bank hadn't raised more capital earlier in the year when its share price was much stronger. If it had done so, then it might have weathered the current storm a lot better.

Shortly after Daniels and Blank had left the building, McKillop and Goodwin of RBS arrived. It was now coming up to noon. They were brought up to a room on the second floor where Myners, Kingman and Charles Randell from Slaughter & May were waiting for them. Myners wasted no time in getting down to business. RBS would have to take £20 billion in new capital from the Government, and perhaps more, giving the state a controlling shareholding in the bank. As controlling shareholder, the Government would be dispensing with the services of its chairman and chief executive. Neither said much in reply. But as he stood up to leave Goodwin, glanced at Myners and Kingman and said with a wry smile: 'You know, that was more like a drive-by shooting than a negotiation'.

Kingman resisted the urge to tell Goodwin that he had never been in any position to negotiate with anyone. But he had to take his hat off to the man and his chutzpah. Here was RBS on life support and this was the chief executive who had put it there. And yet he still believed he had enough leverage to bargain with its rescuer. The game was up but he still felt a burning sense of injustice. No-one present that day would forget the encounter.

A message was sent to Darling in Washington relaying the outcome of the Lloyds and RBS meetings. Myners was warming to his task but the bankers on the other side of the table did not appear to be having quite such an enjoyable time. 'Paul seems to be getting into his stride. He rather likes being on the other side of the fence,' Darling commented to Rosenfield.

Although Daniels had been reassured Barclays' CEO was also in the building receiving the same treatment, he was in fact nowhere near Whitehall. Varley was sat in his car in a service station on the A46 half-way between Winchester and Newbury. It was now lunchtime on Saturday and he was having a pre-arranged call with Myners and Shriti Vadera. Two down, one to go.

The purpose of the call was to apply the thumbscrews to Varley and persuade him that Barclays had no real option but to take part in the Government's scheme. But Varley, a keen cricket fan and member of the MCC, opened the discussion by bowling an unexpected googly. Far from taking capital from the Treasury, why didn't Barclays do the Treasury a favour by buying RBS? To paraphrase Fred Goodwin, it would be the mercy killing to end all mercy killings and it would take one giant headache off the Government's hands. Varley suggested separating RBS into a good bank and a bad bank, much as the Government had done with Bradford & Bingley. Barclays would then acquire the 'good' bit of the bank but leave the 'bad' bit – its hard to value and high-risk assets and loans with the taxpayer. The putative takeover had not been formally considered by the Barclays board, nor had Barclays approached RBS or held any discussion about the price it might pay. It was purely a sighting shot to test whether there was any appetite within government for such an audacious move. Varley was flying a kite. Myners and Vadera were temporarily stunned into silence by Varley's suggestion. By now they had been joined by Kingman. The three of them looked at each other and then Myners shot Varley's kite out of the sky. It was the kind of idea that needed to be closed down, and as quickly as possible.

The conversation then turned back to whether Barclays would take capital from the taxpayer. The tone was polite but menacing. The two ministers told Varley that Barclays had better join the government rescue or it would be sorry. If the bank declined to take part now but then discovered it could not raise sufficient capital on its own and asked to be admitted later, the price of doing business with HMG would be considerably higher. A high degree of mutual suspicion existed between Barclays and the Government. It was not a theological necessity that the bank took capital from the taxpayer. But ministers did not believe that Barclays was being transparent about the quality of the assets on its balance sheet. They also worried that Barclays would find it difficult to raise the requisite amount on its own. If it ran into trouble, then it risked creating a second spike in the crisis and contaminating the rest of the banking sector. Finally, they were concerned that a number of the bank's directors were motivated more by political opposition to the Labour Government and less by business considerations.

Vadera told Varley in no uncertain terms that the 'loyal thing' to do was to take the Government's money. She had a prickly relationship with Barclays and made no secret of her view that she thought the bank was acting badly. Varley was in no doubt that this was a direct message from Brown and Vadera was the messenger. Varley listened to the ministerial threats but declined to give an answer. He concluded they were softening Barclays up in the expectation of delivering the coup de grace on Sunday.

What Varley did not mention on the call was that Bob Diamond, the chairman of Barclays Capital, and Roger Jenkins, chairman of its Middle East investment banking division, had flown out of Farnborough airport earlier that morning by private jet en route to the Gulf. They landed late that afternoon in Doha where they would spend the next 24 hours with Qatar's Prime Minister Sheikh Hamad bin Jassim agreeing the terms of a £7 billion capital injection. This was the visit that Varley had been due to make himself on the Wednesday had the Government's announcement that day not kept him in London. By the time it had reached the weekend, Varley knew he would have to remain in the UK. The Qataris liked to be flattered and would have been disappointed that the CEO was not there in person to negotiate with their Prime Minister. But Diamond was not a bad stand-in. He would, after all, become CEO of Barclays himself less than three years later.

It was now late morning in Washington, late afternoon in London. Darling and his officials had returned to the embassy residence for a spot of early lunch before joining a conference call. With Darling were Spence, Pickford, MacLeod and Rosenfield, all dialled in on their mobile phones as they wandered around the gardens of the embassy compound enjoying the autumn sunshine. Huddled around the bat phone in the Treasury were Myners, Yvette Cooper, Kingman, Scholar and Rathi.

The purpose of the call was for the Chancellor to be given the latest news on how the discussions with the bank CEOs were going. Kingman, Scholar and Rathi began with an update on RBS, Barclays and Lloyds respectively. But then Cooper interjected to say they were having a problem with Vadera – she was demanding to be let into progress meetings between Treasury ministers and officials. They were also concerned that Vadera was giving the banks the impression that she had been authorised by the Prime Minister to negotiate on behalf of the Government. Darling took the view that the Treasury owned the recapitalisation plan and should therefore be left to get on with it without Number Ten looking over its shoulder. Number Ten took the view that Vadera was the true architect of the plan and therefore not only deserved but demanded a seat at the table. Anyway, Myners and Kingman would struggle to manage it if Vadera was not on hand. Eventually Darling reluctantly agreed that she could sit in on the meetings but added: 'The Prime Minister has made it clear that you [Kingman] are in charge of the negotiations.'

The call ended with a brief roll call of the remaining banks. Standard Chartered and Santander were not an issue. Nor was HSBC. Turner had met its chairman Stephen Green in Washington that morning to discuss the Government's plans and briefed Darling on their conversation. Green had explained to Turner that the bank was concerned about the damage that could be done to its credit worthiness in Asia by being seen to take capital from the British taxpayer. There was also the matter of how much capital to raise – too much would signal that the Government thought there was something seriously wrong with the bank but too little would make no difference. He reassured Turner, as he had reassured Brown, that although HSBC would not take part in the Government scheme, it would raise a token amount of capital on its own as a demonstration of its support.

As soon as the call with Darling had ended, Myners made his way back down the corridor to his office in the company of Kingman for their last and most difficult meeting of the day. Myners had also asked the Treasury's senior legal adviser, Randell from Slaughter & May, to attend. Waiting for them were McKillop, Goodwin and Scott of RBS. By now Goodwin and McKillop knew they would be parting company with the bank but there was a long list of conditions attached to the recapitalisation of RBS which would have a major impact on those directors who had survived the cull. Myners told the RBS trio that no executive bonuses would be paid that year, even though £1 billion had been set aside by the bank to reward traders in its global banking and markets division. He also said that the bank's future remuneration policy would be overhauled to ensure that there could be no 'rewards for failure' or incentives for its executives to maximise their bonuses by taking undue risks.

Myners and Kingman found Goodwin to be strikingly business-like and unemotional as they set out how badly the bank had been run under his watch and how they expected it to be managed in the future. On some psychological level, he had faced up the scale of the bank's failure and knew the game was up. RBS was going to be nationalised in large part, he was going to be fired and his career was over. But McKillop was still in a state of dazed denial. It was only as Myners went methodically through everything that was about to happen to the bank, that the full enormity of the catastrophe he had presided over began to dawn on McKillop. A few days earlier, he had sat at the pinnacle of the Scottish business establishment. Now he was about to take the rap for the country's biggest corporate calamity. The look on McKillop's face – shock rather than anger – would remain with Kingman for a long time.

Goodwin got up and left the building but McKillop and Scott stayed on for a smaller side meeting with Myners and Randell lasting 15 minutes. The minister wanted to discuss the specific terms on which Goodwin would be leaving the bank. Myners said McKillop should persuade Goodwin 'to make a gesture' in relation to his pay-off. Stevenson and Hornby would be leaving HBOS without compensation for loss of office. Goodwin should do likewise. Scott replied that Goodwin was 'not the sort of person to give things up'. He also told Myners that Goodwin's pension entitlement would be 'enormous'. However, neither he nor McKillop mentioned that RBS was planning to exercise a discretion that would have the effect of doubling Goodwin's pension entitlement to £703,000 a year.

With the help of his personal lawyers, Maclay, Murray and Spens, Goodwin spent the weekend negotiating a 'compromise agreement' with McKillop, Scott and the bank's HR director Neil Roden. Under the agreement, Goodwin agreed to forego his entitlement to one year's salary in return for the enhanced pension. The agreement was subsequently approved by the bank's remuneration committee the following day.

After RBS had left the building, Myners and Kingman met Stevenson and Hornby of HBOS just before 7pm and explained to both of them that they would need to step down as part of the rescue of the bank. Hornby would be entitled, however, to his pension of £240,000 a year. The discussion with Blank and Daniels of Lloyds did not focus on the leadership of Lloyds as neither man was in the same position as their counterparts at RBS and Lloyds. At the request of Stevenson, Daniels did, however, make the case for Hornby remaining with the business once Lloyds had swallowed up HBOS. Hornby might not have had a profound understanding of how to run a bank or what constituted acceptable levels of risk. But he had integrity and superb retail skills as well as an ability to talk to clients and galvanise staff. Lloyds thought he had a future in the retail arm of the enlarged bank. Myners and Kingman did not agree.

Whilst Goodwin was being despatched, his successor Stephen Hester was locked in negotiations over the terms on which he would take up the job as CEO in another part of the building, well away from the bloodbath taking place on the second-floor. His appointment had been agreed but not his remuneration.

Hester said he was happy to lead the bank but less pleased with the way the Government was proposing to recapitalise it. The Treasury proposed that the taxpayer's stake in RBS should take the form of ordinary shares and preference shares. The latter would carry a high rate of fixed interest and were designed to provide a kicker for the Government, enabling it to recoup some of its enormous financial outlay more speedily. Hester did not like this arrangement, arguing that it would hamper his ability to return the bank to financial health. Knowing that Vadera had the ear of the Prime Minister, he rang her and asked if she could speak to Brown to persuade him to change the terms of the recapitalisation. The Treasury was duly asked if it would look again at the share arrangement. It consulted Leigh-Pemberton who advised the Treasury to stick to its guns. The preference share element remained in place.

But it was yet another example of how Darling and his officials felt they were being second-guessed in Downing Street and being forced to deal with objections raised by Number 10 or think of different ways to execute the bailout when there was so little time to make changes and so much still to do.

Baker, who was leading the Treasury team working on the recapitalisation of RBS together with her colleague Jeremy Pocklington, was as relieved as anyone that more work was not been created for the team. She had been looking forward to flying to Reykjavik that weekend to patch up relationships with the Icelandic government until she was told she would be working 20-hour back to back stints on the third floor of the Treasury.

She had two other bits of good news that night. First, the UK and Iceland issued a joint declaration saying they intended to reach 'a mutually satisfactory solution' to their differences. Second Myners rang her just as he was leaving the building. Would she like the use of his ministerial car and driver so she could get back to her home in west London and grab a few hours' sleep? The bruiser who delighted in beating up Britain's bankers was human after all.

Day 17 – Sunday 12 October

Who Blinks First

Darling arrived back at Heathrow early on the Sunday morning having taken an overnight flight from Washington. As the Chancellor made his way into Downing Street the Prime Minister was passing him on his way out. Brown had been asked back to Paris again by President Sarkozy to address the heads of member states in the Eurozone on the UK's solution to the banking crisis. It was the first time any leader of a non-Eurozone country had been invited to speak to a formal meeting of the Eurozone since the launch of the single currency in 1999.

Brown, of course, was making one last push to persuade his European counterparts to follow the UK's lead and recapitalise their banking systems. Before addressing the full meeting of Eurozone leaders Brown met in private session with Sarkozy, the European Commission President José Manuel Barroso, the chairman of the European Central Bank Jean-Claude Trichet and Prime Minister Juncker of Luxembourg. He wanted to underline the perilous position that Europe's banks were in and the reason why the financial crisis was not restricted to the US, even if it had begun there. The UK government, he said, estimated that European banks held around $2 trillion worth of US-originating assets of which $400 billion or a fifth were 'toxic'. He also pointed out that not only were Europe's banks more highly leveraged than their US counterparts, but

Europe's economies were in turn more exposed to the balance sheet risks that their banks were carrying. In France, Germany and Ireland, bank assets exceeded national output by a three to one. In Spain and Italy they were 280 per cent and 150 per cent greater respectively. Because a large proportion of those assets were of extremely poor quality, the banks in question were badly under-capitalised.

Back in London, a succession of punch-drunk UK banking chiefs prepared themselves for the final showdown with Myners and Kingman. Vadera had also reported for duty at the Treasury. However, the spat the previous day over her involvement had left a whiff of cordite in the air so Darling had given instructions overnight that she should be excluded from the final round of meetings. They were to be conducted by Myners and Kingman alone.

Leigh-Pemberton's team at Credit Suisse had arrived at the Treasury at 9am and presented them with the ammunition they needed to win any shoot-out that the banks might be tempted to enter. RBS would need to accept £20 billion in capital from the Government – twice Goodwin's worst-case assumption – HBOS £11.5 billion and Lloyds £5.5 billion. As a result, the taxpayer would end up owning 57 per cent of RBS and 43 per cent of a combined Lloyds/HBOS.

In addition to restrictions on the dividends and executive bonuses the three banks would be allowed to pay, the Government had also decided that they would be required to increase lending to their retail and business customers if they wanted access to the special liquidity and credit guarantee schemes the Government was providing alongside the capital injections.

Each of the meetings followed the same format. As the executives filed into his office, Myners told them that he would not put up with any 'banker's crap', the offer on the table was non-negotiable and, in the case of RBS and HBOS, non-acceptance was likely to result in both institutions being fully-nationalised.

RBS was first to be given the Myners treatment. Goodwin and McKillop were so weary from the working over they had received on the previous two evenings that they accepted the Government's strictures without much of a fight.

Lloyds was next up. Blank and Daniels had been told to get to the Treasury for 11am. They arrived 15 minutes early and gathered in a huddle in St James' Park together with Tookey and the bank's lawyer Jeremy Parr, senior partner with the magic law firm Linklaters, so the chain-smoking Daniels could settle his nerves with a cigarette. Myners and Kingman spotted them out of a window in the Treasury. It was one of their few moments of light relief – they always knew when Lloyds was preparing to enter the building because a gaggle of smartly-dressed City gents could be found standing on the grass outside with a plume of cigarette smoke drifting upwards from their midst.

It was 11.30am by the time Blank and his colleagues were shown up to Myners's office. They sought to extract explicit promises that Lloyds would be able to maintain its commercial freedom, allowing its management to run the bank and set executive remuneration as they saw fit free from interference by the UK government and Brussels. They received no such guarantees and were told that such matters would have to be ironed out once the recapitalisation had been agreed. Myners was in no mood to take prisoners, nor agree compromises. Blank and Daniels were told very bluntly that there was no room left for talking. Myners also said Lloyds would be required to remove the Material Adverse Change clause from its merger agreement with HBOS to prevent the bank from later using the government capital injection as an excuse to back out of the transaction.

Myners and Kingman had one further piece of unwelcome news for Lloyds. If the merger did not take place, then both banks would have to raise even more capital – £7 billion in the case of Lloyds and £13 billion in the case of HBOS. The Lloyds executives looked at each other and then at Myners and Kingman in stunned miscomprehension. How could Lloyds, a conservatively-run and financed bank, be forced to raise more capital if it chose to remain a standalone bank and yet be allowed to raise less capital if it took on a high-risk bank such as HBOS. Where was the logic in that?

Kingman replied that was just the way it was. If Lloyds thought it could raise new capital elsewhere it was welcome to do so but it would have to have firm commitments in place by 6pm that evening. Likewise, the bank was welcome to see if it could renegotiate the price of the HBOS purchase but, again, it would have to be in a position to announce the revised terms by 7am the following morning.

The Lloyds team trooped out of the building, realising for the first time that they had been well and truly shanghaied and there was nothing they could so about it. They retired to Gresham Street to review their options. Tookey immediately picked up the phone to Sants, who was still at home in Oxfordshire, demanding to know where the new numbers had come from. Sants said he didn't really know but suggested it was part and parcel of the Government's desire to build a 'confidence premium' into the bank's capital ratios.

In fact, it was a mixture of that plus two other considerations: one was Leigh-Pemberton's application of the 'Mayhew principle' – if you are going to raise new capital, go big. The other was a calculation by the Credit Suisse team that if the merger took place then Lloyds would be able to squeeze as much as £1.5 billion in savings from the combined business which would, in turn, reduce the amount of new capital that it would be required to raise.

Blank, being a pragmatist, put the best gloss he could on the outcome and decided the bank needed to look on the bright side. Lloyds would still get to complete its once-in-a-generation transformative deal, it was having to raise a lot of new money but less than it would otherwise need to and the Government was buying its shares at a much smaller discount than Lloyds would have to offer other investors, even supposing the market was open, which it wasn't.

And there was one further arrow in Lloyds's quiver – it was going to pay less for HBOS than originally agreed. Work to re-cut the terms of the takeover had already begun a few days earlier and the investment bankers representing the two merger partners – Merrill Lynch's Matthew Greenburgh for Lloyds and Morgan Stanley's Simon Robey for HBOS – would spend the rest of the day and night negotiating the new takeover price.

In Washington, meanwhile, it was 9am and Paulson, Bernanke and Geithner of the New York Federal Reserve were meeting in great secrecy to finalise the terms of the US Government's recapitalisation of its banks. An hour later the heads of America's leading banks were called to a meeting at the US Treasury to be told of the plan. Some $250 billion earmarked for TARP was going to be spent instead on buying shares in their banks.

Whilst Lloyds was arm-wrestling unsuccessfully with Myners and Kingman in the Treasury, the board of Barclays was locked in session on the 31st floor of the bank's Canary Wharf headquarters. Of the 36 meetings the board held that year, it would be the most crucial. The bank's entire strategy for the next five years would depend on it. Diamond and Jenkins came on the line to say that their negotiations in Doha had gone well and the Qataris were good for the money. Varley also told his fellow directors that the bank had received the results of the stress test that the FSA had been carrying out over the previous 48 hours on the Barclays balance sheet. It showed that although Barclays needed more than the £7 billion the bank had calculated it required, it would not have to raise anywhere near the £13 billion the Government had warned would be necessary.

Armed with the news from Doha and the FSA and buoyed by the strong backing of his board, Varley felt confident of going into battle with Myners. He had two one-to-one conversations with the minister that day. The first took place late morning and was in the manner of a 'sighting shot'. Everyone else is taking capital, come on down, was Myners's line. The second and crunch conversation took place around 5pm. By now Myners's tone had become far more menacing. Varley was told that Barclays was drinking in the last chance saloon and would regret it if the bank refused to participate. Should it wish to come back at a later stage and take advantage of the Government's recapitalisation fund, then it would be a lot more expensive and painful for the bank. Varley stood his ground.

At the precise same moment that Varley was on the telephone to Myners, the remuneration committee of the RBS board was meeting under the chairmanship of Scott. Many of its members were phoning in from their country homes or else airport lounges in various parts of the world. The committee's job was to approve the financial terms on which Goodwin would step down as chief executive and Hester would be appointed to succeed him. Had Goodwin been dismissed he would have received a pension worth £416,000 a year when he reached the age of 60. Had RBS not been rescued by the Government and gone into administration, his pension would have been capped at £27,770 under the rules of the Pension Protection Fund. But because of the 'compromise agreement' that Goodwin had agreed with the company, he was allowed to take an immediate and undiscounted pension from the next day worth £703,000 a year. At the time he was 53.

Scott had spoken to Myners by telephone earlier in the day, mindful of the minister's warning that there should not be any 'rewards for failure' when RBS executives stood down. Scott told him that Goodwin's pension pot was estimated to be worth somewhere between £15 million and £20 million, based on the agreed terms of his departure. There has since been much argument about what ministers were and were not told about Goodwin's severance terms and whether they were aware that RBS was exercising its discretion in giving him the maximum pension possible. There has even been debate about whether the non-executives themselves knew what they were agreeing to when they approved his pay-off. Because of the public outcry, Goodwin volunteered nine months later to halve his pension. Three years after that he was stripped of his knighthood.

Although Vadera had been excluded from the bank meetings, she still had an important role to play in the agreements they would each sign. As far as Brown had been concerned, the central purpose behind recapitalising the banks was to bring the credit freeze to an end, enabling them to start lending once again to private and business customers alike and thus save the real economy from being plunged into a depression. However, the agreements being drawn up with the banks contained no lending requirements. Brown told Vadera to remedy this. She grabbed a spare desk on the second floor and with the aid of the Treasury's Director of Financial Services Alison Cottrell set about inserting the appropriate clauses into the individual agreements. RBS would be required to lend an additional £25 billion to retail mortgage and small business customers in the following year and Lloyds an extra £14 billion.

It was now early evening. Brown was on his way back from Paris. As his car was approaching Downing Street, he took a call from Bush. He was ringing to tell him that the US bank recapitalisation programme had been agreed and would be announced in full the following Tuesday.

There was less good news for Brown a few miles to the east, however. Negotiations in the offices of Merrill Lynch and Morgan Stanley over the revised terms of the Lloyds/HBOS merger were dragging on without an agreement in sight. If there was no merger, then the whole recapitalisation plan would fall apart so the two banks were playing for the highest of stakes. Informed of the stand-off in the talks, Stevenson and Horny briefly considered the option of abandoning the merger and asking the Government for more capital so HBOS could continue as a standalone bank. But the idea was rejected as quickly as it was suggested. Myners thought about asking Credit Suisse to intervene but Leigh-Pemberton told him this was one area in which the bank was not capable of providing advice. HBOS's advisers were becoming nervous too. At one point, Robey of Morgan Stanley reportedly pleaded with Greenburgh of Merrill Lynch to think of the 'national interest' only to be told that he was negotiating on behalf of his client, not the national interest.

By 9pm, the two sets of advisers were still at loggerheads. With time running out, Blank spoke to Daniels and said they had to finalise terms that night. At 9.30pm, agreement was finally reached. Lloyds would pay 0.598p a share for HBOS – a reduction of 25 per cent on its offer three weeks earlier. Blank called Downing Street to let them know that a deal had been struck. Half an hour later, Robert Peston reported the news on the BBC Ten O'clock News.

When the news filtered through to Kingman that Lloyds had agreed revised terms to buy HBOS, there was huge relief that the deal was going ahead. But it was matched by surprise that Lloyds was still offering to pay £6 billion for a bank that was effectively bust. Kingman wondered why Lloyds hadn't cut the price to a nominal one penny, given that the alternative staring HBOS directors in the face was 100 per cent nationalisation. He concluded that whilst Stevenson and Hornby might not have been great shakes at running a bank, they were quite adept at running a negotiation. To have extracted any price from Lloyds was an achievement.

Lloyds, unsurprisingly, did not see it that way. In buying HBOS it was trying to catch a falling sword but it could only take decisions based on the information it had on the day. It had thought about being much more aggressive on price but the priority was to get the deal done and that meant giving HBOS a stake in the combined business that was big enough to convince the bank's directors to support the deal and persuade its shareholders to vote for it. Daniels, personally, was also acutely conscious that, in Lloyds, he had the fate of a 250-year-old institution in his hands and he was its current custodian. The absolute priority was not to do anything that would imperil the bank. Others might demur, but he remained convinced that Lloyds's heritage – and its future – was best protected by seizing the once in a lifetime opportunity that HBOS represented.

There were still some loose ends to tie up. One of them was Hornby. Robey, his adviser at Morgan Stanley, was still batting for his client and so he went over to Daniels's office in Gresham Street late in the evening to ask whether there was any prospect of Hornby securing a role in the enlarged bank. Daniels sympathised with him but said that horse had already bolted. Myners was not in the mood to be magnanimous.

Another was executive bonuses. As he was making his way to his home to Hampstead Garden Suburb, Blank received a call from Myners to say that Lloyds executives would not be allowed to receive any bonuses in cash that year – they would all have to be taken in the form of shares. Blank knew this would infuriate Daniels even further so he called him with the news. Daniels erupted but agreed to consult his fellow directors. A short while later, he called back reluctantly agreeing to the Treasury's latest demand.

If they thought that was the end of the drama for the night, they would be wrong.

Day 18 – Monday 13 October

Where the Hell is Victor?

Brown arrived back from Paris at 12.30am and half an hour later he was tucked up in bed in the family flat in Number 11. Darling had retired earlier and was already asleep in the smaller flat above Number 10. Neither man had any reason to suppose there was anything left that could jeopardise their bailout of Britain's banking system. They would wake early, sign off on the statement that had been prepared ready for release to the London Stock Exchange at 7am and allow themselves a small smile of satisfaction that the Doomsday clock had been stopped at five minutes to midnight. Cross-party support for their action was assured in the Commons later that day. More significantly, governments across the developed world had agreed to follow the UK's lead. What the Prime Minister and Chancellor could not know was that Lloyds's merger with HBOS was still hanging in the balance, threatening to hole their recapitalisation plan below the waterline.

As the two men slumbered, the final act was taking place in the corporate life of Fred Goodwin. At 12.40am the RBS chairman's committee convened by conference call. After a brief discussion of a confidential company initiative codenamed Project Blade, the bank's departing chief executive and its CEO-designate left the call whilst the 14 remaining non-executives approved the former's pay-off and the latter's remuneration.

At 3am Goodwin agreed to the terms of his departure and at 3.30am he was relieved of his RBS pass and left 280 Bishopsgate for the last time, disappearing on foot into the night.

Varley was still awake too. The rumour mill was in full swing, fed from Whitehall, and it was still saying that Barclays would be taking £7 billion of capital from the Government. Varley was fielding calls from colleagues in far-flung parts of the globe expecting to walk into the office to discover they were working for a bank that had been part-nationalised.

As Goodwin was leaving RBS's London headquarters, bankers and government advisers were frantically descending on the Treasury. Myners was still in the building and had been told by lawyers acting for HBOS that there was a small discrepancy in their merger agreement which would have the effect of favouring Lloyds by a few million pounds. This had to be corrected. That, in turn, would affect the wording of the Treasury statement that was due to go out simultaneously in less than four hours' time. Unless it was resolved, neither statement could be issued and neither bank would be able to open its doors in the morning.

What follows is sixty minutes of mayhem. Robey of Morgan Stanley is woken at home by a call from Greenburgh at Merrill Lynch insisting that the discrepancy has to be sorted out before the deal can be signed. One of Robey's team, William Chalmers, puts a call into Maddison at Credit Suisse asking if he can resolve the problem. Maddison said he's 'only the traffic cop' and there is nothing he can do. But he calls his boss Leigh-Pemberton who had only just got into bed in his Marsham Street flat, and tells him he has to get back to the Treasury because the Lloyds/HBOS deal is being renegotiated at the last minute. On his way in Leigh-Pemberton calls Randell at Slaughter & May, who has been shuttling back and forth between the Whitehall and Bunhill Row for the past hour trying to work out what on earth is going on. It appears that lawyers and underwriters for the two banks are slowing the whole process down further by making inconsequential comments on documents which there is no longer any time to change.

Daniels is still in Lloyds headquarters in Gresham Street. He takes a phone call from Hornby at HBOS who says it has a problem because the deal he had presented to his board earlier in the evening for approval is not the one the two banks are about to announce. Daniels tells him there isn't time to get the HBOS directors back in to vote all over again. Stasis rules. Until Myners finally explodes inside the Treasury. 'Everyone else is still up. Where the hell is Victor?', he demands to know. Told that the Lloyds chairman is in bed at home, Myners replies: 'Then get him out of bed and down here. In his pyjamas if necessary.' Blank gets out of bed and out of his pyjamas. He climbs into his G-Wiz and drives to the Treasury. Lloyds agrees to stick to the version of the agreement that HBOS directors thought they had approved. The merger terms are tweaked and the price rises from 0.598 to 0.602 of a Lloyds share for each HBOS share. It is 4.15am and the deal is finally signed.

At 5am there was a disturbance outside the Prime Minister's bedroom door. Someone was stumbling around for the light switch and had tripped over a tricycle. Brown woke up thinking it was his son John. His wife Sarah went to the door and told him to go back to bed and let his father sleep. The voice on the other side of the door whispered in reply: 'Sorry Sarah, it's Shriti.'

Vadera had been sent upstairs from the study in Number 11 where she, Darling, Macpherson and Scholar were looking over the final announcements that were about to be made. They were all dog-tired and operating off a short fuse and the mood was ill-tempered. Because the amount of capital going into RBS was so colossal, the state would end up effectively controlling the bank. The Chancellor wanted the Prime Minister's hands dipped in the blood. He would need to see and personally approve the decision. Vadera said testily that there wasn't really a decision to take. It was a simple matter of mathematics for anyone who could count. The simmering resentment that had been building for many days between the two factions – the Treasury and Number Ten – spilled over into a furious row. It ended with Vadera being sent upstairs to wake Brown. He said he was perfectly aware what the consequences would be of injecting so much capital into RBS and had been so for a number of days. But, yes, he would come down. As it happened, there was also a small technicality that necessitated his presence. The contracts which would bring RBS under government control were massive and complicated and by law they had to be signed by two Lord Commissioners of the Treasury. The Chancellor was one. The Prime Minister was another.

At 6am, Brown joined Darling downstairs and together they signed the documentation. What a supreme irony that two architects of New Labour, two modernisers of the party, were doing what Michael Foot, Tony Benn and a legion of former left-wing ministers could only have dreamt of: nationalising Britain's biggest bank.

At 7am, the statements went out. The Government was injecting £20 billion into RBS in return for a 57 per cent stake (later to rise to 70 per cent following a further capital injection), £11.5 billion into HBOS, giving it a 58 per cent stake, and £5.5 billion into Lloyds. Once Lloyds completed its purchase of HBOS, the Government stake in the enlarged bank would be 43 per cent. In total, the Government would eventually spend £76 billion buying shares in the three banks. Barclays meanwhile announced that it had agreed to increase its capital by £8 billion. Of this at least £6.5 billion would come from Qatar and Abu Dhabi and a further £1.5 billion would be generated from operational efficiencies and balance sheet management. Amanda Staveley advised the Abu Dhabi royal family on its £3.5 billion investment in Barclays. She went on to sue Barclays for £1.6 billion, claiming the fees she received were only a fraction of those paid to secure the investment from Qatar.

In addition to the capital injection, the Government was making an additional £100 billion of liquidity available to all UK banks and introducing a £250 billion loan guarantee facility. Three months later it would launch its own version of TARP, offering to insure RBS and Lloyds against potential losses on £280 billion worth of assets.

The galvanising effect of the UK's decisive action was seen later that day as, one by one, its European counterparts followed suit. Germany unveiled a €100 billion bank recapitalisation scheme and €400 billion of credit guarantees, France pumped €320 billion of loan guarantees and €40 billion of capital into its banks and Italy committed the same amount of new capital and pledged 'as much as necessary' in credit guarantees. The

Netherlands said it would provide €200 billion in loan guarantees to its banks and Spain and Austria pledged €100 billion each.

But for now the moment and the glory belonged to Darling and Brown – with a little help from a galaxy of Treasury officials and external advisers. One of them, James Leigh-Pemberton, was going to enjoy a well-earned rest after spending the past five days chained to a desk in the Treasury. The announcement out of the way, he headed in the direction of Canary Wharf and Credit Suisse's headquarters, unshaven and still dressed for the weekend. Arriving at the building he took the lift and a few seconds later emerged onto the bank's share trading floor and began to make his way across the vast room to his office in the far corner. As he did so he noticed a copy of *The Sun* lying on a trader's desk and glanced down at the front page. 'Cashier No 10 please' said the tongue-in-cheek headline.

Well, you had to see the funny side, didn't you?

After the Storm

The day after Britain's banks were rescued, America followed suit. The Bush administration announced an even more sweeping programme of recapitalisation and loan guarantees, buying stakes in the country's top eight banks in the form of preference shares and warrants giving it the right to buy ordinary shares. The US would not negotiate with individual banks but insisted on taking an industry-wide approach. It would not allow any major bank to escape. Mervyn King, the Bank of England Governor, could only look on with envy.

Bank of America Merrill Lynch, JP Morgan Chase, Citigroup and Wells Fargo were each required to take $25 billion in capital from the US taxpayer. Goldman Sachs and Morgan Stanley were made to take $10 billion each and Bank of New York Mellon and State Street $5 billion each.

America's protectionist tendencies and the reluctance of successive administrations of either political stripe, Republican or Democrat, to allow foreign ownership of strategic US companies meant that Wall Street was not allowed to take its additional capital from anywhere else and certainly not from state-controlled sovereign wealth funds in the Gulf, Far East or China, as Barclays had done in the UK. The US applied the same strictures to ownership of its defence manufacturers and port operators and the banks were no different.

In the UK, policymakers quickly discovered that the £37 billion of capital they had injected into RBS and Lloyds/HBOS would not be enough to strengthen their balance sheets sufficiently. By December that year the total amount of taxpayers' capital injected into the three banks had risen to £67 billion. As for Barclays, it successfully raised the money it needed from the Gulf, launching a £7.3 billion capital raising offer on 31 October. The effect would be to give the royal families of Qatar and Abu Dhabi a combined 29 per cent stake in the bank.

The recapitalisation schemes implemented across the UK, mainland Europe and the US ensured that a global banking crisis had been met by a global response from policymakers. Capital was the vaccine that had stopped the financial pandemic in its tracks. But the injection of that vaccine really only marked the end of the beginning. A global depression had been averted but it would take the world's economies a long time to return to full health.

Although immunised against the contagion caused by years of reckless lending and excessive risk taking, the world's banks were still in a perilously fragile condition and they still had enormous quantities of under-performing loans on their books. Something had to be done with these illiquid and difficult to value assets, otherwise the banks might very quickly find themselves back where they had been at the start of October.

The US had dealt with the problem through Paulson's TARP programme. Although $700 billion had been earmarked originally for the scheme, the budget was reduced a year later to $475 billion. When the scheme was finally wound up in 2014 the US government had spent $431 billion, including the cost of buying shares in the top eight banks. All banks taking part in TARP were also required to impose new and tougher curbs on executive remuneration, including the abolition of controversial 'golden parachute' payments to departing executives which often had the effect of rewarding them for failure.

In January 2009, the UK launched the Asset Protection Scheme. Its purpose was similar to TARP, but it differed in that it involved insuring the banks against losses on their questionable assets rather than the purchase and re-sale of them. The scheme was open to RBS and Lloyds. However, there was one major complication: both banks found it very difficult to provide the Treasury with reliable and accurate data on the quality of their assets. In some cases they struggled even to establish whether they were the legal owners. As a result, the Treasury refused to allow some assets to be included in the scheme or else took a worst-case view of the potential losses. In the end, RBS placed £280 billion of assets into the scheme, rather than the £325 billion originally envisaged. It agreed to bear the first £60 billion of losses whilst the Treasury met 90 per cent of losses above and beyond that. RBS also paid an annual insurance premium subject to a minimum exit fee of £2.5 billion.

Lloyds initially agreed to place £250 billion of assets into the scheme (largely ones inherited through the HBOS takeover) and pay a participation fee of £15.6 billion in the form of preference shares allocated to the Government. Ten months later, it bought itself out of the scheme, paying a £2.5 billion exit fee.

The insurance scheme dealt with the bad assets within the banks. But there was still a need to ensure that the amount of capital they held – their financial buffer against any future catastrophe – did not sink back into dangerous territory. Financial regulators and central banks dealt with this through the Basel Committee on Banking Supervision – the body which sets the banking rules for the world's 28 leading economies. Today, all banks are required to hold capital in the form of equity and reserves equal to at least 8 per cent of their 'risk-weighted assets'. It is what is known as a bank's capital ratio. Before the crash, Royal Bank of Scotland's capital ratio was just 2.9 per cent. In the US, the Federal Reserve imposes even higher capital requirements on what it terms Systemically Important Financial Institutions (SIFIs) – what in common parlance are known as 'too-big-to-fail' banks.

Alongside tougher capital ratios and regular stress testing of balance sheets, a panoply of new rules was introduced to improve banking supervision and discourage risk-taking. And, inevitably, there were changes in the leadership of the banks. In the UK, Goodwin and McKillop had already gone from RBS, as had Stevenson and Hornby from HBOS. By 2012, there had been a complete change of the guard at Britain's other leading banks. Sir Victor Blank stepped down as Lloyds chairman in May 2009 and his CEO Eric Daniels followed him out of the bank a year later. Stephen Green stepped down as chairman of HSBC just before Christmas 2010 – albeit to take up a post as trade and industry minister in the new coalition government. Barclays's CEO John Varley retired in January 2011 and his chairman Marcus Agius did likewise 18 months later. Varley was replaced by Bob Diamond, the head of Barclays Capital, but he lasted only a year in the CEO's job until he was forced to resign over the Libor interest rate-setting scandal by the Bank Governor King. Eighteen months after leaving Barclays, Diamond and the entrepreneur Ashish Thakkar founded Atlas Mara, a financial services group with a mission to become sub-Saharan Africa's biggest bank. It floated on London's Alternative Investment Market in December 2013. By June 2020, the shares had lost 95 per cent of their value.

After a period of purdah lasting just nine months, Hornby re-entered corporate life in July 2009 as chief executive of the chemist's chain Alliance Boots on a basic salary of £800,000. He stepped down after only two years citing a need to recover from the stress of 'an intense five years'. Three months later he resurfaced as chief executive of the betting group Coral. He is now chief executive of the Restaurant Group, owner of the Wagamama, Frankie & Benny's and Garfunkel chains.

Most of the big US banks repaid their taxpayer's capital within 12 months. Goldman Sachs bought back all $10 billion worth in April 2009, JP Morgan bought back $13 billion in November 2009 and Citigroup repaid $20 billion of capital a month later. It is taking the UK's banks rather longer. Lloyds did not return to full private ownership until May 2017 and while the Government has begun the process of selling its stake in RBS the taxpayer still owns 61.92 per cent of the bank.

Although the banks had been prevented from dragging the rest of the British economy into a depression, the impact of the financial crisis was nonetheless enormous. The Bank of England reacted to the rapidly slowing UK economy by pulling two big monetary levers. First, it cut interest rates dramatically from 4.5 per cent in October 2008 to 3 per cent the next month and 2 per cent in December. By March 2009 – six months after the bank rescue – they had fallen to 0.5 per cent. When the Bank could not cut rates much further it turned to Quantitative Easing or QE to stimulate the economy. Sometimes referred to as the digital equivalent of printing money, QE is the mechanism by which central banks buy assets such as government bonds and mortgage-backed securities from private financial institutions such as pension funds. That has two effects: first, it pushes down interest rates on mortgages and business loans, making it cheaper for homeowners and companies to borrow money; second, it puts cash in the hands of those pension funds to then re-invest in other assets such as company shares and bonds, thus providing funds for investment.

The Bank of England's QE programme began in November 2009 when it injected an initial £200 billion into the system. By March 2020 it stood at £645 billion, including a further £210 billion to combat the economic downturn caused by the Covid-19 pandemic. In the US, the Federal Reserve's QE programme stands at just under $5 trillion, including $700 billion to counter the coronavirus.

After leading the international effort to resolve the banking crisis, Brown remained in Downing Street for a further 17 months. His government fought hard to rescue the economy from the after-effects of the banking crisis. Alongside QE, Darling introduced a variety of other supply side measures such as a temporary cut in VAT and a car scrappage scheme to revitalise the motor industry. But in the face of a recession, the only way to reflate the economy was through an increase in public spending and so in his first post-crisis Budget, Darling forecast that the UK economy would shrink by 3.5 per cent in 2009 while borrowing would rise to £175 billion or some 12.4 per cent of GDP.

If it is 'the economy, stupid' that determines election outcomes, then that old adage was demonstrated in spades in May 2010 when David Cameron swept to power at the head of a coalition between the Conservatives and Liberal Democrats. Brown left office believing that the job of rescuing the world's advanced economies was only half finished. Darling stayed on as shadow Chancellor on the Opposition benches until retiring from front-line politics too in October 2010. Many of those nations that had joined together in 2008 to avert the financial crisis had reverted to their national silos. International cooperation had been abandoned and much of Europe was reconciled to a long and painful period of low economic growth. The safety nets and early warning systems that the world economy needed after 2010 were not in place and the threat posed by the unofficial or shadow banking system had not gone away – it was simply lying dormant.

If QE was the carrot that the Bank of England dangled as it sought to reflate the UK's economy in the aftermath of the financial crisis, then austerity would be the stick that the coalition government relied upon to beat the nation's ravaged public finances back into shape. A year before his election victory, Cameron had presaged what was in store for the nation should the Tories regain office when he warned that 'the age of irresponsibility is giving way to the age of austerity'.

The charge of 'irresponsibility' was levelled at the Labour government and it referred to the explosion in public expenditure which had occurred during the Brown years. It could just as easily have applied to the bankers who had so nearly brought the economy crashing down. There was no doubt, however, about which sector of society would bear the brunt of 'austerity' – it was those at the bottom of the pile and least able to afford it. The banks had been saved and financial disaster averted but the rest of the economy would pay the price in the shape of a long, slow and extremely painful adjustment.

In his first Budget in June 2010, the new Chancellor George Osborne immediately set about eliminating the nation's structural budget deficit with a five-year austerity plan designed to save £110 billion – largely through cuts in public spending. By 2015 it had fallen by a half and so a new plan was unveiled to get rid of the deficit entirely by 2020.

Between 2010 and 2020 public spending fell in real terms by 14 per cent. The effects of that austerity were very real and were there for all to see in almost every region of the country and sector of the economy from housebuilding and transport to education and public services. Public sector employment fell to its lowest since the Second World War, police numbers declined by 20,000 and public sector wages were frozen. Private sector employment actually grew (largely through an increase in poorly-paid, part-time service sector jobs). But food banks and pay day loan companies proliferated, infant mortality rates rose for the first time in two generations, the rate of increase in life expectancy halved between 2010 and 2017 and child poverty reached its highest level since 1945 as state spending per child fell.

Libraries closed, bus subsidies were slashed, the building of homes for social rent collapsed from 40,000 a year in 2009-10 to 1,000 by 2015-16, testing by the Food Standards Agency fell by 58 per cent, rough sleeping increased, homelessness rose and by 2018 some 50,000 families were being forced in live in bed & breakfast accommodation. Between 2010 and 2020 there was a 60 per cent decrease in central government funding for local authorities and in 2018 one of them, Northamptonshire County, actually declared itself insolvent. Home ownership declined but average household debt rose. Real wages did not return to their pre-crisis 2008 levels until January 2020. The number of over-65s grew by a quarter but the pressing need to overhaul the social care system was pushed repeatedly into the long grass. Just about the only thing that survived the decade of austerity intact was the state pension, protected as it was by the triple-lock.

The economic carnage being wrought by Covid-19 differs from that which we experienced 12 years ago in one important respect: the cause of the 2008 crisis was a collapse in demand, today's crisis has been caused by a collapse in supply. And whereas it was the reckless behaviour of the banking sector 12 years ago that threatened the stability of the world economy, it is the banking sector which promises to be one of the victims of the Coved-driven economic collapse, as can be seen by the multi-billion pound write offs the banks are already being forced to make against loans they know will never be repaid.

When the financial crisis struck, the most exposed countries were those which lacked adequate infrastructure. Banks were required to hold too little capital, regulatory supervision of financial services was too lenient, depositor protection schemes were underfunded and mechanisms for dealing with failing banks did not exist.

Fast forward to 2020 and those countries which have dealt least well with Covid-19 have also been those which lacked adequate infrastructure at the outset – whether it be test and tracing capacity, supplies of PPE, sufficient numbers of environmental health officers or an integrated strategy for dealing with infection across hospitals, care homes and the community.

We do not yet know what the full human, social and economic cost of the Covid-19 pandemic will be. In monetary terms alone it seems certain to dwarf the amount that governments around the world spent to avert the banking collapse that so nearly befell advanced capitalism 12 years ago, threatening to plunge much of the global economy into depression.

But here is one reason to be hopeful. A year after the financial crash, the National Audit Office estimated its cost to the UK taxpayer at £1.162 trillion – approaching £15,500 per head of the population. (The total bill globally reached $15 trillion). The NAO's figure was made up of £133 billion in direct spending – predominantly the cost of buying shares in failing banks – and £1,029 billion in credit guarantees, liquidity support and insurance cover extended to the banking system by government. In 2019, Robert Chote, the chairman of the Office for Budget Responsibility, revisited those figures to take account of the money recouped for the taxpayer over the years through the subsequent sale of bank shareholdings and assets exchanged by banks for liquidity support together with the premiums charged to banks in return for insuring their high-risk assets. The OBR's revised cost estimate: £27 billion.

No such revisionism awaits the banking boss who more than any other became the poster boy for the 2008 financial crash. The pent-up anger at the age of austerity Fred Goodwin had helped to usher in found its expression in March 2009 when his former marital home in the Grange neighbourhood of Edinburgh was attacked. Windows were smashed and cars vandalised. Three months later, RBS announced that, following negotiations, its former CEO had agreed to halve the amount he takes out of his £16 million pension pot. Goodwin now scrapes by on £342,500 a year and will be eligible for his state pension in August 2024. When he is not counting his millions, Goodwin spends his time restoring classic cars, playing golf and attempting to keep out of the public limelight.

Where are they now?

Then	Now
Gordon Brown UK Prime Minister	UN Special Envoy for Global Education
Alistair Darling UK Chancellor of the Exchequer	Lord Darling of Roulanish, Non-executive Director Morgan Stanley
Lord Paul Myners Financial Services Secretary, HM Treasury	Chairman, Edelman UK. Chancellor, University of Exeter
Dame Shriti Vadera Parliamentary Under-Secretary of State for Economic Competitiveness, Small Business and the Cabinet Office	Chairman, Santander UK. Non-executive Director and Chairman-designate, Prudential Senior Independent Director, BHP Group
Mervyn King Governor of the Bank of England	Lord King of Lothbury, Professor of Economics and Law, Stern School of Business and Law, New York
Adair Turner Chairman, Financial Services Authority	Lord Turner of Ecchinswell, Chairman, Energy Transitions Commission, Chubb Europe. Trustee of British Museum
Hector Sants Chief Executive, Financial Services Authority	Sir Hector Sants Chairman, Money and Pensions Service. Trustee of Just Finance
Nicholas Macpherson Permanent Secretary, HM Treasury	Lord Macpherson of Earl's Court Chairman C Hoare & Co. Non-executive Director of British Land, Scottish American Investment Trust

John Kingman Second Permanent Secretary, HM Treasury	Sir John Kingman Chairman, Legal & General. Deputy Chairman, National Gallery. Chairman, UK Research and Innovation. Non-executive Director, Tesco Bank
Tom Scholar Director General for Financial Services, HM Treasury	Sir Tom Scholar, Permanent Secretary, HM Treasury
Nikhil Rathi Head of Financial Stability, HM Treasury	Chief Executive, Financial Conduct Authority
Dan Rosenfield Principal Private Secretary to Alistair Darling	Chief of Staff 10 Downing Street. Chairman of World Jewish Relief
Kirstin Baker Finance and Commercial Director, HM Treasury	Panel Enquiry Chair and Non-executive Director, Competition & Markets Authority
Sir Tom McKillop Chairman, Royal Bank of Scotland	Non-executive Director, Almirall SA
Fred Goodwin Chief Executive, Royal Bank of Scotland	Retired
Marcus Agius Chairman, Barclays	Deputy Chairman, PA Consulting
John Varley Chief Executive, Barclays	Member, MCC Finance Committee
Bob Diamond Chief Executive, Barclays Capital	Founder and Non-Executive Director, Atlas Mara
Sir Victor Blank Chairman, Lloyds Bank	Chairman of Social Mobility Foundation, Rothschild Foundation Europe, Wellbeing of Women. Senior Adviser, TPG

Eric Daniels
Chief Executive, Lloyds

Non-executive director,
Funding Circle, Russell Reynolds.
Senior adviser to Workday, CVC,
Mitheridge Capital. Partner in
Abako Inc. Adviser to
Leaders Futures Inc

Lord Dennis Stevenson of Coddenham
Chairman, HBOS

Retired

Andy Hornby
Chief Executive, HBOS

Chief Executive,
The Restaurant Group

Antonio Horta-Osório
Chief Executive, Santander UK

Chief Executive
Lloyds Banking Group.
Non-executive Director
EXOR NV.
Chairman of Wallace Collection

Graham Beale
Chief Executive, Nationwide

Retired

Stephen Green
Executive Chairman, HSBC

Lord Green of Hurstpierpoint
Retired. Ordained Priest

Stephen Hester
Chief Executive-designate,
Royal Bank of Scotland

Group Chief Executive, RSA.
Non-executive Director,
Centrica

Peter Sands
Chief Executive, Standard
Chartered Bank

Executive Director,
The Global Fund

Charles Randell
Senior Partner, Slaughter & May

Chairman, Financial Conduct
Authority

James Leigh-Pemberton
Chief Executive, Credit Suisse UK

Sir James Leigh-Pemberton
Chairman, RIT Capital Partners.
Deputy Chairman, UK Government
Investments. Receiver General of
The Duchy of Cornwall

David Mayhew
Chairman, JP Morgan Cazenove

Retired

Robin Budenberg
Head of Corporate Finance, UBS

Chairman, The Crown Estate
London, Centerview
Partners. Acting Chairman of Big
Society Trust. Senior Independent
Director, Charity Bank Limited

David Soanes
Head of Global Capital Markets
EMEA, UBS

UK Country Head, UBS.
Chairman, Business in the
Community Education Team

Hank Paulson
US Treasury Secretary

Founder of the Paulson Institute.
Leader, Climate Leadership
Council

George W Bush
US President

Retired. Portrait Painter

Bibliography

Back from the Brink: 1000 Days at Number 11 by Alistair Darling, published by Atlantic Books, London, 2011

Black Horse Ride: The Inside Story of Lloyds and the Banking Crisis by Ivan Fallon, published by The Robson Press (Backbite Publishing Limited), 2015

My Life, Our Times by Gordon Brown, published by The Bodley Head, London 2017

Beyond the Crash – Overcoming the First Crisis of Globalisation by Gordon Brown, published by Simon & Schuster, 2010

Bad Banks by Alex Brummer, published by Random House Business Books, London 2015

House of Cards by William D Cohan, first published in the United States by Doubleday, 2009 (Great Britain by Allen Lane, 2009, Penguin Book, 2010)

Making it Happen: Fred Goodwin, RBS and the Men Who Blew Up the British Economy by Iain Martin, published by Simon & Schuster, 2013

Acknowledgements

My thanks to all those who gave generously of their time, consulted their diaries, dredged their memories and worked their Rolodexes to help make this book possible. The research began with a two-day visit to Edinburgh in October 2019 to talk to Alistair Darling and ended in a blizzard of lockdown interviews on Zoom. My special appreciation, therefore, to Alistair for his assistance and patience. For their insights, reflections and recollections, many thanks also to Gordon Brown, Mervyn King, Shriti Vadera, Nick Macpherson, Tom Scholar, John Kingman, Dan Rosenfield, Nikhil Rathi, Kirstin Baker, Adair Turner, John Varley, Victor Blank, Eric Daniels, James Leigh-Pemberton and Charles Randell. My thanks also to Alan Parker, Andrew Fenwick and Andrew Porter for their generous help, to Andy Bone for his sublime design skills and technical support and finally to Fiona for her diligent proof-reading and attention to detail. Without Charlie Viney's inspiration, the project would never have begun. Without the support and encouragement of my family, it would never have been completed.

Michael Harrison

November 2020

Index

ABN Amro 6,
Abu Dhabi 144, 157, 193-6
Agius, Marcus 59, 103, 110, 126, 198, 204
Aitkenhead, Decca 20
Alliance & Leicester 8, 17-18, 42
Alliance Boots 198
Argos 18
Asset Protection Scheme 148, 196
AstraZeneca 131
Atlas Mara 198, 204
Austerity, age of 200-202
Ayling, Robert 7, 20
Bailey, Andrew 44, 52, 55, 116, 118-19
Baker McKenzie 102
Baker, Kirstin 43-44, 48, 60-61, 99, 115, 135, 152, 169, 180, 204
Balls, Ed 10-11, 83
Balti Bailout 130, 133
Bank of England 1, 5, 8, 10-11, 13-14, 16-17, 20-3, 28-30, 42-4, 63, 72-9, 85, 88, 95, 104-05, 108, 113, 116, 118-20, 131
Bank of New York Mellon 5, 195
Barclays:
    June 2008 capital raising 17
    Interest in buying Lehman Brothers 23
    Approached to rescue Bradford and Bingley 48-9
    Share placing September 2008 126
    Capital raising discussions with Qatar 126, 144, 155
    FSA stress test of capital requirements 155

    Growth Strategy 156
    Offer to buy RBS 175
    Capital raising from Qatar and Abu Dhabi 176, 186, 193, 196
Barroso, Jose Manuel 15, 91, 163, 182
Beale, Graham 50, 51, 108, 109, 128
Bear Sterns 15, 16
Begbies Traynor 101
Bellany, John 69
Benn, Tony 193
Berlusconi, Silvio 91, 92, 141
Bernanke, Ben 10, 142, 162, 185
Bismarck, Nilufer von 53
Blair, Sir Ian 79, 82
Blair, Tony 47
Blank, Sir Victor 18, 23, 24-5, 57-9, 85, 87-9, 103-05, 125, 144, 153, 166, 173-4, 179, 183-5, 188-9, 192, 198, 204
Blankfein, Lloyd 35, 57
Boardman, Nigel 53
Bond, John 103
Boss, Wouter 65
Bowler, James 45
Bowman, Mark 73, 79
Bradford & Bingley 17, 28, 33, 40-2, 46, 48, 55, 60-1, 63
Brown, George 32
Brown, Gordon:
    Readiness for the crisis 2-3
    Early diagnosis of the challenge 9, 18, 19
    Bank crisis simulations 10-11
    Euro summit, January 2008 15
    Tensions with Alistair Darling 20, 21, 73, 80

Proposal for Special Liquidity
Scheme 16
At Spencer House reception 23
Backing for Lloyds/HBOS
merger 24
Visit from Swedish Central Bank
Governor 32
Approach to recapitalisation of
banks 34, 41
Visit to UN General Assembly,
September 2008 34, 35
Meetings with George W Bush
and Tim Geithner 36-40
Agreement with Darling on
recapitalisation 40-1, 47-8
Telephone call with Irish
Taoiseach 65
Relationship with Shriti Vadera
65-6, 77
Authorises emergency liquidity
for HBOS 72
Authorises emergency liquidity
for RBS 118
View of Fred Goodwin 74-5
Intervenes in HBOS crisis 89
Receives bailout plan from
Vadera 77
Cabinet reshuffle 81-3
Paris meeting with EU leaders
91-2
Launch of National Economic
Council 102-03
Advice from Michael Klein 106,
151
Telephone call from Sir Tom
McKillop 130
Call to Qatar Prime Minister
125-26
Announces bailout deal 137-40
View of Barclays 155-57

Visit to Cheltenham Literature
Festival 163-4
Address to Eurozone leaders
182
Departure from office 199
Brown, Sarah 35, 135, 192
Browne, John 121
Brummer, Alex 108
Brunswick Group 103
Budenberg, Robin 45, 57, 65, 75,
98-9, 102, 206
Buffett, Warren 22
Burns, Terry 50-51
Bush, George W 32, 36-9, 40-1, 48,
76, 127, 132, 170, 187, 195, 206
Cable, Vince 68, 94, 139, 143
Cameron, David 26, 67, 85-6, 199,
200
Cameron, Johnny 162
Capital ratios 12, 26, 58, 148, 185,
197
Cardiff, Kevin 64
Carter, Stephen 103
Cass Business School 61, 138
Chalmers, William 191
Charterhouse Bank 18
Chase Manhattan Bank 25
Chote, Robert 202
Churchill Insurance 16
Citigroup 19, 23, 105, 195, 198
Clasper, Mike 67
Clifford Chance 18
Collateralised Debt Obligations
(CDOs) 4-6, 13, 15-16, 58
Commerzbank 90
Confederation of British Industry
(CBI) 24-5, 27
Cooper, Yvette 48, 121, 177
Corfugate 93
Cottrell, Alison 187

Covid-19 199, 201-02
Cowen, Brian 63
Credit Suisse 122-23, 146-48, 151,
153-55, 164, 166, 169, 174, 183, 185,
188, 191, 194
Cummings, Peter 8, 85, 90
Cunliffe, John 35-6, 92
Curtice, Ruth 153
Curtice, John 153
Daniels, Eric 49-51, 5-58, 68, 70,
74, 85, 88, 90, 104-05, 108-10, 124-
25, 128, 143-44, 153, 166-67, 173-
75, 179, 183-84, 188-89, 192, 198,
205
Darling, Alistair
    Telephone call with Sir Tom
    McKillop 1, 117,
    Readiness for crisis 2-3
    Home visit from Fred Goodwin
    12-13
    Guardian Interview 20-21
    Refusal to rescue Lehman
    Brothers 23
    Orders Tripartite to begin work
    on bailout 28
    Move into Chancellor's office 32
    Rescue of Bradford and Bingley
    41, 48-50, 54, 55
    Formation of Tripartite bailout
    team 43-4
    Bradford and Bingley lifeboat 48
    Irish bank guarantee crisis 63-5
    Approach to UK bank crisis 65-
    6
    Icelandic bank crisis 66-7
    Relations with Shriti Vadera 66
    First meeting with bank CEOs
    68-70
    Authorises emergency liquidity
    for HBOS 72
    Authorises emergency liquidity
    for RBS 118
    Relations with Christine Lagarde
    74
    Telephone call with Icelandic
    PM 79, 84
    Press speculation about position
    as Chancellor 82-3
    Visit from Peter Mandelson 83
    Defuses Icelandic 'timebomb' 83
    Visit to Balerno music festival
    85, 92
    Andrew Marr interview 94-5
    Failed attempt to calm financial
    markets 107
    View of National Economic
    Council 103
    Dismisses Klein bailout plan 106
    Second meeting with bank
    CEOs 107-11
    Attends media reception 108
    Attends EU finance ministers
    meeting in Luxembourg 112-17
    Return to London to oversee
    bailout 121
    Third meeting with bank CEOs
    128-29
    Ultimatum to bank CEOs 129
    Announces bailout 137-40
    Overrules Permanent Secretary
    on Iceland 145-46
    At Washington G7 meeting
    161-62, 169, 172
    Signs off final bailout plan 193
    Departure from office 199
Darling, Anna 42, 61, 150
Darling, Margaret 12-13, 42, 47
Darroch, Kim 116-17
Darzi, Ara 97
Davies, Gavyn 19

Debt Management Office 60
Deripaska, Oleg 93
Dexia 90
Diamond, Bob 59, 110, 156, 158, 176-77, 186, 198, 204
Dickinson, Alan 119
Direct Line 16
Dougan, Brady 147
Drayson, Paul 103
Dresdner Bank 17, 90
Ellam, Michael 41, 140
Emergency Liquidity Assistance 15, 72, 105, 113, 116, 119, 131
European Central Bank 14, 91, 142, 182
Fanny Mae 22
Feldman, Andrew 94
Field, Steve 70, 135
Fillon, Francois 91
Financial Services Authority 6, 10, 12, 14, 17-18, 23, 25-6, 28-9, 32-3, 39, 41, 45, 58-9, 63, 66, 83-4, 86, 89, 98, 107, 109, 113-14, 120, 122, 143, 145, 152, 154-55, 165-66, 174, 186
Financial Services Compensation Scheme (FSCS) 66, 84
Financial Stability Forum 153
Financial Times 9, 37, 70, 71, 78, 87, 100, 151
Fletcher, Tom 35-6, 45, 141
Flint, Douglas 108
FME 120
Foot, Michael 193
Fortis 6, 55, 61, 90
Freddie Mac 22
Gartmore 82
Geithner, Tim 23, 36, 39, 75, 185
Gieve, John 32, 44, 59, 118, 166-67
Giles, Chris 78
Glasgow Herald 20, 112

Glitnir 61, 138
Gnodde, Richard 57
Goldman Sachs 19, 22, 35, 57, 102, 111, 195, 198
Goodwin, Fred 6-7, 12-13, 16, 50, 56, 60, 68-70, 74-5, 108-09, 111, 113, 115-19, 123-24, 127-30, 134, 138, 142, 154, 161-62, 167, 169, 173-75, 178-80, 183, 186-87, 190-91, 197, 202, 204
Great Universal Stores 18
Green, Philip 81
Green, Stephen 58, 69, 178, 198, 205
Greenburgh, Matthew 113, 144, 185, 188, 191
Grigg, Sebastian 123, 146, 148, 154
Group of Four (G4) 87, 92, 106-07
Group of Seven (G7) 16, 35, 39, 141, 151, 153, 158, 161-62, 169, 172
Guardian 20, 71, 100, 113, 151, 172
Guardian Media Group 82
Haarde, Geir 79, 84, 145
Haldane, Andy 45, 120
Hamad Bin Jassim Bin Jabr Al-Thani, Sheikh 110, 125, 144, 177
Hamleys 62
Hampton, Sir Philip 6, 103, 161
Hancock, Matt 85-6, 95
HBOS:
    Creation of 7
    Failure of 2008 rights issue 16-17
    Search for a buyer 17-18
    Merger discussions with Lloyds 18
    Announcement of merger with Lloyds 24
    Codename for 42
    Bid for Bradford and Bingley 51-2, 54

Receipt of Emergency Liquidity Assistance 72

Weekend liquidity crisis 88-9

Due diligence by Lloyds 105

Capital requirements 147, 173-74, 183-84

Revised merger terms 144, 188, 191-92

Government shareholding in 193

Hedge, Mridul 122-23, 146-47

Henrion, Jerome 148, 154

Heseltine, Michael 60

Hester, Stephen 161-62, 168, 180, 186, 190, 205

Heywood, Jeremy 19, 54, 63, 79, 96-7, 102, 161, 168

Hinduja family 87

HM Treasury 10, 19-24, 32-5, 39-46, 48-53, 55, 58-61, 63, 65-8, 72-5, 78-86, 94-110, 114-15, 117, 120-26, 128-130, 132, 134-37, 139-41, 143, 145-49, 151-55, 158, 162, 165-69, 171-75, 177, 180, 183-86, 191-94, 197

Homebase 18

Hornby, Andy 50, 88, 90, 108-09, 128-29, 131, 161, 165, 179, 188, 189, 192, 197-98, 205

Horta-Osorio, Antonio 50, 69-70, 108-09, 128, 205

Hosie, Stuart 68

HSBC 1, 5, 31, 33, 34, 48, 57-9, 69, 103, 126, 129, 160, 167, 178, 198

Huertes, Thomas 154

Hunter, Archie 162

Hutton, Will 151

Hypo Real Estate 61, 96, 98

Icesave 66, 84, 99, 120, 137, 145-46, 151

Independent 82, 100, 137

Ingves, Stefan 32

International Monetary Fund 21, 43, 141, 151-53, 158

J P Morgan Cazenove 98, 102, 111, 124

Jenkins, Roger 144, 176, 186

John, Dyfrig 50, 69, 128-29

Johnson, Boris 79

Jones, Digby 24

JP Morgan Chase 15, 119, 195

Juncker, Jean-Claude 182

Kaletsky, Anatole 71

Kaupthing 62, 67, 99, 114, 137-38, 145, 151

Kaupthing Edge 151, 66, 83

Kelly, Gavin 45

Khan, Lowri 43-4, 48, 97-8

Kheraj, Naguib 102

King, Mervyn:

View of investment bankers 29, 127

War gaming bank collapse 11

Relationship with Callum McCarthy 14

Dinner with Adair Turner 29

Assessment of Brown and Darling 30-1

Warns Darling over under-capitalised banks 30

Refuses further liquidity for Bradford and Bingley 41

Urges compulsory recapitalisation 33-4, 79

Meeting with George Osborne 85-6, 95

Provides emergency liquidity to RBS 116, 118

Coordinated cut in interest rates 142

View of Barclays 157-58
At IMF/G7 meeting in
Washington 163
Attitude towards Icelandic banks
145-46
Kingman, John 121-122, 124, 129,
132, 134, 146, 152-53, 161, 165-68,
172-80, 183-84, 186, 188, 204
Kinnock, Neil 138
Klein, Michael 19, 105-06, 151
Kroes, Neelie 65
Krugman, Paul 35
Kudrin, Alexei 162
Lagarde, Christine 65, 74, 78, 101-
02, 115, 162, 170
Landsbanki 62, 66-7, 84, 99, 114,
120, 138, 146
Leeson, Nick 30
Lehman Brothers 1, 22-3, 25, 110, 118
Leigh-Pemberton, James 122-23,
146-49, 151, 153-54, 165-67, 169,
180, 183, 185, 188, 191, 194, 205
Leigh-Pemberton, Robin 123
Lenihan, Brian 63-4
Linklaters 184
Lloyds Banking Group:
Interest in buying Abbey
National and Northern Rock 18
Announcement of HBOS
merger 24
Codename for 42
Management clear out 50
View of Tripartite 58
Business model 58, 70, 110
Strategic options 103-04
Due diligence on HBOS 105
Removal of MAC clause from
HBOS deal 124
Renegotiation of HBOS terms
144, 185, 188, 191-92

Capital requirements 143, 166,
173-74, 183-84
Banning of cash bonuses 189
Participation in Asset Protection
Scheme 197
Return to private ownership 198
Lord Mayor's Banquet 13
Lula, Luiz Inacio da Silva 36
Macintyre, Ben 164
Maclay, Murray & Spens 179
MacLeod, Catherine 20, 112, 138,
158, 177
Macpherson, Nicholas 42-3, 50-1,
56-60, 64, 66, 69-70, 77, 79-80, 95,
97-8, 102, 106, 108, 111, 118, 121-
23, 125, 131-32, 134-35, 139, 146,
152, 157, 168, 192, 203
Maddison, George 148, 153, 164,
191
Mandelson, Peter 81-3, 87, 93-4,
97, 103
Mansur Bin Zayed Al Nahyan,
Sheikh 106
Marks & Spencer 81
Marr, Andrew 94-95
Mathewson, Sir George 6
Mathiesen, Arni 120-21
Maxwell, Clive 52, 55
Mayhew, David 98-99, 102, 124,
130, 167, 185, 205
McBride, Damian 21, 83, 136
McCarthy, Callum 14, 17, 23, 25,
29
McKillop, Sir Tom 1, 116-17, 130-
31, 138, 161-62, 167-69, 174, 178-
79, 183, 197, 204
McKinsey 25-6
McLean, Miller 162
Meddings, Richard 75
Menezes, Jean Charles de 79

Merkel, Angela 15, 39, 64-5, 91-2, 96, 98, 141, 163

Merrill Lynch 113, 115, 144, 185, 188, 191, 195

Miles, Colin 45, 120

Miliband, David 26, 65, 103

Mirror Group Newspapers 18

Mitsubishi 22

Morgan Stanley 22, 48, 51, 54, 111, 144, 188-89, 191, 195, 203

Murphy, Paul 115

Murray, Andy 7

Myners, Paul 48, 59, 81-2, 97-9, 103, 105, 120-21, 123-25, 129, 131-32, 134, 148, 151, 165-67, 169, 171-81, 183-84, 186-89, 191-92, 203

National Audit Office 55, 202

National Economic Council 102

National Economic Development Council 32

Nationwide Building Society 48, 50-1, 69, 108-09

New York Federal Reserve 10, 15, 23, 75, 118, 185

Ng, Tom 153

Nicklaus, Jack 7

Northern Rock 1, 8-9, 12, 14, 17-18, 24, 42, 44, 52, 55, 58, 60, 72, 83, 117-18, 121, 131, 145, 154, 162

O'Donnell, Gus 73, 97

Odey, Crispin 49

Office for Budget Responsibility 202

Olver, Dick 103

Orna, Turner 26

Osborne, George 68, 85-6, 93-6, 139, 200

Parker, John 113, 116

Parr, Jeremy 184

Pascoe-Watson, George 82

Paterson, Sarah 53

Paulson, Hank 10, 16, 22-3, 25, 32, 37, 39, 48, 55, 101, 127, 162, 170, 172, 185, 206

Peat Marwick 42

Peston, Robert 8, 55, 111, 114, 188

Pickford, Stephen 121, 158, 177

Pocklington, Jeremy 180

Posen, Adam 35

Pratley, Nils 151

Prodi, Romano 15

Qatar 17, 111, 125, 144, 155, 157, 193, 196

Qatar Holding 111

Quantitative Easing 19, 199

Randall, Jeff 138

Randell, Charles 52-3, 169, 174, 178-9, 191, 205

Rankin, Ian 12

Rathi, Nikhil 43-44, 48, 52, 60, 74, 115, 130, 135, 148, 152, 168-169, 177, 204

Restaurant Group 198

Robey, Simon 144, 185, 188-89, 191

Robinson, Geoffrey 87

Robson, Steve 162

Roden, Neil 179

Rodgers, Ivan 43

Rosenfield, Dan 50, 55, 61, 69, 73, 79, 84, 95, 97, 108, 112, 114, 116-117, 120, 129, 134-35, 138, 140, 158, 167, 172, 175, 177, 204

Rosyth dockyard 74-75

Rothschild, Nat 94

Rowling, JK 12

Royal Bank of Scotland:
    Capital ratios 13, 142, 147
    Purchase of Citizens Bank 5
    Purchase of Mellon Bank retail operations 5
    Acquisition of NatWest 5
    Acquisition of ABN Amro 6

Ambassadors for 7
2008 rights issue 16-17
Sale of Direct Line and
Churchill 16
Codename for 42
Gogarburn headquarters 7, 56
Orphan assets 75
Provision of Emergency
Liquidity Assistance 116,
118-19
Board meetings to discuss
Goodwin pension and departure
179, 186-87, 190
Government purchases shares in
167, 183, 193
Participation in Asset Protection
Scheme 197
Rudd, Sir Nigel 156
Ruddock, Joan 163
Sands, Peter 45, 65, 69-70, 75, 77,
108-09, 111, 128, 205
Santander Bank 6, 8, 17-18, 50-2,
54-5, 60, 69, 108-09, 143, 178, 203
Sants, Hector 26, 32, 45, 59, 155,
163, 165-66, 173, 185, 203
Sarkozy, Nicholas 15, 39, 84, 91, 96,
141, 163, 182
Sawer, John 36
Scholar, Fabiola 43
Scholar, Tom 43-46, 52, 55, 57-60,
65-6, 75, 77, 79, 83, 97-8, 105-06,
121, 124, 129, 132, 134-36, 146-48,
151-53, 159, 161, 165-67, 169-73,
177, 192, 204
Scott, Bob 162, 178, 186-87
Scottish Widows 166, 104, 105
Securities and Exchange
Commission 10
Seligman, George 53
Silvia, John 161

Skinner, Paul 103
Slaughter & May 52-54, 84, 148,
169, 174, 178, 191
Smith, David 54
Smith, Kevin 103
Soanes, David 45, 57, 65, 75, 102
Special Liquidity Scheme 16, 22, 44,
70, 72, 102, 118, 120, 137-38
Spence, Geoffrey 69, 112, 114-17,
121, 158, 167, 177
Spencer House 23
Spencer, Diana 23
Stamen, Robert 60
Standard Chartered Bank 45, 65, 69,
75, 108-09, 111, 143, 160, 167, 178
State Street 195
Staveley, Amanda 105-06, 193
Steinbrueck, Peer 65, 79, 101
Stevenson, Dennis 88, 90, 131, 161,
179, 188, 197, 205
Stevenson, Ewen 123, 146, 148
Stewart, Jackie 7
Stiglitz, Joseph 35
Strauss-Kahn, Dominic 162
Sub-prime mortgages 4-5, 7, 12, 16, 91
Sutherland, Peter 162
Thakkar, Ashish 198
The Sun 82, 150, 194
The Sunday Times 54, 93, 138
The Times 20, 71, 100, 151, 163-64
Tobin, Matthew 53
Tookey, Tim 166, 173-74, 184-85
Touche Ross 75
Treasury Quartet 161-67, 169
Treasury Select Committee 105, 158
Tremonti, Giulio 101, 162
Trichet, Jean-Claude 91, 182
Tripartite, the 10, 14-15, 28, 32, 40-
1, 44-5, 55, 58, 69-70, 77, 89, 98,
101, 108-10, 122, 127

Troubled Assets Relief Programme
(TARP) 22-3, 25, 32, 35-40, 48, 55,
60, 62, 69, 75-6, 78, 104, 163, 170,
172-73, 186, 193, 196
Trump, Donald 117
Tucker, Paul 45, 59, 90, 95, 116,
118-19
Tullet, Louise 169
Turner, Adair 25-6, 28-33, 40-2,
47, 59, 68-9, 83, 89, 99, 107-09,
113-14, 116, 126-27, 129, 132,
145, 163, 178, 203
US Federal Reserve 10, 14-15,
142, 162, 197
Vadera, Shriti 9, 18-19, 22, 34-8,
40, 45, 53, 57, 65-66, 75, 77, 79,
82, 89-91, 96-8, 102, 120-123,
126-27, 131-32, 140-42, 175-77,
180, 183, 187, 192, 203
Vanhanen, Matti 141
Varley, John 48-9, 51, 59, 68-70,
108-10, 115, 126, 128-29, 144,
155-58, 165-66, 175-77, 186, 191,
198, 204
Wachovia 62, 161
Waples, John 54
Warner, Jeremy 137
Weidmann, Jens 91
Wells Fargo 62, 195
Weymarn, Ian de 44, 120
Whelan, Charlie 83
Whelan, Kevin 130
Whittaker, Guy 116
Wilkinson, Jim 172
Williams, Rowan 74
Winters, Bill 102, 119
Wolf, Martin 71
Zapatero, Jose Louis Rodriguez
107

About the Author

Michael Harrison is a former financial journalist and corporate adviser. He was one of the founder members of *The Independent* in 1986, going on to become the newspaper's Business Editor. He was also Deputy City Editor of the *London Evening Standard*. He was named Business Journalist of the Year in the 2001 UK Press Awards and shortlisted for the award on two further occasions. During his career in financial journalism he covered some of the biggest stories of the day including Black Monday in 1987, the dot.com crash, the collapse of Barings Bank and the demise of MG Rover. In 2007 he joined the corporate advisory firm Brunswick where he worked with some of Britain's largest companies on crisis communications and corporate reputation. His first book, *Mr Charming: The Life and Crimes of Felix Vossen*, was published in 2019 by Amberley Publishing. Michael lives in Brighton.

Printed in Great Britain
by Amazon

26571457R00131